WORKING CLASS RADICALS

WEST VIRGINIA AND APPALACHIA Volume 14

Ronald L. Lewis, Ken Fones-Wolf, and Kevin Barksdale, Series Editors

TITLES IN THE SERIES

"They'll Cut Off Your Project:" A Mingo County Chronicle
Huey Perry

*An Appalachian Reawakening:
West Virginia and the Perils of the New Machine Age, 1945–1972*
Jerry Bruce Thomas

An Appalachian New Deal: West Virginia in the Great Depression
Jerry Bruce Thomas

Culture, Class, and Politics in Modern Appalachia
Edited by Jennifer Egolf, Ken Fones-Wolf, and Louis C. Martin

Governor William E. Glasscock and Progressive Politics in West Virginia
Gary Jackson Tucker

Matewan Before the Massacre
Rebecca J. Bailey

Sectionalism in Virginia from 1776 to 1881
Second Edition by Charles Ambler; Introduction by Barbara Rasmussen

Monongah: The Tragic Story of the 1907 Monongah Mine Disaster
Davitt McAteer

Bringing Down the Mountains
Shirley Stewart Burns

Afflicting the Comfortable
Thomas F. Stafford

Clash of Loyalties
John Shaffer

The Blackwater Chronicle
By Philip Pendleton Kennedy; Edited by Timothy Sweet

Transnational West Virginia
Edited by Ken Fones-Wolf and Ronald L. Lewis

WORKING CLASS RADICALS

The Socialist Party in West Virginia, 1898-1920

FREDERICK A. BARKEY

WITH A FOREWORD BY KEN FONES-WOLF

MORGANTOWN 2012

West Virginia University Press, Morgantown 26506
Copyright 2012 by West Virginia University Press

All rights reserved
First edition published 2012 by West Virginia University Press
Printed in the United States of America

20 19 18 17 16 15 14 13 12   9 8 7 6 5 4 3 2 1

Cloth: 978-1-935978-44-2
Paper: 978-1-935978-45-9
PDF: 978-1-935978-46-6

Library of Congress Cataloguing-in-Publication Data

Barkey, Frederick A., 1933–

Working class radicals : the Socialist Party in West Virginia, 1898–1920 / by Frederick A. Barkey—(West Virginia and Appalachia ; v. 14)
Includes bibliographical references and index.
ISBN-13: 978-1-935978-44-2 (cloth : alk. paper)
ISBN-10: 1-935978-44-6 (cloth : alk. paper)
ISBN-13: 978-1-935978-45-9 (pbk. : alk. paper)
ISBN-10: 1-935978-45-4 (pbk. : alk. paper)
[etc.]
1. Socialism--West Virginia--History. 2. Socialist parties--West Virginia--History. I. Title.
HX91.W4B37 2012
324.2754'074--dc23
Library of Congress Control Number: 2011042250
Book Design by Than Saffel
Cover image: Socialists in Union Square, New York City, May 1, 1912. George Grantham Bain Collection, Library of Congress. Reproduction number LC-USZ62-56285

This book is dedicated to the memory of my late son,
Timothy Allen Barkey.

Contents

Foreword: West Virginia's Socialists:
Recovering A Radical Working Class
By Kenneth Fones-Wolf ix
Acknowledgments xli
Introduction 1

I. The Origins of West Virginia
Socialism: 1898–1904 7
II. The Growth and Appeal of the West Virginia
Socialist Movement: 1905–1911 33
III. The Susceptibility of the West Virginia
Working-Class Leadership to the Appeal
Of Socialism 61
IV. "We Had The Revolution": The West Virginia
Socialist Party At Its Peak: 1912–1915 78
V. The Decline Of The West Virginia
Socialist Party: 1915–1920 124
VI. Technological Change And The Decline
Of Trade Union Strength For The West Virginia
Socialist Party 159
Conclusion 167

A Forty-Year Retrospective: An Interview
with Dr. Fred Barkey *By Gordon Simmons* 171
Appendix A: Socialist And Non-Socialist
Working-Class Leadership Sample 177
Appendix B: Socialist Voting Patterns
In West Virginia 191
Notes 206
Bibliography 252
Index 264

Foreword
West Virginia's Socialists: Recovering a Radical Working Class
By Kenneth Fones-Wolf

I have rediscovered and admired Fred Barkey's dissertation on the Socialist Party in West Virginia numerous times. The passion generated by the new labor history in the 1970s was one of the reasons I became a historian. Influenced by the New Left and the capacity of social movements for democratic social change, studies of workers, minorities, immigrants, women, and the poor seemed to offer possibilities for recapturing a hidden democratic spirit that resided below the surface of American society.[1] Rescuing the lives, thoughts, and actions of the historically voiceless from the "enormous condescension of history," many of us believed, might provide a useable past for progressive social change. As a graduate student, I gravitated toward others who studied the American working class, including my future wife, and my friend Dave Corbin, who was studying West Virginia's mine wars. Knowing my interest in working-class politics, Corbin introduced me to Barkey's dissertation, completed at the University of Pittsburgh in 1971.

Barkey studied under one of the giants of the new labor history, David Montgomery. Like his mentor, he wrote about the state's Socialist movement as the expression of a genuine, home-grown, working-class radicalism, a refreshing change from scholarship that had emphasized the national party, its leaders, and their ideas.[2] Of course, that scholarship was in the process of undergoing a major change. Already, books chronicled the Socialist movement in Massachusetts, New York City, and a handful of labor unions. Studies of the Haymarket Affair, the Seattle General Strike, the suppression of the Industrial Workers of the World, and radical leaders such as Eugene Debs and Big Bill Haywood gave insight into American workers and their radicalism.³ Concurrent with or shortly after Barkey finished his dissertation, articles and books were published on the Socialists in states such as Oklahoma, Arkansas, Iowa, and Maine, and in cities such as Rochester and Milwaukee. By the end of the 1970s, the virtual cottage industry of scholarship on the local context and Americanness of Socialism achieved maturity with the publication of James R. Green's study of southwestern Socialists and Nick Salvatore's Bancroft Prize-winning biography of Eugene V. Debs.⁴

The subsequent decade was a time of great excitement in the field of labor history. The journal *Labor History* published some of the most innovative scholarship in social history; the North American Labor History Conference, held annually at Wayne State University, provided a central gathering place every fall; the Walter Reuther Library doled out generous research grants; labor archives sprouted in Georgia, Texas, Pennsylvania, and California, and many older repositories embarked on programs (often with generous funding from the National Endowment for the Humanities or the National Historic Publications and Records Commission) to collect the records of labor organizations or record the memories of workers; and the University of Illinois Press began a distinguished series of books, "The Working Class in American History," which included Dave Corbin's book on the West Virginia mine wars.⁵ Barkey's dissertation should have been a part of that flowering, but teaching obligations, family responsibilities, and a quest for perfection that frequently accompanies such a labor of love prevented him from getting the dissertation into print. By the early 1990s, the field of labor history was no longer "new," and the concerns of working-class historians had moved far from the goal of recovering the hidden struggles for democratic social change from below. New directions emerged in part due to the labor movement's rapidly declining influence but also from influential scholarship that turned the field sharply toward cultural history and exposed the racism and misogyny that undermined working-class quests for power.⁶ A profile and chronicle that focused on the men, mostly white, who promoted the Socialist Party in West Virginia was increasingly out of step with the fashions of the historical profession, even a portion as specialized as working-class history.

What, then, accounts for a renewed interest in Barkey's dissertation? First, the intrinsically interesting story of the appeal of Socialism and the impact that Socialists made in West Virginia and as part of the nation's Progressive Era. It is a distinctive part of the story of the mine wars, and yet something more at the same time. The strength of the Socialist Party vote, especially in 1912, helped temporarily reshape the politics of the southern West Virginia coalfields, the upper Monongahela River Valley, and the state's delegation to Congress. Forty years later, no one else has told that story or described the fervor that such a vision of social democracy inspired. Second, none of the literature on Socialism has reconstructed the sources of Socialist votes with the same detail available in Barkey's work. He went, literally and figuratively, into the hollows to reveal the local bases of Socialist support, allowing the reader to see the rise and decline of Socialism in incredible detail and specificity.

A third reason to make this work more widely available is the resource base that Barkey used to tell the story of West Virginia's home-grown radicals. Barkey developed a wonderful rapport with Socialist veterans and their children in the course of his research, and conducted more than one hundred interviews. Most of these interviews were conducted without the benefit of a tape recorder, and they comprise, in many cases, the only recounting of the ideas and attitudes of Socialist Party activists, and the only version of events from their perspective.[7] Since Socialists were key actors in momentous conflicts, historians have plumbed Barkey's pages for insights. Making the text more widely accessible will encourage a new generation to reconsider how we think about West Virginia's and the nation's histories during a critical era of reform. In addition, Barkey's statistical evidence anticipated current themes in Appalachian scholarship by refuting the essentialist perspective that the region was an isolated and homogeneous place defying the main currents of American history.

Finally, Barkey's study has relevance to the state and the coalfields of today. As I write this introduction, hundreds of marchers have descended upon Blair Mountain, wearing the red bandanas that the coal miners wore on their rebellious march ninety years ago. Back then, with the help of leaders who drew upon the ideas and fighting spirit of the Socialist Party, the first marchers to Blair Mountain fought to bring the promises of American freedom and citizenship to the southern West Virginia miners. In 2011, marchers included labor unionists who have watched the near destruction of the United Mine Workers of America (U.M.W.A.) and one of its most sacred places, local citizens who have witnessed coal slurry impoundments threatening their water and their land, and environmental activists who fear the destruction of the unique biodiversity and ecosystems that are the bounty of Appalachia and a national resource.[8] In much the same way that the freedom of coal miners bowed to powerful outside corporations and their agents in state and national governments, today's activist alliance faces absentee energy companies and unresponsive government bureaucrats who stripped Blair Mountain of its designation as a protected historic site. Barkey's Socialists would undoubtedly have much to say to 2011 marchers. Not since the Gilded Age has there been such a need for remembering the different and more humane vision for American society offered by Barkey's protagonists.

How would the past forty years lead Barkey to write a different book today? In his introduction, Barkey felt the need to reassert the fact that Socialists were an essential and vital force in the labor movement. In the highly charged atmosphere of New Left activism and anti-Vietnam War protesting, unions seemed to some progressives to "have always been the bulwarks of the status quo" and never more so than in "the recent spectacle" when hard-hatted construction workers defended "Wall Street against young people bent on radical social change." Subsequent scholarship and events have complicated that assertion.[9] Moreover, Barkey's long and supportive relationship with the labor movement in West Virginia, as well as his admiration of labor's intrepid struggle to protect worker rights in the most inhospitable political environment since the 1920s, would encourage him to recast that statement in 2011. In the remainder of my foreword, I will move back and forth between an appreciation of Barkey's contributions to the historical literature on Socialism, West Virginia, and coal mining to an acknowledgment of the changing scholarship of the past generation and some suggestions about opportunities for additional research. In some cases, I will use Barkey's own ongoing scholarship to plug holes in work he did at the outset of his career.

Roots of Socialism in West Virginia

New scholarship provides background on the factors that made West Virginia ripe for Socialism. As Barkey notes, Eugene V. Debs helped create West Virginia's first chapters of what would become the Socialist Party of America during the coal strike of 1897. After leading the American Railway Union to challenge a federal injunction during a strike and boycott of the Pullman Car Company in 1894, Debs became a nationally known figure. His actions landed him in jail, where he began a journey toward Socialism. In 1897, when Debs arrived in Wheeling as part of a national speaking tour, he had only recently abandoned his hope for Populism, a casualty of William Jennings Bryan's defeat in the 1896 presidential election. At that time, the most influential versions of Socialism were the doctrinaire Socialist Labor Party, the Social Democrats who advocated for a Marxist class analysis of politics, and a large group of cooperative colonizationists, with whom Debs was allied when he visited Wheeling in 1897. A year later, Debs sided with the Social Democracy faction, which became the Socialist Party of America in 1901.[10]

Unlike Debs, the Wheeling citizens attracted to Socialism leaned toward the Social Democrat faction. They were mostly German immigrants and their adult children, small businessmen, and workers already distressed by "the unfair relation capital bears to labor."[11]

Industrialization was altering social relationships in the state, as Barkey notes, and Wheeling was West Virginia's most advanced industrial center. No other place in the state rivaled the city's concentration of industries, its multi-ethnic working class, or its numbers of skilled craftsmen, the workers who typically provided the backbone of labor unions and independent leftist politics.[12] Thus, Debs naturally provided a spark there for the formation of a Socialist Party chapter.

Subsequent historical work also notes that working-class political radicalism had longer antecedents in West Virginia. In the 1880s, a vigorous Greenback-Labor Party captured a number of seats in the state legislature and the presidency of the state senate. Although ostensibly an alliance of farmers and workers clamoring for a currency reform that would help those in debt, the path of Greenback-Labor success grew alongside industrial development, which followed the railroad, especially in the Ohio and Kanawha River valleys, suggesting the influence of the labor part of the equation.[13] In the most industrialized city in the state, Wheeling, debates over independent, class-based political action began dividing the Ohio Valley Trades and Labor Assembly during the deep depression of 1893–97, and continued for the next twenty years. The arrival of the first chapters of the Socialist Party only provided a consistent party orientation to the ongoing dispute.[14]

We also now have a better understanding of how the emergence of Socialism in West Virginia was shaped by major political realignments in the state and the nation. Mountain State Republicans rose to power in the wake of the Panic of 1893 and the ensuing depression. The Republican platform, in trumpeting high tariffs leading to high wages, became instrumental in the political change. The party carried the most heavily industrialized counties in the northern panhandle and the Monongahela and Kanawha river valleys.[15] West Virginia's shift to the Republican column helped break a national deadlock, resulting in the party's dominance over much of the next forty years. Workers, who had supported Republicans in the 1890s in anticipation of a government more friendly to labor, were quickly disappointed. They found the Republican legislature totally unsympathetic to their lobbying efforts and the struggles of workers during the depression. By 1899, the lobbyists that the Ohio Valley Trades and Labor Assembly sent to Charleston complained of the "alarming state of corruption" in the Republican legislature.[16] The snubbing of labor by the Republicans energized Wheeling's (and the state's) working-class radicals to insist on independent political action, an option that the return of Debs to Wheeling in 1900 made more palatable and seemingly more attainable. Increasingly confident, Debs wrote to "Mother" Jones in January 1901, "Ah, but Socialism cannot be kept out [of] a Labor organization any more than the rays of the rising sun can be prevented from dispelling the lists of darkness."[17]

As Barkey demonstrates throughout his discussion of Socialism's roots, leftist ideas spread in tandem with organized labor. Railroad unions carried radicalism along the various lines that traversed the state, especially in the hubs and repair shops that emerged. As the highly unionized glassworkers followed the development of the industry into the state, they imbibed the Socialist principles of men such as Tommy Rowe of the Flint Glass Workers or the Belgian and French immigrants who brought their ideas of worker-owned cooperatives complementing the *Parti Ouvrier* (Workers' Party) with them to West Virginia.[18] Increasingly influential was the growth in the southern coalfields.

Despite successfully planting Socialism in West Virginia's working class, Debs was premature in his prediction of rapid fruition. Many skilled industrial workers hoped that the incoming Republican government might yet deliver some benefits to the state's union members. Republican high tariffs, which theoretically protected high wages, were certainly on the minds of iron, tinplate, glass, and pottery artisans in the northern end of the state. In addition, reform-minded Republican governors, A. B. White and William M. O. Dawson, promised a major overhaul of the state's tax system, one that would promote manufacturing, modernize the state's infrastructure, and benefit working people and their children.[19] Even timber and coal baron Henry Gassaway Davis applauded the reformers' desire to help the state. He wrote to his fellow Tax Commission member, William Hubbard, about the unfair returns recouped by oil, gas, and coal operators, "especially as a large proportion of those who reap the benefit of the mining of coal, and the production of oil and gas, live out of the State and pay practically no taxes in West Virginia."[20] For several years, tax reform monopolized the state's political agenda, and Republicans succeeded in using the issue to maintain the support of workers. Even a bitter coal strike in 1902 did not dislodge many workers from the existing two-party system. In fact, coal miner success in the Kanawha River Valley seemed to solidify support for the Republicans. Only among the defeated New River miners did Socialism continue to thrive. Thus, when Debs ran for president in 1904, he competed for support against a progressive Republican program in the centers of iron, tinplate, glass, and pottery production, holding the Socialist vote in check.

Growth and Appeal

By 1906, as Barkey notes, Socialist support was expanding beyond its urban roots. Particularly in the coalfields, the dynamics of the resource extraction economy exposed the most exploitative and socially destructive aspects of capitalism and the complicity of governments. According to historian Thomas Andrews, this was true not only in West Virginia, but in places such as Ludlow, Colorado.[21] Perhaps the greatest advances in scholarship since Barkey's dissertation have come in the area of analyzing the state's coal-oriented political economy. Although they would agree with the general outlines of Barkey's argument, historians John Alexander Williams, Ronald Eller, and David Corbin posit a more theoretical understanding that emphasizes the colonial-like nature of West Virginia's economy. The state's coal, oil, timber, and natural gas industries, so the argument goes, came under the control of absentee corporations that exploited the state's valuable resources for the benefit of a national capitalist class. Using their access to investment capital and political influence, absentee corporations treated West Virginia like an "internal colony," drawing upon a carefully controlled supply of cheap labor to provide carbon fuels for the nation's industry. Capitalists leveraged control over state politicians in both parties through campaign contributions, and incorporated local businessmen as junior partners. Williams called these local elites *compradors*, equating them with the complicit native officials who worked with colonial empires.[22]

Gradually, this interpretation has given way to a more complex and sophisticated analysis of the operation of world capitalist systems. Jettisoning inapt aspects of the colonial analogy, scholars such as Richard Simon, David Walls, and Ronald Lewis wrote of West Virginia as a peripheral region whose economic well-being was subjugated to and dependent upon the metropolitan cores of national and global capitalism. For example, historian Michael Workman effectively demonstrates that the north-central West Virginia coalfields were developed by local rather than outside capital, but the results, in terms of labor policies and the positions of coal operators on political issues, were much the same.[23]

This scholarship adds a more theoretical grounding to Barkey's description of the social and economic changes that produced worker disillusion with the two-party political system. No matter which model one applies, West Virginia's political economy seemed weighted against workers and left them without influence. Even when organized labor elected pro-labor candidates on the Democrat or Republican tickets, the legislators typically confronted mostly antagonistic delegates. Most discouraging by far were the cases of such men as John Nugent. After rapidly rising to the presidency of United Mine Workers District 17 and the West Virginia Federation of Labor and winning election with union support to the House of Delegates, he defected to become the State Commissioner of Immigration, a position paid by a coal company. This was a betrayal of epic proportions.[24] Meanwhile, session after session of the West Virginia legislature passed with few gains for organized labor, leading some unionists to support an independent working-class party but others to talk about abandoning politics altogether. Ironically, as Barkey points out, the Socialists' belief in American democracy enabled them between 1906 and 1910 to gain control over the key labor institutions in the state. Labor newspapers, city labor federations, and union locals increasingly came under the sway of Socialists who promised improvements for workers if they would only unite behind their party's political program.

Barkey reminds us that another source of Socialist growth occurred as a result of the barriers to the full exercise of citizenship erected by the coal operators through their company towns. His many interviews with former residents of the coalfields revealed the carefully crafted control that company-owned towns exerted over miners and their families. Nowhere was the percentage of miners who lived in company towns higher than in West Virginia, where nearly eight of every ten miners were subject to such control. In these towns, operators maintained the law enforcement and educational institutions; they mandated that miners shop at company-owned stores at company-dictated prices using company-specific currency (scrip), live in company-owned houses, and even worship at churches paid for by the company. When trouble arose, operators' private guards evicted miners from their homes or cut off credit at the store. Operators, determined to thwart any expression of shared interest, purposely filled their mines and company towns with a "judicious mixture" of local farm boys, African-American migrants from the South, and southern and eastern European immigrants. Miners dared not voice any dissent or try to enjoy the basic citizenship rights that the United States promised. American Federation of Labor President Samuel Gompers famously called "feudal" West Virginia "the last remains of industrial autocracy in America."[25]

While many of Barkey's Socialists attributed their political odyssey to the notorious brutality of mine guards and the lack of freedom they experienced growing up in company towns, this picture of company towns has undergone some revision. Most notably, historian Crandall Shifflett and economist Price Fishback portray a rosier picture of coal miners' options. Fishback asserts that non-unionized coalfields were not the feudal domains portrayed by most labor and social historians. He claims that overall earnings rivaled those in union fields because non-union operations typically offered steadier employment; the company stores and rent in company housing at times accommodated falling wages; and that miners offset company authority and poor conditions with their feet—that is, they moved frequently.[26]

More balanced is the work of Crandall Shifflett, which charts the evolution of coal towns through various stages. He argues that early company towns did resemble some of the most unflattering portraits, but as they reached a more mature phase, during which operators competed for labor, the towns provided more substantial housing, better schools and recreation facilities, and a healthier environment. However, when the United States Coal Commission reported on its survey of company towns in 1922–23, its findings reflected the substandard nature of housing, sanitation, and health conditions in many towns nearly two decades after Socialists began their agitation.[27] "Mother" Jones, the "miners' angel," still referred to the state as "Medieval West Virginia." Not surprisingly, a range of oral history collections attest to Barkey's assertion that company towns played a significant role in provoking a radical outlook among many who grew up in them.[28]

The state's political economy and the hardships experienced in company towns drove future Socialists from the two-party system, but what did the Socialist Party promise? In election programs, the party broadcast political reforms such as the initiative, referendum, and recall as well as home rule for cities that would allow for greater citizen participation. They also promised general reforms such as public ownership of utilities and improved municipal services that aimed at more efficient public services, especially for working-class neighborhoods. Many of these ideas were part of a broader political program supported by many stripes of progressives. The Socialists differed most from other progressives in their solution to the era's most vexing problem, "the labor question." While many middle-class progressives rejected the necessity of a class struggle, Socialists believed that it was an inevitable situation that required a political solution or it would lead to violence and rebellion.[29] Barkey notes that they underscored the need to guarantee wage earners the same rights, options, and fairness that the political system gave employers and corporations.

Mountain State Socialists looked backward and forward. They propounded ideas from older "producerist" politics, such as the labor theory of value and worker ownership of the means of production, and gave these ideas a distinctly American flavor, coupling them with all due respect for private property, the Protestant Social Gospel, and notions of liberty and freedom stretching back to the American Revolution.[30] At the same time, they pursued arguments for a fairer distribution of the profits accruing as a result of the tremendous productivity of American industrial capitalism. To accomplish this, the Socialist Party pledged to enact laws that would protect the rights of workers to join unions and organize for their own protection.

Such a promise resonated with West Virginia's coal miners, enmeshed in company towns. After 1907, protection of worker rights took on a special significance in the state when a federal District Court judge—Alston G. Dayton of West Virginia—issued a broad injunction against union organizing, citing the existence of "yellow dog" contracts. The U.M.W. had been trying to organize the Hitchman Coal and Coke Company in the state's northern panhandle, but the company had forced its miners to sign individual employment contracts stipulating that they would not join a union for the duration of their employment with the company. Dayton, citing the contracts, issued a sweeping order forbidding the union from any contact with the company's miners. This case pointed the way for other coal companies to legally combat the rights of miners to freely join unions and engage in collective bargaining, and threatened the U.M.W. with indictments. Eventually upheld by the U.S. Supreme Court, Dayton's decision had national importance until the 1930s.[31]

The Socialists' vow to protect the freedom of coal miners against such a ruling had a powerful influence in a state in which one-sixth of the workforce was engaged in mining in 1910. It is not surprising, then, that the Socialist vote grew most rapidly in the coalfields, but the denial of basic freedom had an impact throughout the state. In a later article, Barkey notes the anarcho-syndicalist tendencies that arose from such callousness on the part of judges like Dayton. Party organizer "Fritz" Merrick, for one, justified support for the most extreme "Red" Socialist faction of the party, even though he lived in Parkersburg. As a result of coal operators' snuffing out of democracy, seemingly with the consent of state officials, others advocated policies more in keeping with the Industrial Workers of the World.[32]

A Socialist Profile: Leaders and Rank and File

Perhaps the most original part of Barkey's dissertation is the profile he constructed of the Socialist and non-Socialist working-class activists, a broader profile than we have for any other state. Based largely upon information gleaned from his numerous interviews, Barkey's profile reveals two strikingly similar cadres. Somewhere around 90 percent of both groups were native-born (some of long-term native stock), reflecting the effectiveness of the party's appeal to American values. In contrast to many places, there were more Americans among West Virginia Socialist leaders than among their non-Socialist counterparts in the labor movement. They were more likely to come from a local farming or artisan background, to be practicing Protestants and lodge members, and to have reaped the benefits of a system of free public education. In most respects, according to Barkey's profile, they resembled the most famous Socialist of the American heartland, Eugene V. Debs, more than the party leaders in New York or Milwaukee.[33]

In the years between writing his dissertation and the present day, Barkey has probably done as much as anyone to create a more inclusive portrait of West Virginia's working-class radicals. Of note were the oral histories that he conducted with Belgian glassworkers, which he eventually pulled together in a monograph that wove in some lengthy excerpts of the transcripts. That work, *Cinderheads in the Hills: The Belgian Window Glass Workers of West Virginia*, points to the transatlantic Socialism that these highly skilled artisans infused into the state's movement. Their Socialism, which emphasized skilled worker control over the means of production, often through cooperatives, was at times exclusionary and apolitical, but it also elicited a strong Socialist Party vote when their control came under attack. The story of this ethnic Socialism certainly complicated Barkey's earlier profile of the Socialists.[34]

More recently, Barkey has looked closely at the Italian radical influence in the West Virginia coalfields. Recognizing that he included few Italian Socialists or their descendants when he conducted his dissertation interviews, Barkey has since then redoubled his efforts. Noting that by the First World War, West Virginia's mine workforce "was the most foreign-born of any southern state," he set out to recover the weighty contributions Italians made to the militancy of the state's miners. Chronicling the passage of Italians from their villages in the *Messogiorno* to towns like Boomer in the Kanawha Valley or Monongah in the Upper Monongahela Valley, Barkey found a remarkable solidarity, often rooted in Socialist and Anarchist ideologies that Italians carried with them wherever they ventured in America.[35] Consequently, while Barkey's profile of West Virginia Socialist Party's leadership cadre stresses the native and German lineages of the group, the rank and file that supplied its voting strength was more multi-ethnic and transnational.

Were he writing his study today, Barkey would undoubtedly have asked more questions about women's roles in the Socialist Party. He includes plenty on "Mother" Jones, the dynamic organizer who ventured to West Virginia so many times, but few other women make appearances. Subsequent scholars have done little to correct this omission.[36] Although there have been a number of studies of the mine wars, few detail the part played by women in sustaining a militant working-class political movement in the region. Denise Giardina's novel, *Storming Heaven*, contains perhaps the best insights about women in the early twentieth-century coalfields.[37]

Today, it would be easier to say more about African Americans in West Virginia. Major works by historians Ronald L. Lewis and Joe William Trotter have added to our knowledge of the racial dynamics in the coalfields as well as the complicated role that African Americans played during strikes and the building of the union. Recognizing the growing numbers of blacks in the state's mines, the United Mine Workers sent George H. Edmunds to help organize. Edmunds was a black Socialist who proselytized for the U.M.W. and the party at the same time. According to Lewis, he maintained "a frenetic speaking schedule at mass meetings" throughout the Kanawha and New Rivers, but as yet we still have insufficient information about his effectiveness in converting black miners to Socialism.[38]

Subsequent scholarship helps us question one aspect of Barkey's characterization of West Virginia working-class Socialists' religious preferences. Although there has been a popular perception that Socialists were opposed to religion, West Virginia's Socialists, like many other American radicals at the time, were not opposed to religion.[39] Among the leadership cadres of the state's working-class, the Socialists were perhaps more religious than their non-Socialist counterparts. However, Barkey contends that one quarter of West Virginia's Socialist leadership was Pentecostal. Pentecostal churches were spreading into the coalfields in the first two decades of the twentieth century, but they did not have that sort of influence.[40] Barkey lumps Holiness, independent Baptist, Seventh Day Adventists, and Disciples of Christ churches under a Pentecostal umbrella. These denominations were outside the mainline Protestant denominations, but they were not necessarily Pentecostal. The largest numbers of those Barkey labels Pentecostals were Campbellites (members of the Disciples of Christ or the Church of Christ). These groups descended from the early nineteenth-century Restoration Movement and they shared some of the Holiness tendencies, but it is inaccurate to claim that they were Pentecostals.[41]

Socialism at High Tide

Although the millennialist spirit contributed to high tide of the Socialist movement, it was the violent turmoil of labor conflict that was critical to the impressive vote totals racked up by Debs in 1912. This Socialist high tide was a result of both the long-lasting and bitter struggle to spread the union in the West Virginia coalfields in 1912, and the smoldering animosity toward capitalism in the tin-plate mills of the northern panhandle and in the glass factories of Clarksburg, Fairmont, and South Charleston. As Barkey's tables reveal, the Socialist vote in the four-county northern panhandle and in several counties of the Upper Monongahela River Valley topped 9 percent. In Kanawha Valley's Fayette County, one of every seven votes was for Debs; in neighboring Kanawha County, nearly one of every five, far surpassing the 6 percent share that Debs received nationwide. Meanwhile, such towns as Adamston, Cameron, and Star City elected Socialist mayors while towns and counties in the state elected Socialist sheriffs, constables, councilmen, and other officials.[42]

The election of 1912 has remained one of the nation's most interesting elections, pitting a regular Republican (William Howard Taft), a Progressive Republican (Theodore Roosevelt), and a Socialist (Debs) against Democrat Woodrow Wilson, who won with under 42 percent of the vote. It came in the middle of what historian Graham Adams called the "Age of Industrial Violence."[43] Nowhere did that seem truer than in the nation's coalfields. West Virginia's miners, as well as those in Pennsylvania, Ohio, Illinois, and southwestern Colorado, returned a disproportionate share of Socialist votes as a referendum on the tumultuous labor relations.[44]

Socialist vote totals, however, instead of achieving intended results, subtracted support from the Republicans and tipped the scales toward the Democrats, a party in West Virginia controlled by a Kanawha statehouse ring and prodevelopment coal barons like Clarence W. Watson of Fairmont. The Socialist press had expressed dismay at the unintended effect of the 1910 election in which the notoriously anti-union Watson received the Democratic state legislature's election to the United States Senate.[45] Nevertheless, the high-water mark of Socialist influence in the state occurred in the 1912 election cycle.

In the spring of 1913, however, controversy surrounded the Socialist presence in the southern West Virginia coalfields, a site of ongoing strife. The Socialist Party sent Eugene Debs, Victor Berger, and Adolph Germer, three of its most important leaders, to investigate and report on the open warfare occurring in the Cabin Creek and Paint Creek strikes, the imposition of martial law by Governor Henry D. Hatfield, which included the arrest of nearly 300 strikers and sympathizers, including "Mother" Jones, and the suppression of the Socialist press in the southern part of the state. The investigating committee did not adequately comprehend the considerable animosity between Socialist miners and the leadership of District 17 of the United Mine Workers of America. Even before the investigating committee could issue its report, statements in the press elicited a storm of protest from an ultraradical group of Socialists who believed that Debs's committee was whitewashing the actions of the governor and betraying the struggle of the miners against the operators and their brutal mine-guard system. The final report proved to be neither as favorable toward the governor as the Socialist miners feared nor as condemnatory of the governor as they had hoped. Meanwhile, many Socialists in the coalfields began to question their support for the party, especially its reformist wing represented by Berger and Germer. They thought that the report erred in condemning the radicals for criticizing U.M.W. leaders over the contract they negotiated under pressure from Governor Hatfield.[46]

Subsequent scholarship has pointed to this episode of "betrayal" as the start of Socialism's decline in the state. Historian David Corbin, for one, points to the fact that the rank-and-file leaders of the Paint Creek and Cabin Creek strikes, including Frank Keeney and Fred Mooney, abandoned the party shortly after the committee's visit for failing to support their more militant position and to demand more from Governor Hatfield. These were the men who, in 1916, successfully ousted the U.M.W.'s District 17 leaders who had negotiated what many believed was a poor contract.[47] Others, most notably historian Roger Fagge, assert that Corbin lays too much blame on Debs, Berger, and Germer. Fagge uses Barkey's dissertation to suggest that ultramilitant followers of the Industrial Workers of the World were the cause of the divisiveness in the U.M.W., and that Debs was right to cooperate with the District 17 leaders and try to build upon the imperfect contract.[48]

Barkey's study, however, does not vindicate either side of the argument. Even if the rank-and-file radical leaders, Frank Keeney and Fred Mooney, abandoned the Socialist Party after Debs's visit, there was little dropoff in Socialist voting in 1914 in the coalfields, and the Socialist Party and Socialist ideas remained forces among the coal miners.[49] Moreover, the miners who put them in power in District 17 still thought of Keeney and Mooney as Socialists who continued to promote Socialist policies. Likewise, "Mother" Jones, who was arrested during the strike, wrote a warm letter to Debs after her release regretting that she was unable to see him when he was in West Virginia.[50] At the same time, Barkey notes that Socialists and miners rejected the conclusions of the report and set about putting their union in the hands of a more radical leadership. He also disagrees with Fagge that the I.W.W. was an important force in the coalfields, even if some of the Wobbly philosophy seeped into the attitudes of local Socialists.

Any study of West Virginia radicalism will undoubtedly spend a good deal of time on the militant actions and the high voter turnout in the southern coalfields from 1912 to 1914. Barkey, however, reminds us that this was not the only scene of note during the high tide of Socialist influence. By surveying the factories of Wheeling, the growing Socialist presence in the glass towns, the growth of cooperative stores in such diverse locations as Star City, Salem, Red Star, Fairmont, and Huntington, and Socialist electoral successes in 1914, he demonstrates that the party was a vibrant and diverse force, not limited to the southern coalfields. However, there were significant gaps in the party's appeal, even during its heyday years. Farmers, by and large, rejected Socialism; African Americans were loath to break with the Republican Party; the Catholic Church resourcefully opposed Socialism; and reform-oriented Republicans and Democrats siphoned off support. In fact, Keeney and Mooney even lent support to the election of reformist Democrat John J. Cornwell in the 1916 gubernatorial race.[51] Damaged, constrained, and limited they may well have been, but West Virginia's Socialists could not be ignored.

Socialism in Decline

The impressive showings in 1912 and 1914 mobilized the opponents of Socialism. At the state level, as Barkey notes, the legislature moved to solidify the two-party system by changing the procedures governing candidate selection by all parties and by making it difficult for the Socialists to pay the exorbitant registration fees and to remain on the ballot. All these actions threatened to dilute party discipline and to open the Socialist Party to opportunists or machinations by outsiders who wanted to weaken the party by nominating men who did not represent Socialist principles. Attacks on Socialist political action also took place at the local level, borrowing from national initiatives to limit working-class political influence. In Clarksburg, for example, Socialists had demonstrated significant strength in working-class wards and won offices in neighboring villages. In response, the city adopted national ideas aimed at restoring elite control and efficiency—it consolidated control over the outlying areas, instituted a city manager form of government, and modified its council elections to a city-wide basis, which lessened the influence that working-class neighborhoods could exert. Although some of these changes meant to curtail the corrupting influence of party politics, they also decimated the Socialist vote.[52]

Equally damaging to the party was the internal dissension generated by the impediments placed on Socialist political activity. In West Virginia, as in the nation generally, Socialists debated the benefits of continuing to emphasize politics as opposed to turning their energies to militant industrial unionism and direct action, efforts that would win gains for workers.[53] As Barkey explains, this debate in West Virginia had immediate implications because of the long campaign to take control of District 17 of the United Mine Workers. Frank Keeney even set up a rival organization, the West Virginia Mine Workers Organization, to force changes within the UMW. He eventually won election as president of the combined districts 17 and 29 of the UMW. This struggle absorbed most of the energies of the radical miners during 1916.

Labor union members encountered an additional dilemma: gains delivered by Democrat Woodrow Wilson's Administration. These gains were particularly tough in a time when the Socialists could not reasonably expect to elect their own candidates. In his first term, with support from Progressive Republicans, the Wilson Administration won amendments to the Constitution authorizing an income tax and providing for the direct election of U.S. Senators; appointed former UMW officer William B. Wilson to the first cabinet-level position for labor; and enacted three important labor laws for which unions had been lobbying for years, the Clayton Act (hailed by unions as "labor's Magna Carta"), the LaFollette Seaman's Act, and the Child Labor Law. The Wilson Administration also created the United States Commission on Industrial Relations, which offered recommendations "more radical than any report upon industrial subjects ever made by any government agency," claims labor historian Melvyn Dubofsky.[54] Surely, Wilson's actions made the Socialist task more daunting, moreso in a year when Eugene Debs chose not to be the party's standard bearer.

In West Virginia, the Democrats could lay claim to being friends of the working class. Barkey says that the bulk of the Socialists supported Democratic candidates in 1916, an assertion that he backs up with a careful reconstruction of the vote totals. In the coalfields, UMW leaders not only threw their support behind John J. Cornwell but also did their best to persuade Republicans and Socialists to get on board. Workers also had a staunch friend in Marion County democrat, Matthew M. Neely. Neely won the support of labor, including many Socialists, when he led a fight to impeach Judge Alston G. Dayton, who had issued the infamous *Hitchman Coal and Coke* injunction. The new Democrat Party attitude even captured the attention of Clarence W. Watson, former U.S. Senator and executive of Consolidation Coal Company. While previously known for his anti-unionism, Watson began the process of negotiating agreements with the U.M.W. in the Fairmont field in 1917, hoping that labor organizations would help return him to the Senate.[55]

The 1916 election marked a turning point in the political fortunes of West Virginia Socialists. At least some of Barkey's interviews hint at the dispiriting impact that Debs's decision not to run had in the coalfields. But Socialism was not dead yet. One of the reasons that Socialists supported Woodrow Wilson's reelection was that he had kept the nation out of war. In 1917, that fact changed, and working-class radicals in West Virginia felt betrayed by politics once again. Led by the indomitable Frank Keeney, Socialists throughout the state joined in the protest against a "capitalist war." Governor Cornwell, who supported the war, asked the Justice Department to have "Mother" Jones removed from the state's coalfields because her antiwar speeches and organizing were wreaking havoc with production.[56]

Within a year, however, West Virginia's Socialists sang a different tune. Labor made significant gains and union membership grew under the protection of war-time agencies, leading many working-class radicals to view the war as an opportunity to push a progressive agenda. At the national level, unionists talked optimistically about a coming "industrial democracy."[57] West Virginia's Socialists got on board, perhaps even more enthusiastically. In U.M.W. District 17, Keeney and "Mother" Jones felt the time had come to organize the non-union southern fields, especially now that the Fairmont field was under contract; in Wheeling's factories, workers improved their wages, shortened their working hours, and voted the Democrat ticket; in the pockets of Socialism that followed the glass industry in the state, skilled craftsmen breathed new life into their cooperatives and turned away from independent political action.[58] Of course some workers were even keener for the war. Belgian window-glass craftsmen, whose homeland was overrun by the Germans, volunteered enthusiastically for the American war effort. Throughout the state, former Socialist strongholds exhibited less enthusiasm for independent politics in 1918 than they had two years earlier, and the vast majority of West Virginia Socialists did not follow the antiwar example of their former hero, Eugene V. Debs.[59]

Not all of the Socialist Party's decline was voluntary, however. Subsequent scholarship has placed a great deal of emphasis on the disruption caused by "red squads" and federal investigators during the war and its aftermath. Barkey concentrates on the southern coalfields, but in north central West Virginia, federal marshal Clarence Edwin Smith employed spies to report the movements of anyone suspected of radical sympathies during the war.[60] After the war, Governor Cornwell and patriotic groups throughout the state used this information to crack down on the activities of labor unions, particularly those with Socialist leanings. For example, in Weirton, a center of tinplate production, the Weirton Vigilance Committee rounded up more than 200 Finnish workers who were trying to organize the plant during the 1919 steel strike, marched them to the center of town, and forced them to kneel and kiss the American flag before banishing them from the town.[61] During the nation's Red Scare in 1919, anything that smacked of sympathy with radicalism or Bolshevism faced repression, even though, as Barkey notes, most West Virginia Socialists were disillusioned with the Russian Revolution.

Barkey also points out that new technology was another factor that contributed to Socialism's decline. His profile of Socialist support made clear that the party owed a great deal to the attitudes of skilled workers. By the end of the war, however, new technology had decimated the control of craftsmen in the glass industry, a group of men who had voted for Socialism before the war. In bottle and window-glass plants, the unions disappeared and skilled workers scrambled for semi-skilled or unskilled jobs that paid far less than their former jobs. Likewise, advancing technology in steel and pottery chipped away at the remaining vestiges of the "craftsman's empire," undercutting the pride, control, and standards of living that had sustained an outlook that included notions of "worker control."[62]

In 2000, political sociologists Seymour Martin Lipset and Gary Marks speculated about why Socialism "didn't happen here." They mentioned the American party system, Socialist factionalism, the large presence of immigrants in the party, poor strategies, and political repression.[63] While those factors contributed to the failure of Socialism in America, Barkey's work makes clear that the story had many variations, and that West Virginia's Socialists made their own unique contribution to that story.

Conclusion

In his argument with David Corbin about whether or not Eugene Debs betrayed and irreparably harmed West Virginia's Socialists in 1913, historian Roger Fagge claims that ultimately the question is moot. He believes that the Socialists had not really made substantial headway among the state's working class.[64] Barkey's work is a reminder of just how much progress had been made. Were the Socialists likely to capture the state any time soon? Even in the best scenarios, it is hard to imagine them winning anything more than a few additional local offices. Neither Fred Barkey nor I, however, are content with a narrative that implies that the history of Socialism in the state was insignificant. Between 1910 and 1914, the Socialist Party disrupted politics as usual in West Virginia. Their critique of the state's industrial development and its inequalities forced both the Democrats and the Republicans to swing to the left. With control of the state and its delegation to the U.S. Congress hanging in the balance, progressive individuals stepped forward to grab the nominations in both parties. Although they largely disappointed the most forward-thinking workers in the state, the legislature passed workmen's compensation and child labor laws, created a public service commission to set reasonable rates for public utilities, ratified the U.S. Constitution amendments on income taxes and the direct election of Senators, and raised state taxes on inheritance and corporations. Then, during the First World War, the state moved to replace the hated mine-guard system with a state police force.[65]

Socialism's ability to influence the existing two-party system was far more limited after the decisions made to support Democrats in 1916. We may do well to speculate about what difference a vigorous Socialist Party might have made when labor conflict resurfaced in 1919 to 1921. Toward the end of his term, Governor Cornwell became an enemy of unions, despite the fact that his supporters had groveled for Socialist votes in 1916. He was against the nationwide steel industry strike in 1919, and he interpreted the resumption of the mine wars in the southern coalfields as unpatriotic.[66] But as the 1920 election approached, there was virtually no Socialist Party presence to hold the balance. Conservative Republicans triumphed, and maintained control over the state for the next decade.

A Socialist presence was important not only in the polling booth, but also in the daily lives of Mountain State workers. It gave them a vision for a society that protected workers' rights and served the people's interests on a range of issues from recreation to resource allocation. It also encouraged working people to view their participation in the democratic process as an essential responsibility. Making Fred Barkey's *Working Class Radicals: The Socialist Party in West Virginia* more widely accessible should help us reflect on this era of promise and possibilities.

Notes

1. Leon Fink, "The Great Escape: How a Field Survived Hard Times," *Labor: Studies in Working-Class History of the Americas* 8:1 (2011): 109.
2. Howard Quint, *The Forging of American Socialism: Origins of a Modern Movement* (Columbia, SC, 1953); David A. Shannon, *The Socialist Party of America* (New York, 1955); Ira Kipnis, *The American Socialist Movement, 1897–1912* (New York, 1952); *Socialism in American Life*, v. 2, ed. by Donald Egbert and Stow Parsons (Princeton, NJ, 1952); James Weinstein, *The Decline of Socialism in America, 1912–1925* (New York, 1967).
3. See, among others, Henry F. Bedford, *Socialism and the Workers in Massachusetts, 1886–1912* (Amherst, MA, 1966); Melvyn Dubofsky, "Success and Failure of Socialism in New York City, 1900–1918," *Labor History* 9 (1968): 361–75; John H. M. Laslett, *Labor and the Left: A Study of Socialist and Radical Influences in the American Labor Movement, 1881–1924* (New York, 1970); Henry David, *The History of the Haymarket Affair: A Study in the American Social-Revolutionary and Labor Movements* (New York, 1963); Robert Friedheim, *The Seattle General Strike* (Seattle, WA, 1964); William Preston, Jr., *Aliens and Dissenters: Federal Suppression of Radicals, 1903–1933* (New York, 1963); Ray Ginger, *Eugene V. Debs: A Biography* (New York, 1962, c1947); Joseph R. Conlin, *Big Bill Haywood and the Radical Union Movement* (Syracuse, NY, 1969).
4. James R. Green, *Grass Roots Socialism: Radical Movements in the Southwest, 1895–1943* (Baton Rouge, LA, 1978); Nick Salvatore, *Eugene V. Debs: Citizen and Socialist* (Urbana, IL, 1982).
5. *The Labor History Reader*, ed. by Daniel J. Leab (Urbana, IL, 1985); *Labor History Archives in the United States: A Guide for Researching and Teaching*, ed. by Daniel J. Leab and Philip P. Mason (Detroit, 1992); *Working-Class America: Essays on Labor, Community, and American Society*, ed. by Michael H. Frisch and Daniel J. Walkowitz (Urbana, IL, 1983); *Labor Histories: Class, Politics, and the Working-Class Experience*, ed.

by Eric Arnesen, Julie Greene, and Bruce Laurie (Urbana, IL, 1998).

6.   Donna T. Haverty-Stacke and Daniel J. Walkowitz, "Introduction," in *Rethinking U.S. Labor History: Essays on the Working-Class Experience, 1756–2009*, ed. by Donna T. Haverty-Stacke and Daniel J. Walkowitz (New York, 2010), p. 5; Fink, "Great Escape," 110.

7.   Jim Green, however, reminded me that there are some scattered examples of these voices remaining; for example, the interviews conducted by Bill Taft with the miner Socialists A. D. Lavinder and Bert Castle are available in the West Virginia and Regional History Collection, West Virginia University, Morgantown, WV.

8.   Alex Bloedel, "Diverse Paths Lead Up Blair Mountain," *Weekly Yonder*, June 15, 2011; *http://www.dailyyonder.com/node/3373* (accessed June 16, 2011).

9.   Peter Levy, *The New Left and Labor in the 1960s* (Urbana, IL., 1994); Joshua B. Freeman, *Working-Class New York: Life and Labor Since World War II* (New York, 2001).

10.   Salvatore, *Eugene V. Debs*, 161–69; Shannon, *Socialist Party of America*, 1–3.

11.   Ohio Valley Trades and Labor Association, "Minutes," Dec. 2, 1895, in OVTLA Records, West Virginia and Regional History Collection, West Virginia University Libraries, Morgantown.

12.   Still an important starting point for understanding the radicalism of craftsmen is David Montgomery, *Workers' Control in America: Studies in the History of Work, Technology, and Labor Struggles* (New York, 1979). For recent work on Wheeling, see W. Hal Gorby, "Subcultures in Conflict in Polonia: Class, Religion, and Ethnic Tensions in the Formation of Wheeling's Polish Community, 1895–1917," *West Virginia History* 4 [new series] (Fall 2010): 1–34.

13.   John Alexander William, *West Virginia and the Captains of Industry* (Morgantown, WV, 1976); Ken Fones-Wolf, "A House Redivided: From Sectionalism to Political Economy in West Virginia," in *Reconstructing Appalachia: The Civil War's Aftermath*, ed. by Andrew L. Slap (Lexington, KY, 2010), 242–43. For an overview of the Greenback-Labor Party nationally, see Mark A. Lause, *The Civil War's Last Campaign: James B. Weaver, the Greenback-Labor Party, and the Politics of Race and Section* (Lanham, MD, 2001).

14.   David T. Javersak, "The Ohio Valley Trades and Labor Assembly: The Formative Years 1882–1915" (Unpublished Ph.D. dissertation, West Virginia University, 1977), 117–30.

15. Fones-Wolf, "House Redivided," 251–53.

16. O.V.T.L.A., "Minutes," February 26, 1899; Javersack, "Ohio Valley Trades and Labor Assembly," 107–10

17. Eugene V. Debs to Mary Harris Jones, January 28, 1901, in *Letters of Eugene V. Debs, Volume 1, 1874–1912*, ed. by J. Robert Constantine (Urbana, IL, 1990), 158.

18. *National Glass Budget*, July 29, 1905, February 10, 1906, June 29, 1901, September 7, 1901.

19. See Williams, *Captains of Industry*, 222–32, and Fones-Wolf, "House Redivided," 256–60, for discussions of the importance of the tax issue in dividing politically the manufacturing and resource extraction sectors of industry in the state. For the appeal of the Republican Party among glassworkers, see Ken Fones-Wolf, *Glass Towns: Industry, Labor, and Political Economy in Appalachia, 1890–1930s* (Urbana, IL, 2007). For examples of the class rhetoric surrounding tax reform, see Parkersburg (WV) News, January 30, 1903; *Grant County Press* (Petersburg, WV), January 30, 1903; *Grafton (WV) Sentinel*, January 30, 1903.

20. Henry Gassaway Davis to William D. Hubbard, January 30, 1904, box 15, Henry Gassaway Davis Papers, W.V.H.R.C.

21. Thomas G. Andrews, *Killing for Coal: America's Deadliest Labor War* (Cambridge, MA, 2008).

22. Williams, *Captains of Industry*, chapter 7; Ronald D. Eller, *Miners, Millhands, and Mountaineers: Industrialization of the Appalachian South, 1880–1930* (Knoxville, TN, 1982), *passim*; Corbin, *Life, Work, and Rebellion*, chapter 1.

23. David S. Walls, "Internal Colony or Internal Periphery? A Critique of Current Models and an Alternative Formulation," in *Colonialism in Modern America: The Appalachian Case*, ed. by Helen Matthews Lewis, Linda Johnson, and Donald Askins (Boone, NC, 1978); Richard M. Simon, "The Development of Underdevelopment: The Coal Industry and Its Effect on the West Virginia Economy, 1880–1930," (Ph.D. dissertation, University of Pittsburgh, 1978); Ronald L. Lewis, *Transforming the Appalachian Countryside: Railroads, Deforestation, and Social Change in West Virginia, 1880–1920* (Chapel Hill, NC, 1998); Michael E. Workman, "Political Culture and the Coal Economy of the Upper Monongahela Region, 1776–1933," (Ph.D. dissertation, West Virginia University, 1995).

24. Barkey later elaborated on the Socialist opposition to Nugent; see Frederick

A. Barkey, "Socialist Influence in the West Virginia State Federation of Labor: The John Nugent Case," *West Virginia History* 38 (July 1977): 275–90. An overview of Nugent's nefarious activities as the State Commissioner of Immigration can be found in Kenneth R. Bailey, "Strange Tongues: West Virginia and Immigrant Labor to 1920," in *Transnational West Virginia: Ethnic Communities and Economic Change, 1840–1940*, ed. by Ken Fones-Wolf and Ronald L. Lewis (Morgantown, WV, 2002), 243–58.

25. Kenneth R. Bailey, "A Judicious Mixture: Negroes and Immigrants in the West Virginia Mines, 1880–1917," West Virginia History 34 (July 1973): 141–61; Corbin, *Life, Work, and Rebellion*, chapter 2.

26. Price V. Fishback, *Soft Coal, Hard Choices: The Economic Welfare of Bituminous Coal Miners, 1880–1930* (New York, NY, 1992).

27. Crandall A. Shiflett, *Coal Towns: Life, Work, and Culture in Company Towns of Southern Appalachia, 1880–1960* (Knoxville, TN, 1995); U.S. Coal Commission, *Report of the United States Coal Commission* (Washington, DC, 1925), Parts 1–5. See also, Ronald G. Garay, *Corporate Paternalism in Appalachia: U.S. Steel and Gary, West Virginia* (Knoxville, TN, 2011); Thomas E. Wagner and Philip Obermiller, *African American Miners and Migrants: The Eastern Kentucky Social Club* (Urbana, IL, 2004).

28. Mary Harris Jones, *The Autobiography of Mother Jones* (Chicago, IL, 1925), 232. For some of the best and most recent work on coal communities, see Richard J. Callahan, Jr., *Work and Faith in the Kentucky Coal Fields: Subject to Dust* (Bloomington, IN, 2009); Alessandro Portelli, *They Say in Harlan County: An Oral History* (New York, 2011); Brian Kelly, *Race, Class, and Power in the Alabama Coalfields, 1908–1921* (Urbana, IL, 2001).

29. For one of the best recent discussions of this difference, see Shelton Stromquist, *Reinventing "the People": The Progressive Movement, the Class Problem, and the Origins of Modern Liberalism* (Urbana, IL, 2006). See also, Robert D. Johnston, *The Radical Middle Class: Populist Democracy and the Question of Capitalism in Progressive Era Portland, Oregon* (Princeton, NJ, 2006). For the dilemma of West Virginia's Progressive Movement when facing the question of class, see Gary Jackson Tucker, *Governor William E. Glasscock and Progressive Politics in West Virginia* (Morgantown, WV., 2008), especially chapter 8.

30. For recent discussions of the producerism of late nineteenth century labor philosophy, see Rosanne Currarino, *The Labor Question in America: Economic Democracy in the Gilded Age* (Urbana, IL, 2011); Ronald Schultz, "The Small-Producer

Tradition and the Moral Origins of Artisan Radicalism in Philadelphia, 1720–1810," *Past and Present* 127 (May 1990): 84–116; and Eric Foner, "Free Labor and Nineteenth-Century Political Ideology," in *The Market Revolution in America: Social, Political, and Religious Expressions, 1800–1880*, ed. by Melvyn Stokes and Stephen Conway (Charlottesville, VA, 1996).

31. For later works that elaborate on the importance of the Hitchman case, see Richard Lunt, *Law and Order vs. the Miners* (Hamden, CT, 1979); William E. Forbath, *Law and the Shaping of the American Labor Movement* (Cambridge, MA, 1991); and Daniel R. Ernst, *Lawyers Against Labor: From Individual Rights to Corporate Liberalism* (Urbana, IL, 1995).

32. Fred Barkey, "Fritz Merrick: Parkersburg Rebel with a Cause," *West Virginia History* 57 (1998): 77–94.

33. Salvatore, *Eugene V. Debs*, Part I. See also, Barkey's subsequent work on the fraternal lodge loyalties of coal miners, "Red Men and Rednecks: The Fraternal Lodge in the Coal Fields," *West Virginia Historical Society Quarterly* 17 (January 2003), accessed on-line at *http://www.wvculture.org/history/wvhs1701.html* (accessed May 8, 2011).

34. Frederick A. Barkey, *Cinderheads in the Hills: The Belgian Window Glass Workers of West Virginia* (Charleston, WV, 1988). See also Robert Lookabill, "The Hand Window Glass Worker in West Virginia: A Study of His Skill, Union Organization, and Life Style," (M.A. thesis, Marshall University, 1971); and Fones-Wolf, *Glass Towns*, especially chapter 5.

35. Frederick A. Barkey, "Here Come the Boomer 'Talys': Italian Immigrants and Industrial Conflict in the Upper Kanawha Valley, 1903–1917," in *Transnational West Virginia*, 161–89. See also, Charles H. McCormick, "The Death of Constable Riggs: Ethnic Conflict in Marion County in the World War I Era," *West Virginia History* 52 (1993): 33–58; William B. Klaus, "Uneven Americanization: Italian Immigration to Marion County, 1900–1925," in *Transnational West Virginia*, 191–214; and Davitt McAteer, *Monongah: The Tragic Story of the 1907 Monongah Mine Disaster* (Morgantown, WV., 2007). See also the important collection, *The Lost World of Italian-American Radicalism*, edited by Philip Cannistraro and Gerald Meyer (Westport, CT, 2003).

36. Still the best study of women in Socialist Party politics is Mary Jo Buhle, *Women and American Socialism, 1870–1920* (Urbana, IL, 1983).

37. Denise Giardina, *Storming Heaven: A Novel* (New York, NY, 1987). For the

dearth of scholarship on women in the mine wars, see Corbin, *Life, Work, and Rebellion*; Lon Savage, *Thunder in the Mountains: The West Virginia Mine War, 1920–21* (Pittsburgh, PA, 1990); Rebecca J. Bailey, *Matewan Before the Massacre: Politics, Coal, and the Roots of Conflict in a West Virginia Mining Community* (Morgantown, WV, 2008).

38. Ronald L. Lewis, *Black Coal Miners in America: Race, Class, and Community Conflict, 1780–1980* (Lexington, KY, 1987); Joe William Trotter, Jr., *Coal, Class, and Color: Blacks in Southern West Virginia, 1915–32* (Urbana, IL, 1990). For Edmunds, see, Ronald L. Lewis, "The Black Presence in the Paint-Cabin Creek Strike, 1912–1913," *West Virginia History* 46 (1985–86): 66.

39. See, for examples, Green, Grass Roots Socialism, chapter 4; Salvatore, *Eugene V. Debs*, 62–65, 311–12; Donald E. Winters, *Soul of the Wobblies: The I.W.W., Religion, and American Culture in the Progressive Era, 1905–1917* (Westport, CT, 1985); Callahan, *Work and Faith in the Kentucky Coal Fields*; Jarod Roll, *Spirit of Rebellion: Labor and Religion in the New Cotton South* (Urbana, IL, 2010); Joe Creech, *Righteous Indignation: Religion and the Populist Revolution* (Urbana, IL, 2006).

40. For the spread of Pentecostalism in the coalfields, see Michael Szpak, "Removing the 'Mark of the Beast': The Church of God (Cleveland, Tennessee) and Organized Labor, 1908–1934," *Labor's Heritage* 6 (Summer 1994): 46–61.

41. Randall Stephens, *The Fire Spreads: Holiness and Pentecostalism in the American South* (Cambridge, MA, 2008); Grant Wacker, *Heaven Below: Early Pentecostals and American Culture* (Cambridge, MA, 2001).

42. Stephen Cresswell, "When the Socialists Ran Star City," *West Virginia History* 52 (1993): 59–72; *Socialists in a Small Town: The Socialist Victory in Adamston, West Virginia* (Buckhannon, WV, 1992); Fones-Wolf, *Glass Towns*.

43. Graham Adams, Jr., *Age of Industrial Violence, 1910–15: The Activities and Findings of the United States Commission on Industrial Relations* (New York, NY, 1966).

44. Lee Morrill Wolfe, "Radical Third-Party Voting among Coal Miners, 1896–1940," (Ph.D. dissertation, University of Michigan, 1976); Michael H. Nash, *Conflict and Accommodation: Coal Miners, Steel Workers, and Socialism, 1890–1920* (Westport, CT, 1982).

45. *Wheeling Majority*, February 16, 1911.

46. Full text of the committee report was published in *West Virginia History*. See "Committee Condemns W. Va. Mine Owners": Debs, Germer, and Berger Report," *West Virginia History* 52 (1993): 19–26.

47. David A. Corbin, "Betrayal in the West Virginia Coal Fields: Eugene V. Debs and the Socialist Party of America, 1912–1914," *Journal of American History* 64 (1978): 987–1009; Corbin, "Appraising Roger Fagge's 'Eugene V. Debs in West Virginia, 1913: A Reappraisal,'" *West Virginia History* 52 (1993): 27–32.

48. Roger Fagge, "Eugene V. Debs in West Virginia, 1913: A Reappraisal," *West Virginia History* 52 (1993): 1–18.

49. Bert Castle interview with Bill Taft, June 19, 1973, W.V.R.H.C. Thanks to Jim Green for calling this interview to my attention.

50. See "Mother" Jones to Eugene V. Debs, July 5, 1913, in *The Correspondence of Mother Jones*, ed. by Edward M. Steele (Pittsburgh, PA, 1985), p. 117. See also, Edward M. Steele, Jr., *The Court-Martial of Mother Jones* (Lexington, KY, 1995), 83.

51. See the forthcoming work by James R. Green on the mine wars and the struggle for democracy in West Virginia, especially chapter 11. I appreciate Jim for letting me see an advance copy of his manuscript and allowing me to mention this fact. See also, Trotter, Jr., *Coal, Class, and Color*, for African Americans, and Gorby, "Subculture in Conflict in *Polonia*," 21–24.

52. Fones-Wolf, *Glass Towns*, p. 139. See especially, Maureen Flanagan, *American Reformed: Progressives and Progressivisms, 1890s–1920s* (New York, NY, 2007). For the use of the city-manager form of municipal government to blunt working-class influence, see James Weinstein, *The Corporate Ideal in the Liberal State, 1900–1918* (Boston, MA, 1968).

53. Shannon, *Socialist Party of America*, chapter 3; Weinstein, *Decline of Socialism*, 110–15.

54. Weinstein, *Decline of Socialism*, 105–06; Melvyn Dubofsky, *The State and Labor in Modern America* (Chapel Hill, NC, 1994), 53–60 (quote from p. 55).

55. Workman, "Political Culture and the Coal Economy," 256–62.

56. Elliott J. Gorn, *Mother Jones: The Most Dangerous Woman in America* (New York, NY, 2001), 244–45.

57. For some of the best of the subsequent literature on this point, see Joseph A. McCartin, *Labor's Great War: The Struggle for Industrial Democracy and the Origins of Modern American Labor Relations, 1912–1921* (Chapel Hill, NC, 1997); David Montgomery, *The Fall of the House of Labor: The Workplace, the State, and American Labor Activism, 1865–1925* (New York, NY, 1987); Alan Dawley, *Struggles for Justice: Social Responsibility and the Liberal State* (Cambridge, MA, 1991); *Industrial Democracy in*

America: The Ambiguous Promise, ed. by Nelson Lichtenstein and Howell John Harris (New York, NY, 1993).

58. *The Speeches and Writings of Mother Jones*, ed. by Edward Steel (Pittsburgh, PA, 1988), 189–91; Fones-Wolf, *Glass Towns*, 139–41.

59. However, when federal officials put Debs in the prison in Moundsville for his anti-war speeches, local Socialists went to considerable effort to make him as comfortable as possible; even the warden of the Moundsville prison gave Debs special privileges. See Salvatore, *Eugene V. Debs*, 308–09.

60. See, for example, Agent 35 to C. E. Smith, October 18, 1919, and Agent 37 to Smith, October 25, 1919, in C. E. Smith Papers, West Virginia and Regional History Collection, West Virginia University, Morgantown, WV. For a broader coverage of this topic, see Charles H. McCormick, *Seeing Reds: Federal Surveillance of Radicals in the Pittsburgh Mill District, 1917–1921* (Pittsburgh, PA, 1997).

61. *New York Times*, October 8, 9, 1919. For more, see John C. Hennen, *The Americanization of West Virginia: Creating a Modern Industrial State, 1916–1925* (Lexington, KY, 1996)

62. The classic statement of the outlook of craftsmen is still found in Montgomery, *Workers' Control in America*.

63. Seymour Martin Lipset and Gary Marks, *It Didn't Happen Here: Why Socialism Failed in the United States* (New York, NY, 2000).

64. Fagge, "Eugene V. Debs in West Virginia," 12–15.

65. Otis K. Rice, *West Virginia: A History* (Lexington, KY, 1985), 212–18. For a more jaded view of Progressivism in West Virginia, see Williams, *Captains of Industry*, chapter 7.

66. See especially, Hennen, *Americanization of West Virginia*.

Acknowledgments

I wish it were possible to recognize each of the many individuals who have contributed directly and indirectly to the completion of this study. Only a few can be noted to whom I here express my gratitude.

My deep appreciation to the late Dr. David Montgomery, Department of History, Yale University, whose wisdom, patience, and encouragement guided my research and whose life and work remain an inspiration to all his students.

I desire to thank the officials and personnel of libraries who gave of their time in the interest of aiding my efforts. Among them were Frank and Joan Badger of the University of Charleston Library; Mrs. E. M. Ashworth, Mrs. C. Bowen, and Ms. J. Brandt of the West Virginia Department of History and Archives; Mrs. Virginia Gray of the Duke University Library; the staff of the Tamiment Institute; and Dr. William Hess and his staff at the West Virginia University Library.

This project would have been almost impossible without the interviews given to me by members, relatives, and friends of the West Virginia workers. In this regard, my specific thanks go to old radicals such as George Glass, Price Williams, Alfred Lavender, Wyatt Thompson, George Harper, and Sylvanus Goff.

I am very grateful to the timeless efforts of my long-suffering typists Ms. Ruby Benson and Ms. Mary Ann McMillian.

And, finally, I am deeply indebted to Dr. Ken Fones-Wolf of the History Department of West Virginia University and Mr. Gordon Simmons, field organizer for the United Electrical Workers Local 170 in West Virginia, for their contribution to the completion of this project.

Introduction

It is difficult to convince most Americans that their country has had a significant Socialist tradition. Since there has been no visible Socialist movement in the United States for a generation or more, it is easy to conclude that this has always been so. Therefore, even educated citizens are startled when they discover that the American Socialist Party before World War I had over 150,000 due-paying members. This party also secured for Eugene Victor Debs almost 1 million votes for the presidency, elected over 2,000 candidates to public office and published hundreds of newspapers and journals. Contemporary Americans are also frequently surprised to discover that Socialist union members once represented a real force to be reckoned with in the labor movement. In the minds of many citizens, labor organizations have always been the bulwarks of the status quo which they are today. Nothing symbolizes this conservative role more than the recent spectacle of hard-hat, blue-collar workers defending Wall Street against young people bent on radical social change.

American scholarship has been partly responsible for the prevailing ignorance of Socialist movements in the United States. Until relatively recent times, little had been done to preserve any heritage that went beyond a capitalistic social system. Ira Kipnis, when he wrote his groundbreaking history of the Socialist Party in 1952, complained that there had been only two articles in the previous thirty years in professional scholarly publications on this subject.[1] However, this picture was gradually changing. Joining Kipnis in the field were Donald Egbert and Stow Persons who edited two volumes containing essays and extensive bibliography that demonstrated the pervasiveness of socialistic thought in American life.[2] Within a few years, scholars had rounded out the history of the Socialist Party at the national level and begun investigations of specific aspects of party activity.³ The extent to which the working-class members of a particular region were influenced by the party has been one area of interest.⁴ It is to add to the latter knowledge that his study of the West Virginia Socialist Party was undertaken.

The Socialist Party's greatest period of growth coincided with the Progressive Movement of the early twentieth century. Research concerning workers interest in socialism can, therefore, provide needed enrichment to standard views of labor's role and attitude during this important era. General histories of these years have tended to relegate the worker to a rather passive role. Even those scholars who were more sensitive to the interests of the laboring classes have only reported the ways in which reformers made workers the object of protective legislation rather than examining the role and outlook of the laborers themselves.⁵ Recognizing this, J. Joseph Huthmacher called for state studies that would develop a fuller perspective in the part played by labor in the accomplishments of this period.⁶

It has not been easy to generate discussion of labor's role in radical and reform movements. A paucity of materials may be partially to blame for the lack of such studies. The orientation of the early labor historian is even more responsible. The original impetus in the field of labor history came with the first two volumes of John R. Commons' *Cooperative History of Labor in the United States*. Commons and those he influenced, such as Selig Perlman, Phillip Taft, and, more recently, Gerald W. Grob, were primarily interested in the ways which the unions of the American Federation of Labor had produced a permanent national organization capable of weathering depressions and the threat of technological displacement. The answer seemed to be, as Selig Perlman called it in *A Theory of the Labor Movement*, a new "job-conscious" unionism. By this, he referred to the pattern established by the American Federation of Labor leaders of accepting the capitalistic system and setting only practical goals.⁷ Most labor historians, therefore, concentrated on the steps taken by those organizations that followed this pragmatic path and gave less attention to the worker's interest in more radical approaches to industrial problems.

The scholarly work done on the history of West Virginia labor conforms to the institutional approach used by the Commons' school. For example, Thomas E. Posey, a student of Selig Perlman, has written of the West Virginia State Federation of Labor:

> ...the internal dissension which characterizes the history of the West Virginia Federation was not due to any ideological differences among the leaders of any fundamental disagreement over policy. The question of Socialist vs. Communist, of left wing vs. right wing, never appeared as an issue.[8]

Several writers have dealt with some of the more sensational strikes of the area.[9] These studies have not usually been placed in a wide enough context to avoid oversimplification of causes and of the reactions of both business and labor. The only local study that has moved far enough beyond the restraints of the institutional approach to even begin to demonstrate the worker's interest in broad social and political questions is Evelyn Harris and Frank Krebs' pioneering history of the West Virginia State Federation of Labor.[10]

The purpose of this study is to examine the character and influence of the West Virginia Socialist Party during the Progressive years. The particular focus will be on the party's appeal to the working class of the area. It is hoped that, within the particular historic, social, and economic context of West Virginia, a more complete understanding of labor's attitudes may be achieved.

The first problem is to obtain a clear picture of the social characteristics of important working-class members of the West Virginia party. This will be partially achieved through discussion of background and experiences of key figures who are scattered throughout the study. However, in order to present a more complete picture, a collective biography will be constructed. The purpose will be to determine if any patterns of common characteristics can be discovered in those West Virginia workers who turned to socialism.

Particular emphasis will be placed on such variables as ethnic origin, religious affiliation, age, trade, education, and political traditions. The characteristics of the radical sample will be compared to a control group consisting of important West Virginia workingmen who remained within the established parties. Wilbur Moore has suggested that such a study may produce no general principles to explain susceptibility to socialism that can be disassociated from the particular circumstances surrounding each case. On the other hand, as Professor Moore admits, "...too little is known concerning the social determinants in adherence to Socialist schemes of reform."[11]

The second problem is to determine the role and influence that the Socialist Party had on the progress of organized labor in West Virginia. National unions, which were greatly influenced by their Socialist members, had strong local organizations in the state. Among these were the brewery workers, machinists, glassworkers, stogie-makers, and miners.[12] This group includes organizations that both industrial and craft in their structure and whose members were both immigrant and native born. This study will attempt to discover the attitudes of the Socialist members of these and other unions in problems affecting their trade. The influence of the radical trade unionists in the West Virginia State Federation of Labor and in several city trades and labor assemblies will also be examined.

Another question is the determination of how local workers viewed the political role of the local Socialist Party. Recent research has been building a case for greater labor political participation and interest in reform issues that had previously been suspected. Irwin Yellowitz has joined J. J. Huthmacher in showing that the working class was actively involved in progressive politics in Massachusetts and New York.[13] Frederick Heath has shown that a similar situation prevailed in Connecticut.[14] A study has suggested that even the American Federation of Labor was active in national politics from 1900 to 1918.[15] Were the workers in West Virginia sincerely interested in issues of municipal ownership of utilities, workmen's compensation, mine and factory inspection, child labor, prohibition, and change in election procedures, which were all part of the political atmosphere of the state? Did the workers see the West Virginia Socialist Party as a vehicle for achieving those reform goals or were the local workers more concerned with revolutionary changes in the social order which the party also promised? The answer to such questions may provide more insight into the synthesis of native American radicalism and some variant of Marxism that appealed to the traditions of Mountain State laboring people.

The final problem is to explain the reasons for the failure of the West Virginia Socialist Party to retain the loyalty of its working-class supporters. Historians have traditionally emphasized that the American Socialist Party started an irreversible decline in 1912 and was all but wiped out by the First World War.[16] More recently, one historian has attacked this standard interpretation by suggesting that the Socialist Party actually grew in power after 1912 and came through the First World War stronger than ever.[17] For the most part, these works have been based upon the actions and attitudes of the Socialist Party's national leaders. By examining the external and internal factors that limited the West Virginia Socialist's attempts to build a working-class base at the local level, some insights may be gained as to why America does not have a viable Socialist Party.

NOTES

1. Kipnis did acknowledge the chapters on the Socialist Party in *Nathan Fine's Labor and Farmer Parties in the United States, 1828–1912*. Ira Kipnis, *The American Socialist Movement, 1897–1912* (New York, 1952), 4–5.

2. Donald Egbert and Stow Parsons, eds., *Socialism in American Life*, Vol. II (Princeton, NJ, 1952).

3. The basic elements that were combined to form the Socialist Party in 1901 are covered in Quint Howard, *The Forging of American Socialism; Origins of a Modern Movement* (Columbia, SC, 1953); David Shannon, *The Socialist Party of America* (New York, 1955), continues the history of the party from 1912 to its demise in 1936.

4. See Henry F. Bedford, *Socialism and the Workers in Massachusetts,*

1886–1912,(Amherst, MA, 1966); H. L. Meredith, "Agrarian Socialism and the Negro in Oklahoma," *Labor History,* II (Summer, 1970), 277–84.

5.   Arthur M. Schlesinger, Jr., *The Crisis of the Old Order* (Boston, 1957), 23–25; James M. Burns, *Roosevelt: The Lion and the Fox* (New York, 1956, 42; Arthur S. Link, *American Epoch* (New York, 1955), 72; George Mowry, *The California Progressives, 1900–1920* (Berkeley, 1951); Charles N. Glaab, "The Failure of North Dakota Progressivism," *Mid-America* XXXIX (October, 1957), 195–203; Richard M. Abrams, *Conservatism in a Progressive Era: Massachusetts Politics, 1900–1912* (Cambridge, 1964).

6.   J. Joseph Huthmacher, "Urban Liberalism and the Age of Reform," *The Mississippi Valley Historical Review* XLIX (September, 1962), 231–41.

7.   Mark Perlman, *Labor Union Theories in America* (New York, 1958), 195–202.

8.   Thomas E. Posey, "The Labor Movement in West Virginia, 1900–1948" (Unpublished doctoral dissertation, University of Wisconsin, 1948), 67–69.

9.   John M. Barb, "Strikes in the Southern West Virginia Coal Fields, 1912–1922" (Unpublished M.A., West Virginia University, 1949); Kyle McCormick, *The New-Kanawha River and the Mine War of West Virginia* (Charleston, 1959); Charles B. Crawford, "The Mine War on Cabin Creek and Paint Creek, West Virginia in 1912–1913" (Unpublished M.A., University of Kentucky, 1939).

10.   Evelyn Harris and Frank Krebs, *From Humble Beginnings: West Virginia State Federation of Labor, 1903–1957* (Charleston, WV, 1960).

11.   Wilbur E. Moore, "Sociological Aspects of American Socialism," in Donald D. Egbert and Stow Parsons, eds., *Socialism in American Life* (Princeton, 1952), I, 554.

12.   Philip Taft, *Organized Labor in American History* (New York, 1964), 323.

13.   Irwin Yellowitz, *Labor and the Progressive Movement in New York State, 1897–1916* (Ithaca, 1965), 2–6.

14.   Frederick M. Heath, "Labor and the Progressive Movement in Connecticut," *Labor History* XII (Winter, 1971), 52–67.

15.   Marc Karson, *American Labor Unions and Politics: 1900–1918* (Carbondale, IL, 1958), ix–xi.

16.   Kipnis, *American Socialist*; David Shannon, *Socialist Party.*

17.   James Weinstein, *The Decline of Socialism in America, 1912–1925* (New York, 1967), vii–xi.

CHAPTER I
The Origins Of West Virginia Socialism: 1898–1904

The first significant Socialist movement in West Virginia was produced during a period of rapid industrial growth. Although this economic transformation had begun much earlier in the century, it was not until the late 1890s that the pace of development so quickened as to disturb the basic patterns of life in several regions of the Mountain State. An increased need for workers brought together groups of skilled and unskilled labor with a variety of both crafts and experiences. Some members of this working force brought with them more than their sweat, muscle, and skill. They also brought a vision of a new social order.

By the early years of the twentieth century, the signs of West Virginia's industrial growth were abundant. The rapid expansion of more main and branch lines had brought about railroad penetration of fifty-one of the fifty-five counties of the state by 1904.[1] This rail network speeded greatly the exploitation of the state's vast store of natural resources, with lumber, oil, coal, and glass production more than doubling between 1890 and 1900.[2]

The railroads also broadened the market possibilities for West Virginia's manufactured goods. Reflecting this potential was the increase of 85 percent in new manufacturing establishments in this period.[3] This industrial expansion was also evident in the trend toward urbanization. The majority of cities with populations of 2,000 experienced an increase ranging from 15 percent to more than 50 percent.[4]

The development of the natural resources of the mountain state, especially its coal and oil fields, had also helped to increase the population from 1890 to 1900 by more than 24 percent.[5] Much of this gain represented 72 percent jump in the number of West Virginia wage earners. A modern labor force was being created that first drew heavily from native, white American stock, but gradually added significant numbers of foreigners and Negroes.[6] In several areas of the state, members of this working force were sowing the seeds of the West Virginia Socialist Movement.

The Wheeling Roots of West Virginia Socialism

The earliest and most impressive Socialist organization in West Virginia centered in the Wheeling area. This might well have been predicted as the so-called "Nail City" as it was the oldest and most industrialized community in the state with a diversity in manufacturing that included important production in iron and steel, pottery, wood, bronze and brass fabricating, glass, cigar making, brewery, and meat packing.[7] Furthermore, by 1902 the skilled labor demands of this business complex had created a well-developed union movement that accounted for 45 percent of the total craft union membership in the state.[8] It would appear, however, that there was no formal Socialist organization until a group of workers and some middle-class allies became interested in the Social Democracy movement.

Much of the impetus for Social Democracy in Wheeling came, as it so often did elsewhere, from the influence of the movement's founder, Eugene V. Debs. At the time of the coal strike of 1897, the threat posed to the miners' national success by the largely unorganized West Virginia coal fields prompted the United Mine Workers of America to dispatch prominent labor leaders to promote unionization of the state. Debs, J. W. Roe, vice president of the Painters and Decorators National Union, Mary "Mother" Jones, and others had tried unsuccessfully to organize the northern West Virginia coal fields. Part of their strategy had been to induce local labor organizations to sponsor a public meeting in order to rally support for the miners and to condemn the mine operator's use of guards and injunctions.[9]

On July 27, 1897, Debs addressed a crowd in downtown Wheeling, estimated at 5,000. After a brief explanation of the strike situation, Debs used the occasion to launch a full-blown exposition of socialism and appealed to the throng to correct the present social and economic conditions by adopting such a system.[10]

The plea of Eugene Debs for a society based more upon socialistic principles was received sympathetically in several quarters in the Wheeling area. Socialist literature had already been circulating among the workers in several of Wheeling's plants.[11] In addition, there is evidence to suggest that informal meetings to discuss "socialism and all its phases" were being held around several of the iron factories.[12] It was exactly this type of atmosphere that produced one of the most important leaders of the earliest formal Wheeling Socialist organization.

Harry Leeds was born in Lancaster County, Pennsylvania, of English and German background. Orphaned at the age of nine, Leeds ran away from an institution when he was fourteen and eventually went to work for the railroad in Pittsburgh. There he became a boilermaker in the Baltimore and Ohio shops and made a good reputation as an intelligent and industrious worker. In about 1892, at the age of thirty, Leeds came to Wheeling as a foreman in the United States Steel Plant at Benwood. Sometime in 1896, Socialist literature was being circulated through the Benwood works. The management wanted the practice stopped. As a result, Harry Leeds was ordered to fire Anthony Osterman, an iron puddler in his crew. Ironically, Leeds had read Osterman's literature, but never realized the truth of the picture of the tenuous status of the workers in the capitalistic industrial system until he refused to follow his superior's directive and was himself let go.[13]

Thus, by the time Debs had made his appeal in July of 1897, Harry Leeds, having read deeply in Socialist literature, was ready to work for a chapter of the Social Democracy.[14] Gradually, a nucleus of Socialists were brought together, and in 1900, the Eugene V. Debs Chapter of the Social Democracy of Wheeling was launched.[15]

Besides Leeds and several other workers, the membership of the Social Democratic Party included a number of small business and professional people. For example, there was Joseph Yahn, an owner of a small stogie-making shop: John L. Bachman, a lawyer; Fred A. Zimmerman, the publisher of the *Benwood Enterprize*; and Dr. George B. Kline.[16] This leadership was almost solidly German in background. Some were like Valentine Reuther in that their families had been forced to flee Europe because of their unorthodox political and economic beliefs.[17] At any rate, though small in numbers, the Wheeling Socialists soon began to make their influence felt.

Good Social Democratic principles taught that if the Cooperative Commonwealth was to be established, the masses had to be thoroughly organized and indoctrinated.[18] The existence of a central body like the Ohio Valley Trades and Labor Assembly provided the Wheeling Socialist with an excellent opportunity for persuading a wider circle of union men to their position. The Assembly had been founded in 1882 and by 1903 represented some forty-two craft unions. Its activities were far ranging and included arbitrating local management—worker disputes, Union label campaigns, and boycotts against unfair employers, and nonunion work. The Assembly also was concerned with securing favorable labor legislation at the local state and national level.[19]

The key offices in the Assembly occupied by Socialists made a warmer reception to the overtures of the local Socialist organization more likely. A comrade, Albert Bauer, occupied the presidency. How Bauer became a Socialist is not clear, but his career had certainly taken him to circles where such doctrines were strong options. After growing up in Wheeling and learning his trade, he worked during the 1880s in both Chicago and Cincinnati. In the latter city he was well known in labor ranks and served as the secretary for the Carpenter's District Council. Bauer later returned to Wheeling in 1892 and moved up very quickly in the central body.[20] Furthermore, in his espousal of the Socialist position, President Bauer could depend on two of his vice presidents: J. T. Hecker, a stogie-maker, and

M. E. Tracey, as well as the Assembly organizer, Louis Hayes.[21] In April of 1900, this group convinced the rest of the Assembly's executive committee that Eugene V. Debs should be secured for a meeting in order to "...promulgate among the working classes knowledge of the power they possess, and the benefits to be derived from their action."[22]

The Debs speech of April 27, 1900 at the Trades and Assembly Hall struck a respondent chord in an audience made up mostly of skilled craftsmen. He painted a placid picture of the times before the era of present industrial conditions. Those were the days of happy toilers when there was no such thing as over-production and where articles were produced for use and not just for profits. It was the machine and mass production, Debs continued, that had changed everything. This wouldn't be so bad if the workers could now at least purchase what they produced. But they could not, and the result was the concentration of wealth in fewer hands and periodic panics, which created that ubiquitous, modern social phenomenon—the tramp.[23]

The Socialists in the Trades Assembly followed up the Debs rally with circulation of literature and soliciting subscriptions for the *Appeal to Reason*.[24] These techniques produced a significant victory in that the Trades and Labor Assembly agreed with one of the major objectives of their more radical brothers. The Social Democrats hoped that socialism in America could be achieved through the gradual nationalization of trusts and municipal ownership of public utilities.[25] In keeping with this goal, Bauer and his comrades succeeded in getting the Trades and Labor Assembly to declare itself in favor of public ownership of all utilities and a thorough reform of these utilities in the interest of the people.[26] Furthermore, Albert Bauer continued to push this issue at every opportunity. Just after his term of office ended in 1901, he urged the Assembly to do all it could to secure the election to municipal office of only those candidates who would pledge themselves to fight the extraordinarily long-term franchise then being demanded of the Wheeling Citizen's Railway Company.[27]

The Wheeling Social Democrats were also making their influence felt politically. They were neither strong enough financially nor sufficiently well organized to promote local candidates, but they did what they could to support the Debs-Harriman candidacy in the presidential campaign of 1900. Harry Leeds organized a pre-election rally for October 25. The turnout at Wheeling's Arvin Hall was good and Debs set forth one of the major tenents of the Social Democratic philosophy. Reflecting the populist and nationalistic background of the movement, he explained that the trend toward economic centralization was inevitable. However, this tendency was "...not an evil but simply a perverted good. The Socialists will convert this question into a blessing by taking it and operating it to the good of the people."[28] Then in a more Marxian vein, Debs pointed out that the contradictions of a capitalistic system where workers secured only one-fifth of the value of what they produced would ultimately bring them to the realization that a cooperative social order must supplant the present competitive one.[29] Though the resultant vote for Debs and Harriman was small, the Social Democrats had at least made themselves the strongest of the minority parties in Ohio County.[30]

In the summer of 1901, the Wheeling chapter of the Social Democratic Party had reconstituted itself as the Eugene V. Debs Chapter of the Socialist Party of America.[31] This development caused some changes in the Wheeling movement. For example, the range of speaking talent it could draw upon was increased. In October of 1901, Louis Hayes chaired a meeting addressed by Max Hayes of Cleveland.[32] Hayes was the editor of the *Cleveland Citizen* and a member of the Rochester faction, which had split away from the Socialist labor party to form the New Socialist Party of the United States in June of 1901.[33] In addition, a winter meeting was scheduled for Father McGrady, a Bellamyite priest, from Bellevue, Kentucky.[34] The most important change, however, was the greater emphasis the local organization would place on political activity.

The new Socialist Party of America was to place much greater emphasis upon winning local and national political activity. Until this was achieved, it saw the old Social Democratic goal of municipal and government ownership only as an additional step in capitalism—albeit a progressive one.[35] Such an approach appears to have made good sense to the Wheeling Socialist not only from the point of view of achieving future objectives but also for safeguarding those victories already won. "There is not lasting gain for the amount of energy expended on the lines that labor unions are working at present," said President Bauer in his annual report to the Trades and Labor Assembly in 1901. "Nor can there be until we recognize the fact that labor is entitled to all it produces and arrange our labor organization with that objective in view, organizing ourselves on the political field as well as on the economic to do away with any system that deprives labor either of brain or hand of its full products."[36]

The Wheeling Socialists launched their drive to convert the Ohio Valley Trades and Labor Assembly to political action under their leadership early in 1902. Their timing appears to have been excellent as the Assembly had been deeply disappointed in the lawmakers of their own city and in the legislative halls of the State Capitol at Charleston. On the surface, it would appear that the State Legislature, which met in 1901, did not have a bad labor record. It had passed a mild industrial accident bill, a bill to protect union labels and trademarks, and created a free public employment bureau.[37] On the other hand, some of the most desirable labor and reform bills were disposed of in what the Wheeling union men felt was a most cavalier fashion. The Humane Institutions Committee killed the Child Labor Bill, the Judiciary Committee ignored a proposal for a State Board of Arbitration and conciliation, corporation lobbies defeated a meaningful Employers' Liability Act, the Factory Inspection Bill was not presented, and someone "lost" the bill to create a State Board of Examiners for Stationary Engineers.[38] Similarly disappointing had been the Assembly's Legislative Committee's joint meeting with the Wheeling Board of Control over such varied matters as keeping the streets cleaned in some efficient manner to greater revenue from city-authorized franchise operations. The discussions on these matters in March of 1902 had produced nothing but "a long protracted struggle."[39]

The Socialists in the Trades and Labor Assembly saw in their fellow workingmen's discontent with the political forces of the day a golden opportunity. The radicals' tactics and attitudes in capitalizing on this atmosphere suggests that early Socialist branches may have been more flexible than their national leadership. Ira Kipnis has pointed out that official Socialist strategy at this time urged party members to create class consciousness by general discussions in union meetings that would lead to support for labor reforms or endorsement of the Socialist Party. On the other hand, good party members were admonished to refuse "to support any attempts by unions to form local or national political parties around the issues of injunctions, labor legislation, political corruption and municipal ownership."[40] However, when the Wheeling radicals failed to obtain endorsement for Socialist candidates from the Trades and Labor Assembly, they did not hesitate to urge a union-sponsored party as a reasonable alternative.

After their frustrating session with the Wheeling Board of Trade, the Socialist-dominated Legislative Committee of the Trades Assembly reported that they felt the Central Labor Body had been negligent in not taking a more active part in municipal affairs; therefore, the Committee proposed that it should be represented on the next city council.[41] Immediately the major obstacles to all such schemes were raised. Delegate John Teufel, a carpenter and an active Catholic layman, requested the floor.[42] He wished the proposal of the legislative committee tabled because the purpose of the Assembly was looking after interests of the workingman. Going into politics would surely bring about the disruption of the central body.[43] Thus, Tuefel evidenced the belief that the central body's major concern ought to be with more practical and immediate demands, and that if partisan issues were raised, members of long-standing political affiliation might withdraw.

At the next meeting of the Trades and Labor Assembly, the Socialists tried to convert that organization to their political position. Jacob Boes, a member of the Typographical Union, was given the floor in order to invite its delegates to be present at a Socialist speech on the twenty-seventh at the Assembly's Hall. Boes used the occasion to urge the Assembly's participation in politics under the Socialist banner.[44] The Assembly's new president, Michael Mahoney, a steelworker, informed Boes that a partisan political argument would not be permitted.[45] The debate, however, went on. Socialists like J. T. Hecker and Mat Greer spoke in favor of Boes's idea while delegate Tuefel was quick to support President Mahoney's position. Tuefel stated that the Garfield Trades and Labor Assembly, which he represented, was opposed to mixing politics with labor matters and that in his opinion, if the question was taken back to the locals, not a half dozen of the representation would be authorized to bring up political matters. Delegate Lyons reduced the level of discussion and accused the Socialists of crass opportunism; "when Republicans are in power, they are Republicans and when the Democrats are in power, they are Democrats."[46]

Although delegates to the Trades and Labor Assembly were not ready to follow the Socialist leadership all the way, they were, nevertheless, interested in political action. Delegate Tuefel moved that questions of political participation be taken back to the local unions for endorsement. This motion was defeated by a 24 to 23 vote.[47] Instead, the delegates worked out an acceptable plan for political participation. The Assembly demanded that the Democrats and Republicans each nominate two laboring men on their House of Delegates ticket in the fall of 1902.[48] At this point, a new Socialist strategy seemed to emerge. This plan, which Socialists felt had a much greater chance for success, was to create an independent labor ticket whose composition would be as radical as possible. In the Assembly's next meeting Albert Bauer pointed out that it was foolish to expect anything from the old political parties; instead the workers should present their own labor ticket.[49] This was followed by a proposal by Comrade S. H. Engle that the Assembly go on record as refusing to endorse any candidate who is opposed to the public ownership of public utilities.[50] Finally, in what must have been a tongue-in-cheek proposal, J. T. Hecker urged that the legislative committee demand that laboring men be given a majority of places on the ballots of both parties for the State Legislature.[51] Although only Engles's proposal appeared to have passed the Assembly, several other Socialists were able to state their position. They said that the Socialist Party would not put its own ticket into the field in the fall but rather would lend its sponsorship to an independent labor ticket for the city election in January.[52]

The action of the major parties in their conventions during the summer of 1902 gave the Trades and Assembly Socialists more ammunition with which to push their proposals. Instead of the two nominees for the House of Delegates requested by the Assembly, the Republican Convention nominated only one, Daniel Moody. The Democratic Convention followed the same course with its nomination of a tin worker, John V. Meken.[53] Jacob Boes led a vigorous attack against the Assembly endorsing these nominations, which he labeled a mere token gesture. However, the forces for endorsement led by John Tuefel carried the day, but not before the delegates were again reminded by the radicals that what was really needed was an independent labor ticket.[54]

Exactly what happened to the Socialist-sponsored labor ticket is difficult to determine since most newspapers in the state only reported their party election returns when they were a real threat to the major parties. At any rate, there is no evidence that the idea was dropped. Nor is there evidence that the Wheeling Socialists were punished, as Ira Kipnis points out, as were the California Socialists for their sponsorship of a similar ticket in 1902.[55] It may well be that the Wheeling Socialist movement was too small to attract the attention of their more doctrinaire counterparts elsewhere. However, it was not long before the Wheeling movement gained more recognition with the national Socialist Party.

In 1903, William Mailly of Massachusetts was elected national secretary of the Socialist Party. Mailly embarked upon a campaign to invigorate the national movement by sending out organizers and lecturers, and by encouraging local affiliates to do the same.[56] The Wheeling area began to reap the benefits of this campaign. The local Socialists received immediate help from John Slayton, a carpenter from Western Pennsylvania who was then organizing for the party around Pittsburgh.[57] In addition, the Wheeling Socialists were promised the assistance of John C. Chase, the ex-mayor of Haverhill, Massachusetts, who was then on a tour of Southern Ohio, and of John M. Ray of Tennessee.[58] The real left organizationally came, however, in July 1903 when Mailly informed his West Virginia Comrades that the National Quorum of the Party had empowered him to select an organizer specifically for West Virginia.[59] For this position, Mailly chose George H. Goebel of New Jersey, who was to become a familiar figure with the Mountain State Socialists up to the time of his election to the National Executive Committee in 1910.[60]

The influx of national organizers into the Wheeling area produced a marked increase in local Socialist activities. With the help of John Slayton, Harry Leeds organized a new local at the nearby community of Moundsville.[61] In the Trades and Labor Assembly, Louis Hayes and H. T. Hecker proposed that the Assembly recommend to the members of its locals that they join the Socialist Clubs of the area.[62] Street meetings became the order of the day, with national leaders showing local Socialists the proper technique.[63] In at least one case, this led to arrest.

On August 24, 1903, *The Wheeling Intelligencer* reported that Harry Leeds brought two "strangers" to the so-called hub on lower Market Street in Wheeling.[64] One of the strangers was Frank O'Hare, who had been holding meetings in the area.[65] Since the only public meetings that could be held in Wheeling on Sundays had to be of a religious nature, Frank O'Hare carried a Bible and proceeded to preach a "Socialist Sermon." The subterfuge did not impress Wheeling police officer Schlick, who broke up the meeting and arrested the speakers.[66]

By 1904, the Socialist movement in the Wheeling area, though still small, continued to gain strength. There were five locals of the party functioning in the area. Besides the two in Wheeling and Moundsville, there were three others in Bridgeport, Bellaire, and Martins Ferry, Ohio, from which they could draw support.[67] There was significant strength among the glassworkers, typographical workers, carpenters, machinists, brewery workers, and, above all, stogie-makers.[68] Furthermore, the Wheeling Socialists had established an executive committee for the State of West Virginia with two of their members, Fred Zimmerman and Dr. George Kline, holding offices of chairman and secretary, respectively. This, in turn, had produced a state ticket in the general election with Socialist candidates for Congress, all major state offices, and the House of Delegates in Ohio County, as well as three other counties in the state.[69] The results of these efforts were gratifying to the Ohio County Socialist Party, which took satisfaction from the fact that in 1904 they were able to increase their vote some 300 percent over 1900.[70]

Individuals of a socialist persuasion were also being drawn into the newly created industrial life of several areas in West Virginia's southern Ohio River Valley. The Cabell County community of Huntington with almost 12,000 inhabitants was well on its way to becoming the fastest-growing city in West Virginia by 1900. This growth was attributable to two major factors. First of all, Huntington's location on the Ohio River allowed it to be the recipient of the greatly increasing river traffic that was accompanying industrial expansion all along the upper Ohio River Valley. Secondly, as the western end of the Chesapeake and Ohio Railroad line, it was one of the major links to West Virginia's extremely rich southern most coal fields.[71] It was this latter development that accounted for an early concentration of Socialists in the Huntington area. To understand more precisely how this happened, it is desirable to examine something of the industrialization process as it began at the eastern end of the state.

The Greenbrier River flows out of the high plateau county of southeastern West Virginia. Along much of its course the Chesapeake and Ohio had been responsible for the creation or expansion of many communities. The railroad's need for timber had transferred Ronceverte, a sleepy little Greenbrier County village of three houses, into a bustling business community by the late 1880s. Similarly, the community of Hinton, some thirty-five miles to the south of Ronceverte owed its existence to the location there of the Chesapeake and Ohio car repair yards and division headquarters.[72]

Into these communities flocked railroad workers following the line's progress from Covington, Virginia, through the mountains of West Virginia. Among the railroad brotherhoods in which their workers held membership, the Socialist position had a substantial following.[73] In the Greenbrier area a few dedicated Socialists carried on agitational activities through personal contact and by circulating the *Appeal to Reason*. Of this early group, the most active and influential was an engineer from Pennsylvania, A. O. Pope.[74]

Socialist agitation on a much greater scale was soon taking place at the larger Chesapeake and Ohio shop and marshalling yards in Huntington. A good deal of this socialism simply moved west with the personnel who had been converted at various stages along the line. Considerably more developed as the size of the workforce needed in these shops drew in workers from Ohio and Kentucky, as well as West Virginia.[75]

Joining the nucleus of Socialists from the railroad shops were building tradespeople and decorators who had come into Huntington to help supply the housing needs of this growing community. The group included such early leaders of the Huntington movement as Fred Eskew, a paperhanger, and Dana Harper, a brickmason.[76] This combined strength was sufficient to justify the establishment of a local of the Socialist Party in Huntington early in 1903.[77]

The Spread of Socialist Politics

The oil and gas boom that had propelled West Virginia to a position of the second largest producer of crude oil in the United States by 1901 also produced incidences of socialism.[78] West Virginia had been a pioneering area in this country's oil industry with many of the drill bits later used by the Drake operations being developed around the Wood Country community of Parkersburg.[79] By the 1890s, important oil fields were opened in counties of Tyler, Wetzel, and Wood, which bordered the Ohio River. At about the same time, other fields were being developed in neighboring counties like Doddridge, Ritchie, and Harrison through which pass streams that empty into the Ohio, and counties like Monongalia and Marion, where oil fields were extensions of the so-called Mount Morris Pool of Greene County, Pennsylvania. In some cases such as Parkersburg, Morgantown, and Fairmont, the oil boom added to an already established industrial economy. However, for other communities like Mannington, St. Marys, and Sistersville, the impact was great enough to characterize them as boom towns. For example, Sistersville became the center of the Tyler County field, which opened in 1892 and just one year later was the world's greatest single producing region. This boom resulted in an increase in Sistersville population from 600 in 1888 to 7,000 by 1898. Almost overnight the Marion County community of Mannington became a shipping and financial center serving surrounding oil well sites.[80]

Though there appears to have been relatively little socialism of unionism among the oil workers, the manner in which the opening of the fields often brought key Socialists into an area may be illustrated by the events that took place in the small Marion County community of Fairview. Located about twelve miles northwest of Fairmont, Fairview was in 1890 a hamlet of a few small businesses and craftsmen who served the nearby farmers. By 1895, the lumber demands of the oil strikes near Mannington made the establishment of a planing mill in Fairview seem an excellent idea. To take advantage of this prospect, the Haneses, a family of carpenters, from nearby Bassnettsville, wrote two of their sons, who were working in the Midwest, to come home.[81]

Alva M. Hanes was born in Fairview in 1858. He had learned his father's carpentry trade and might have continued to ply it in Marion County had not the panic of 1872–73 forced him to seek work elsewhere. He tried a little bit of everything from working in a mine to cooking on a riverboat and finally ended up working for the Baltimore and Ohio Railroad in the shops in Wheeling.[82] In about 1882, the Baltimore and Ohio sent him to their shops in Chicago to be supervisor of the carpentry crews. There he married and started his family. By 1892, he was working as a patternmaker for Calumet and Blue Island Railroad. In 1895 Hanes and his brother, David, returned to Fairview to open a planing mill and began "working for ourselves and not for a boss, thank God."[83]

Hanes had been eyewitness to the events leading up to the Pullman Strike of 1894. The blanket injunctions, arbitrary firings, and arrest of union agitators apparently convinced him of the truth of the claims of the Socialist agitators of Chicago who were arguing that the works could not receive justice under the prevailing industrial system. He returned to Fairview considering himself a Social Democrat and running as a presidential elector for Debs and Harriman in 1900. He continued to work toward the organization of a local of the Socialist Party of America.[84]

The economic expansion resulting from the oil development also produced an early Socialist movement in the Wood County community of Parkersburg. From this small group of radicals emerged two of the most important Socialists to come out of West Virginia. The first of these was Fred "Fritz" Merrick, who published an early Socialist newspaper called *The Social Rebel* in Parkersburg and later edited an even more radical publication in Pittsburgh, *The Justice*.[85] Of more importance was Harold W. Houston, who became well known to two generations of West Virginia miners and whose name became synonymous with socialism.

Harold Houston's father had migrated as a young man from New York State to Freedom in Noble County, Ohio. There, Samuel W. Houston (named for the famous member of the Texas branch of the family) grew to manhood, married, and served as a lieutenant in the 35th Ohio Infantry. In 1874, two years after the birth of their third son, Harold, the family moved to Jackson County, West Virginia and established a small lumber business.[86] By 1890, the family had moved to Charleston, where Harold graduated from Charleston High School and then went on the West Virginia University to complete a law degree. By 1900, the expanding oil business around Parkersburg seemed an excellent place for a young lawyer to make a place for himself.[87]

Houston's conversion to socialism appears to have been largely an intellectual experience. His receptivity to such a view, however, was probably prepared by his nonconforming parents. Whatever the cause, this prematurely gray, handsome, and highly articulate gentleman became one of the acknowledged spokesmen of the Socialist Party in West Virginia.[88]

The tapping of West Virginia's oil resources also accelerated the development of the state's glass production. The glass industry of the Mountain State dates back to the 1820s, when it was recognized that large quantities of the finest silica sand would make the state a potential producer of all sorts of glass products. However, the real spurt in production came with the commercialization of natural gas, which had previously been wasted.[89] This development, along with the continued discovery of new gas fields, increased the potential of many West Virginia communities as sites for glass factories. This trend was reflected in the fact that from 1890 to 1900, the number of glass-producing establishments grew from six to sixteen and the number of employees engaged in the industry jumped over 300 hundred percent.[90]

Most of the firms that moved into West Virginia came from communities in Indiana, like Gas City, Muncie, Elmwood, Fort Wayne, Hartford, Kokomo, Sheridan, and Sherman, where the supply of natural gas was being rapidly depleted. As the daughter of one of the Midwest founders of a West Virginia glass firm put it, "Those people really thought they had plenty of gas. I remember a farmer who had gas lights all around his house. It was so cheap that you didn't have gas meters, just paid a quarter an outlet. Well, those lights just got dimmer and dimmer until there was nothing but air coming out so we had to move."[91] Joining this influx were skilled workers from older glass communities like Toledo, Mt. Vernon, and Findley in Ohio, and McKeesport, Charleroi, Glassport, Kane, Mount Jewett, and Jeanette in Western Pennsylvania.[92]

These glassworkers were among the most highly organized union men in the country. At the turn of the century they were formed into three national unions; the Bottle Blowers, the American Flint Glass Workers, and the Local Assembly 300 made up of skilled window glassworkers.[93] By 1902, West Virginia had a least ten locals of the American Flints, eight locals of the Local Assembly 300, and three locals of the Glass Bottle Blowers.[94] Although the Protective Tariff policies of the Republican Party attracted a majority of the glassworkers, there was considerable Socialist sentiment in their ranks.

There is evidence to suggest that wherever they went, the glassworkers were one of the major elements of a Socialist fusion. For instance, strong Socialist voting trends and even political control existed in many midwestern and Pennsylvania cities with large glassworker population.[95] Furthermore, interviews with these craftsmen in West Virginia indicate that even some of the official organizers of their unions were also strong Socialists.[96]

The best indication of the Socialist infiltration of the West Virginia glassworkers is that the two substantial municipalities captured by the Socialists were essentially created by the glass trade. The communities of Adamston, which today is part of Clarksburg and Star City, a suburb of Morgantown, had much in common. At the turn of the century both were farm villages close to large industrial centers and mining sites. Into both communities came a great number of glassworkers around 1900 to 1903. A number of these glassworkers formed Socialist political organization.[97] These parties were both political and cultural in that they offered a broad reform program and also gave a sense of identity to the glassworkers as the existing political organizations were in the hands of the natives who often looked down on the glassworkers.[98]

Coal Miners Adopt the Red Flag

The most important segment of the Mountain State's economic growth was the increase in coal production. During the 1890s, the tonnage increase of 200 percent moved West Virginia past Ohio to become the nation's third greatest producer of coal.[99] In part, this growth was due to certain technical improvements such as a greater introduction of cutting machines and an upgraded system of inside haulage, which was replacing mine mules. Even more important were improved transportation facilities. Completion of railroad main branch lines were bringing additional areas into production. Furthermore, marketing possibilities were being improved by the River and Harbor Act of 1896, which helped to make West Virginia rivers more navigable to large coal barges. Finally, there was a sharp rise in coke production, especially in the New River, Pocahontas, and Fairmont coal fields.[100]

Because expansion of coal production was not confined to any one section of West Virginia, its impact was even more far-reaching than that of glass or oil. Mining communities, with their hillside tipples, steaming job piles, and small clusters of company houses began to dot the hollows of most remote areas of the state. Established communities grew because of their location as centers of banking, processing, and wholesale mercantile businesses serving the surrounding mining development. Thus, by 1895 West Virginia's capitol city of Charleston was assured a period of great expansion by the rapid development of the surrounding coal fields in Kanawha, Putnam, and Boone counties. The Fayette County community of

Montgomery, some thirty miles to the south, had become the shipping center for characterized cities like Elkins in Randolph County and Logan in Logan County.[101] Into the new coal camps and nearby feeder communities were drawn the state's largest labor force.

By opening year of the twentieth century some 32,386 men were employed in coal and coke production.[102] Unfortunately for the progress of the laboring man in West Virginia and the nation, relatively few of the state's miners were organized.[103] The leaders of the United Mine Workers of America had long realized the need to organize West Virginia, but the events of the 1890s made that need imperative. During the Coal Strikes of 1894 and 1897, West Virginia coal production not only continued, but even increased.[104] Moreover, West Virginia operators had rather consistently refused to attend any interstate contract conventions.[105] Therefore, the operators of the central competitive fields of Illinois, Indiana, and Ohio also put pressure on the United Mine Workers to organize West Virginia.[106]

Beginning in 1897, District 17 of the United Mine Workers, with the backing of all organized labor, made serious attempts to organize West Virginia. The most successful of these early drives was initiated late in 1900 and early 1901 when national organizers were sent all over the state.[107] United Mine Workers representatives like W. D. Vanhorn, William Morgan, Tom Haggerty, W. S. Wilson, and, above all, Mary "Mother" Jones were able to establish eighty new locals and recruit some 5,000 miners.[108] This obvious success achieved by these national figures can be partially attributed to the increasing efforts of a core of dedicated local union men.

Many miners in West Virginia saw the need to organize themselves for very practical and immediate reasons. The wages in 1897 averaged about $275 per year, the lowest in the nation, with the possible exception of the Pittsburgh area, where cheap immigrant labor was available.[109] Furthermore, wages were based upon a confusing patchwork of payment in which some men were paid on a long ton basis while others received payment per short ton.[110] To this were added such persistent complaints as high rent, exorbitant prices charged at the company store, and the general paternalistic practice common to isolated coal communities.

Several local Socialists became active in the concentrated national effort to organize the West Virginia miners at the turn of the century. The best known of this group were David Morgan, Clarence Griffith, Rome Mitchell, and A. D. Lavinder. Morgan, a Welsh immigrant who had migrated to West Virginia in 1886 via Pennsylvania and Ohio, was most active in the union activities around Montgomery in Fayette County.[111] Griffith and Mitchell, native Kanawha Countians, and second-generation miners, were well indoctrinated in the need of unionization since their fathers had been involved in earlier organizational attempts of Mountain State miners. All of these men had become Socialist prior to 1900, but the details of their actual conversions is only known in the case of A. D. Lavinder.[112]

Lavinder, a lad of fifteen, left his father's farm in Rocky Mount, Virginia, to work in a mine owned by the Norfolk and Western Railroad at Popular Hill near Pearisburg, Virginia. Here as a Knight of Labor, he first heard of socialism from an old German, the master workman of his lodge. But it was Debs's conversion after the Pullman Strike of 1894 that really piqued his interest. Curious about Socialist principles, he began to read widely and became convinced that the "brute-like conditions" of the workingman could be changed. After working several years in the Southern Illinois coal fields, Lavinder came to West Virginia in 1900 to help open the Kaymoor Mine, located just outside of Payetteville, the county seat of Fayette County.

It was in this setting near Fayetteville that Lavinder and others met on hilltops in old school buildings at night and eventually established a local union. When the United Mine Workers launched their organizing campaign in 1901, they recognized the abilities of Griffith, Mitchell, Lavinder, and other local individuals and recruited them as paid representatives.[113] However, it was not until the Coal Strike of 1902 in the Kanawha and New River coal fields that an atmosphere was created in which the occasional socialistic arguments of Lavinder and others for a cooperative society became more widely appreciated.

Coal Strike of 1902

The peace in the coal industry in 1900 and 1901, which allowed much of West Virginia to be organized, was due to the campaign needs of the Republican Party. Their campaign slogan, "the full dinner pail," was not to be challenged. Bowing to such pressure, the country's hard coal operators concluded an unwritten agreement, which guaranteed their employees a 10 percent wage increase. Nevertheless, by 1902, the hard coal miners remained discouraged with the low pay scale, high accident rate, and the feudal-like system of company-owned towns and felt these conditions required correction. When the miners presented their demands, the employers became determined not to be pressured into any further concessions. This belligerent position of the operator brought about a nationwide coal strike in June 1902.[114]

The building tension in the anthracite regions, with the strong possibility of a strike, stimulated mining in the soft coal areas to discuss possible supporting action. A West Virginia convention on this question, held in late May in Huntington, overrode opposition from some of the more conservative officials and promised a sympathy stroke if no agreement could be reached in the hard coal fields.[115] Consequently, a strike in West Virginia was called on June 7, 1902 and some 16,000 miners from a fifteen-county area walked out, closing down 180 of the 408 active mines across the state.[116]

The Coal Strike of 1902 was successful in the Kanawha County coal fields. A fairly thorough unionization of the field was achieved and a contract negotiated, which covered some 7,000 miners.[117] The contract provided for a nine-hour day, a reduction in the cost of powder, the right to trade at a non-company store, and the promise of no discrimination if gains in Kanawha were offset by heavy losses in union organization in the Fairmont, Logan, Williamson, Winding Gulf, Pocahontas, and New River fields.[118]

Many of the events that took place in the miners' losing struggle in the New River field fit the pattern often pictured by the Socialist of powerful capitalists using all the weight of the courts, the government, and the police to deny the workingman a decent existence. Injunctions were granted to prevent miners and their organizers from attempting to close down the mines. Armed guards were brought in to protect mine property and strike breakers. At the Justin Collins operation at Glen Jean in Fayette County, these guards were stationed at iron gates, which were erected to keep the strikers out and protect those who were working.[119]

In conformity with an all too familiar pattern in which the company is not only the employer but also the landlord, evictions began. This activity, more than anything else, embittered the miner because it struck so directly at his family and what few possessions he had been able to purchase from his hard toil at the coal bank. A *Charleston Gazette* reporter caught the pathos of such a situation precisely when he wrote, "Most of them haven't much more furniture than a good stout man could carry out at one load, and there it sat out in the weather, the wife busy trying to cook a little handful of grub they got at the Commissary."[120]

Interviews with several of those who became Socialists in the New River area suggest that such evictions fixed indelibly on their minds the helplessness of the miner. Although the example is doubtless an extreme one, the case of a young German immigrant makes the point well. Gustave Frisk was born and raised in Poznan, Poland. He had come to the mines of Fayette County after working for a few years in the peninsula section of Michigan. During the strike of 1902, Frisk contracted typhoid fever. Despite the warning of the coal company doctor, Frisk was thrown out of his house and onto the public highway. In a tent colony, where he fought a desperate fight against the disease, he became convinced that the American ideal of decency and human dignity could not be achieved under a capitalistic economic system.[121] In such camps as "Sweetrod Hollow" or "Camp Israel" there was much talk of the absolute necessity of unions, "and now and then a dab about socialism."[122]

The overwhelming power on the side of the mine operators provoked violence from the miners. At Stanniford near Beckley in Raleigh County, the miners lost lives in a pitched battle with guards.[123] Gunfire also erupted at Willis Branch near Mount Hope, at Elverton, and at other spots along the New River.[124] The sniping that took place at the Whipple Mine on Loup Creek brought a request from the operators for State Militia.[125] The arrival of the troops marked the beginning of the end for the miners' efforts to keep their hold on the New River fields.

Their defeat in the New River field caused many of the more active union miners to seek out areas that would be considered safer ground. They often found their way to small communities where the coal companies owned little or no property and had less control.[126] Small farm towns like Hilltop near Oak Hill and Gatewood near Fayetteville are good examples. In both of these communities were men who owned small farms, but also worked from time to time in the mines.

In these communities the union men often joined with the farmers who knew from the disaster of 1902 that control of politics was a necessary step in improving the existing industrial conditions. Thus, the suggestions of newly allied radical miners for a working-class political organization were well received. In Gatewood, for example, a Socialist Club was formed early in 1903 by such local people as Benjamin Hunt, H. L. Rodes, John Gatherum, and by more recent arrivals, O. B. Chewning and Sylvanus Goff.[127] A similar situation developed at the small incorporated town of Hilltop. Here the Socialist storekeeper and schoolteacher, Daniel Argabright, with his brother, Phillip, were joined by Rhier King, a Scotch coal miner, in the formation of a local.[128]

Other union men retreated into the still unionized districts of the Kanawha Valley. There they often added to a nucleus of radicals in agitating for a Socialist local. A. D. Lavinder, for example, found his way to Crown Hill, some twenty miles from Charleston on the South Side of the Kanawha River. He found a nucleus of a strong Socialist organization consisting of miners like Rome Mitchell and George T. Parsons.[129]

The atmosphere in Crown Hill was the prevailing mood all over Kanawha County. So disgruntled, in fact, were the miners and workingmen in general, that they met in Charleston in September of 1902 to place their own labor ticket on the ballot in the fall. Their platform urged the popular election of United States senators, immigration restriction, government ownership of railroads, telegraph lines, and all public works. Furthermore, they denounced the employer's use of injunctions, black lists, and evictions as un-American and un-Christian. And although they endorsed one Republican candidate, they chastised "… both the Republican and Democratic Parties as tools of the wealthy."[130] Seeing this, the Charleston Socialists hoped to be able to take advantage of such independence.

A few of the miners displaced by the Strike of 1902 moved into larger cities like Oak Hill, Mount Hope, and even Charleston. Here, they came in contact with Socialists who were anxious to talk to someone from the strike zone and, of course, to push the Cooperative Commonwealth. This was the experience of Wyatt Thompson whose family first came to the Kanawha Valley to engage in the salt drillings in the Malden area near Charleston. Later they became miners. Thompson was looking for work early in 1903 and found it as a combination errand boy and custodian at Moses W. Donnally's Printing Company in Charleston. Thompson possessed an inquisitive mind and had "kept up on his reading." Bellamy's *Looking Backward* had already made an impression on him. However, it was not until his move to Charleston that he was exposed to Scientific Socialism.[131]

The center of much of Charleston's small Socialist group was the tailor shop of George Gherken. This little tailor had left his native Hamburg in 1887 and settled in Elmira, New York, in 1892. He moved to Charleston and became the center of a group including both immigrants like himself and native West Virginian radicals like Tom Swinburn, J. T. Lewis, Otis Stant, and George Rathburn.[132] Gherkin's shop became known as the congregating place for workingmen coming into Charleston. It was in this shop that Wyatt Thompson and others first heard much about Scientific Socialism, and where important links were forged between Charleston's Socialists and their coal-mining comrades.[133]

The National Executive Committee of the Socialist Party encouraged the activities of the local radicals in the southern West Virginia coal regions. William Mailly recruited Mary "Mother" Jones as a speaker and organizer. She was apparently upset with the look of aggressiveness displayed by John Mitchell and other officers of the United Mine Workers in the Coal Strike of 1902. Therefore, "Mother" Jones was anxious to be of help in creating an aggressive spirit among the West Virginia coal miners.[134] The joint efforts of national and state organizers began producing results as evidenced by the fact that Kanawha and Fayette counties joined several Ohio River counties in fielding candidates for state and local offices in 1904.[135]

The Socialist locals of Kanawha and Fayette counties became important additions to West Virginia's small but growing radical movement. The strategy of this new movement was clear. By helping to fight the day-to-day struggle within the existing unions, they had hoped to create a class consciousness that would be reflected in political support to their party. Failing this, their social democratic background caused them to believe that independent political action was at least a step in the right direction.

By 1904, there were Socialist branches in fifteen of the state's fifty-five counties. Most of these were located in the western section of West Virginia where the greater industrial growth had occurred.[136] The nascent Socialist organizations appealed not only to the middle-class radical and skilled tradesman who had recently moved to the state to work, but also to the native farmer and small villager who sought new jobs in these industrial centers.

Unfortunately, comparatively few workers were yet convinced that a Socialist society offered them a chance for economic and social well-being. On the other hand, most did agree that some drastic changes needed to be made in the existing system.[137] The young Socialist movement hoped to broaden this discontent by converting simple reform into more revolutionary action for all classes in society.

CHAPTER II
The Growth And Appeal Of The West Virginia Socialist Movement: 1905–1911

Charleston's Socialist newspaper, *The Labor Argus*, believed the results of the general election in 1910 demonstrated that the future of the party in West Virginia was full of promise. If the Kanawha County situation was any indication, Socialists in the rest of the state might look forward to capturing political offices in the near future. As an example of what could be done with more agitation, more organization, and poll watching, the party in Kanawha County had elected S. O. Johnston, Justice of the Peace, and Frank H. Stephenson, Constable in Washington district. They had also made significant inroads in the large mining district of Cabin Creek by electing Anthony Neff as Constable. *The Labor Argus* further pointed out that the vote would have been higher had many corrupt precinct officials not thrown out legitimate votes. Nevertheless, the fight had been a good one with the Kanawha Socialists more than tripling their vote in 1908.[1]

The optimism of the Kanawha County Socialists was shared by many of their comrades elsewhere. A Putnam County radical noted the change from the situation in 1905 when "he had tried to show others the folly of voting the old ticket put up by mine owners and other corporations, and was laughed at for my pains." By contrast, the reception of his efforts just five years later proved that "socialism is fast gaining ground among those who had been taking the politician's word for everything."[2] The increasing popularity of their position demonstrated that West Virginia Socialists had been able not only to capitalize on the Mountain State workingman's discontent with many existing institutions, but also to present their philosophy of a better society in an appealing fashion.

Responding to a New World of Work

Much of the growing dissatisfaction felt by the West Virginia laborers appeared to stem from a change in the scale of production that took place in the state's industrial complex. For example, although the industrial labor force increased from 43,758 in 1904 to 63,893 by 1909, the number of factories decreased and the number of employees per factory rose from 20.7 to 56.3.[3] The period was also marked by some notable consolidations of mining properties. From 1905 to 1908, firms such as Carbon Fuel and Cabin Creek Consolidated were bringing together many mining operations on the southside of the Kanawha River. In 1906, consolidations were taking place in the coal fields of Fayette County, where Samuel Dixon had formed the New River Fuel Company and in Pocahontas and McDowell County, where Justin Collins was putting together his rather extensive coal properties. A similar development in the Fairmont coal fields in northern West Virginia was being masterminded by George T. Watson.[4]

The increasing size of industrial operations often created additional problems in labor-management relations. Contacts between the actual owners or operators and the workingman were fewer. This trend was as true of mining operations as it was in the factories. For example, many miners and their families who worked at Mucklow on Paint Creek lamented the fact that these properties left the hands of the family for whom the community was named. As a wife of one miner put it, "The Mucklows were good people to work for. No one was ever better about the store and they wouldn't throw people out of their houses. They were friendly and would stop and give you a 'howdy-do.'"[5] In many cases the transfer of ownership meant a policy of stricter discipline by company representatives. For instance, when the Winifrede Coal Company purchased the

Belmont Mine, a few miles above the present city of East Bank, they hired a foreman from the non-union New River fields. The new boss attempted to get rid of the check weighman and establish a five-day vacate provision in the leases for company houses. This certainly was not characteristic of the Winifrede Coal Company. When Brandt Scott, future Socialist justice of the peace, puzzled over these new policies, he noted, "I am unwilling to believe that the company is aware of the action of the superintendent . . . they have always been fair when dealing with men."[6] West Virginia workers also believed that the political influence of many business interests had grown to ominous proportions.[7] These policies provoked a mass protest meeting at Tomsburg on Paint Creek, where the foreman pushed his men too far by posting "No Trespass" notices and using the local constable to make numerous arrests.[8]

Attempts to enforce stricter policies also became more vigorous in the non-union districts. Additional mine guards were brought in to tighten rules, protest property, and keep out union agitators. At the upper reaches of unorganized Cabin Creek, many Italian miners were employed. One of them described conditions around 1906 as ". . . bad, because so many of them Baldwins (Baldwin-Felts Guards) people were here. They rode horses and wouldn't let anyone they didn't like walk on the railroad tracks. Worse though, you couldn't go into the office and tell about mistakes or complain about the store. They would just kick you off the porch."[9] Such treatment was even more galling to the experienced native-born miner as it contrasted so much with the independence he had enjoyed on the job. As Professor Carter Goodrich demonstrated in this classic work, *The Miner's Freedom*, the coal miner and his buddy made all the key decisions in their own room and were rarely even visited by a foreman.[10] It was the lack of freedom off the job that made one of Huntington's leading Socialist become a radical union organizer. Until he left the mines in 1910, Henry Franklin had worked in the non-union fields of McDowell and Logan counties. "They paid him well enough and he didn't mind the work itself," his daughter recalled, "but he often stated that a man couldn't call his soul his own in those communities."[11] Complaints of these conditions prompted even conservative labor spokesmen to characterize the suffering of the West Virginia miners as worse than that of Colorado or Siberia. The recurrent theme was that the traditional independence of the self-reliant mountaineer had disappeared and that the only freedom left was that of being ". . . driven about by armed thugs who are protected by state and county officials at the behest of such soulless and inhuman interests as the Dixon-Fairmont-Cabin Creek Syndicate."[12]

Only a little less serious were the complaints of the urban workingmen. Many of their grievances dealt with city policies that they felt bore upon job conditions. The union men in every large municipality wanted the city to set an example by enforcing an eight-hour day, refraining from using convict labor, and employing resident workers on more projects directly supervised by public officials.[13]

Other objections concerned the quality of life in cities where public services could not keep pace with rapid growth. The laboring man felt somehow that it was always his section that was inadequately lighted or became a quagmire after a rain because there were not enough paved streets and sidewalks. Added to this was the lack of public recreation, toilet facilities, and a generally unsanitary environment. Furthermore, the worker often felt that he shouldered the major burden of payment for the few improvements that were made; thus the union men of both Charleston and Wheeling criticized the high utility rates and demanded the construction of toll bridges into their cities.[14]

It was maintained that coal barons, whether Democrat or Republican, dominated the counties in which their operations were located. George Watson, owner of the Fairmont Coal Company, controlled Marion County for the Democratic Party. On the other hand, in Fayette County, "King Samuel" Dixon of the New River Company kept the Republicans victorious. In most cases, the method of business control was similar. The technique consisted of such devices as influence in obtaining citizenship papers for prospective voters; extensive use of floaters in elections; the frequent passage of so-called "ripper bills," which usually gerrymandered election districts; and the careful use of patronage.[15]

Prior to the passage of the West Virginia Prohibition Act in 1911, a very important source of patronage was the granting of liquor licenses. The law required that both saloon keepers and liquor distributors be approved by the county court.[16] The retail permits were often granted or withheld on the basis of direct financial support of the controlling political organization or the patronizing of party-approved wholesalers. For instance, in Fayette County the wise saloon owner purchased his whiskey from the Fayette Liquor Company at Beury. It was widely recognized that such practices were a major source of corruption. Those individuals drawn from more stable, rural counties seem especially shocked by the conditions. One of them complained,

From the tranquility of Monroe, I came to Fayette County into a boom in the coal fields, and a political condition so completely un-American as to be almost unspeakable. . . . Most coal mines and villages were guarded by deputies or hired detectives whose salaries were said to have been subsidized by various people, and business, and perhaps, the county court. There were saloons up every hollow in this valley which had to buy their liquor (from the right place) or hear from the political ring.[17]

By late 1905, the union men in West Virginia viewed their situation as serious enough to require some coordinated political activity. This tendency was reflected in a call to action by President John Nugent before the State Federation of Labor at its fall convention in Clarksburg. He reminded the delegates that one of the prime reasons for the founding of the Federation in 1903 had been to secure laws from both the local and state legislative bodies that would improve the conditions of the wage earner. The delegates were in a mood to take up President Nugent's challenge. They instructed the Federation's legislative committee to obtain a stronger child labor law, a compulsory school attendance law, a longer school term, and higher salaries for teachers. In addition, the union men were urged to build up sentiment in their respective communities for the popular election of United States senators, advisory initiative, and referendum. Furthermore at its Wheeling convention, in the spring of 1906, the Federation added an endorsement of women's suffrage and began earnest discussions on participating in elections.[18]

The West Virginia Socialists believed that they might obtain some advantage from the labor discontent. Enthusiastic conventions were held all through the summer of 1906 in Ohio, Fayette, and Kanawha counties. In the latter, the Socialist convention drew over 400 delegates to the community of Coalburg.[19] Full slates of candidates were nominated for state and county offices, and party platforms were formulated to appeal to as many of the specific grievances of the worker as possible. For instance, locals in Charleston called for proposals ranging from general political and economic reforms such as city-owned utilities, home rule, initiative, referendum and recall, to the specific desires of Charleston workingmen, such as an eight-hour day for city employees, moving stables out of the residential districts, public baths, toilets, waiting rooms, and a new free bridge across the Kanawha River.[20] It was hoped that these programs in the various county communities would bring many converts. Failing this, the Socialists hoped they could at least persuade their fellow union men to follow an active and independent political course.

In the summer of 1906, there were strong indications that West Virginia union organizations might very well adopt the strategy of forming an independent labor party. It was pointed out that the workingmen of Bluefield had already followed that approach in a recent municipal election.[21] The Charleston *Labor Argus*, not yet in the hands of the Socialists, argued that trying to influence the regular party organizations was foolish as experience had shown that the laboring men had never been given anything like fair representation on these tickets.[22] No less a personage than John Nugent, a strong

Republican, admitted that he might be willing, "If these parties fail to nominate men from our ranks . . . (to) provide the means to have our own men nominated and see to it that they are elected."²³

However, by October of 1906, the issue of West Virginia's labor political participation was decided in favor of the non-partisan approach. It appears that the A. F. of L.'s promised entrance into the summer and fall campaigns threw great weight to those who had been arguing for the idea of "reward your friends and punish your enemies." Although the *A.F. of L. Campaign Programme* did stipulate that if no Republican or Democrat friends could be found, a straight labor candidate could be nominated, its overwhelming emphasis was on the success of the non-partisan technique.²⁴ West Virginia workers were informed as early as July of 1906 that the influence of union men had been the deciding factor in preventing the re-nomination of Representative Grosvenor of Ohio's tenth congressional district and had played a significant part in preventing Congressman Blackburn from getting control of the Republican Party in North Carolina. It was also promised that Speaker of the House, Joseph Cannon, was marked for defeat because of the active opposition of the large number of union voters, especially mine workers, in his district.²⁵

West Virginia union men followed what they felt as the approach favored by the A. F. of L. For example, Ohio Valley Trades and Labor Assembly distributed a questionnaire to all candidates from their county requesting opinions on many desirable reforms such as popular elections of senators, initiative, referendum and recall, universal suffrage, no child labor, home rule for cities, enforcement of the eight-hour day, anti-convict labor, immigration restrictions, anti-injunctions, right of petition of grievances for state employees, a city-owned toll-free bridge to Wheeling Island, and a city-owned light plant. On the basis of replies and other statements, the Trades Assembly found William P. Hubbard, a candidate for Congress, "most antagonistic toward labor," and Lee Woods, a House of Delegates candidate, as "anything but friendly."²⁶ Whether such techniques had any significant bearing on the outcome of the elections or not, West Virginia union men felt they had made an impact with their non-partisan methods. They claimed as victories the election to the state Senate of Adam Littlepage, a Democrat from Kanawha County, and Samuel B. Montgomery, a Preston County Republican. In addition, John Nugent, as a Republican from Kanawha County, had won a seat in the House of Delegates.[27]

In the 1907 legislation, Senators Montgomery and Littlepage were diligent at representing the union men of the State of West Virginia. Senator Montgomery introduced two bills that were important to labor. One measure was designed to prevent workers from being brought into the state under false representations and assurances. The second measure struck at the hated guard system by proposing that the employer be held liable for any unlawful acts committed by security police or detectives whom he might hire.[28] Adam Littlepage was tireless in his efforts to bring Senator Montgomery's measures out of committee where the Senate leadership kept them buried for more than thirty days. Littlepage did succeed in getting the Guard Bill out for the second reading, but the session was drawing quickly to a close. In desperation, Senator Montgomery moved for a suspension of the Constitutional requirements that bills have full and distinct readings on three separate days. This move failed when only eight senators could be mustered to support his tactic.[29] This defeat came as a real shock to the West Virginia union men because their hopes for the 1907 Legislature had been especially high.

The Socialists were, of course, disappointed that the State Federation and City central bodies had not fielded an independent labor ticket; however, they had tried to salvage what they could from the situation. Wheeling Socialists insisted that non-partisan be defined as broadly as possible. Radical members of the Ohio Valley Trades and Labor Assembly pushed for a mass meeting to which *all* political organizations would send representatives to explain precisely what their party would do to improve the status of labor.[30] Furthermore, the Wheeling Socialists hoped to keep union men in the state informed on the proceedings of the West Virginia House and Senate through a Socialist publication. Accordingly, the suggestion was made that the Ohio Valley Trades and labor Assembly appropriate $500 to enlarge Fritz Merrick's *Social Rebel* from four to eight pages so that he could cover the news of the legislative sessions.[31] Though such efforts were not too productive, the Socialists did have more success in capitalizing on the workers' disappointment over the failure of their legislative program.

It was clear that in the spring of 1907, any West Virginia labor circles were taking a hard look at the record of their legislative representatives. The general feeling in Wheeling was that someone had not done their job, and therefore the working class must demand a "strict accounting of stewardship from those favored few who sat in the high places."[32] Similarly, many Charleston union men felt that promises by the politicians had not been kept.[33] The Socialists believed they had at least part of the answer and spearheaded a movement to expose a "sell out" by John Nugent.

Capturing the Labor Movement

On the surface, John Nugent appeared to be an unlikely target for charge of disloyalty to the causes of organized labor. He was a real veteran of the miner's organization, having not only represented the Knights of Labor of the Hocking Coal Fields at the 1890 Miner's Unity Convention in Columbus, Ohio, but also made the motion that formed the United Mine Workers of America. Nugent was sent into West Virginia in 1902 from Michigan, where he had been a national organizer. His rise to the top ranks of the Mountain State labor movement was nothing short of spectacular. Within four years, he had been elected president of District 17 of the United Mine Workers (1904), president of the State Federation of Labor (1905), and a Republican representative from Kanawha County to the House of Delegates serving from 1907 to 1909.[34]

The historians of the State Federation of Labor attributed the opposition to John Nugent to the North–South rivalries that have been so much a part of West Virginia's history. In this case, the Wheeling area, represented by William Welch and Albert Bauer, the first vice president and secretary, respectively, resented the disproportionate influence in the State Federation by Charleston. It seemed that the capitol city controlled the presidency and desired more of the executive offices. After threatening to split the State Federation, these differences were settled with great difficulty. Yet, as Professors Harris and Krebs admit, basic antagonisms had not been resolved.[35] The disagreements of the members were ideological as well as sectional.

Radical union men objected to Nugent's leadership for several reasons. He had been chairman of the Labor Committee of the House of Delegates in the 1907 session, but did not use his position to support the Federation's legislative campaign.[36] Just as significant were the charges that he was too conservative and too friendly with employers. Socialists were among the first to object to the tone of his address to the Clarksburg Convention of the State Federation where he admonished delegates to keep in mind "the fact that the interests of each class depends largely upon the success of all classes and that success is determined by the social and business relations between them. . . ."[37] More specifically, Nugent's own union felt that he was too cozy with the coal operators, For example, in May 1907 Nugent had blamed an explosion at White Oak Fuel Company's Whipple Mine in Fayette County on a poorly placed explosive charge. The Charleston labor paper disputed Nugent's judgment, claiming instead that the Whipple Mine was well known for being excessively dry, and therefore a real generator of mine gas.[38]

All doubt as to Nugent's true sympathies was removed from the minds of the union miners when he resigned as president of District 17 of the United Mine Workers of America to accept the position of Commissioner of Immigration for the State of West Virginia. These workers were allegedly needed because they had great experience with mines that possessed all types of dangerous gasses; therefore their arrival would mean a new period of progressive, safe mining in the Mountain State.[39] Nugent's critics disputed his motives. Whether deliberately or not, he had become the agent of a union-breaking plot by such mine operators as Sam Dixon. The proof lay in the fact that the salary of the Immigration Commissioner was paid by the New River Coal Company. Such firms were willing to bear this expense because their anti-union policies had made it difficult for them to secure skilled miners.[40]

The mounting evidence against John Nugent lent greater prestige to the Socialists who had been among the first to be critical of his policies. Even in Wheeling there had been much reluctance to follow the lead of the Socialists in the matter. As late as the middle of October 1908, Albert Bauer could produce no more than a tie vote for his motion to condemn Nugent; however, by the end of the month, the radicals produced a letter from Frank Snyder, the editor of the *Labor Argus*, stating that proof of Nugent's guilt had been sent to Charleston by John Mitchell. With this encouragement from the other end of the state, the Wheeling Socialists had little trouble getting the Executive Board of Trades and Labor Assembly to officially prefer charges and allow hearings on the allegations in its meeting hall.[41]

Nugent rejected the charges placed against him. He pointed out that by the constitution of the State Federation of Labor only he could call a meeting of the Executive Board to hear such complaints. Then the irate Federation president pinpointed the source of the opposition to him as the Ohio Valley Trades and Labor Assembly, which "is not a bona fide labor organization but is largely a body of Socialists and obligated to no authority in union labor ranks. It has only been tolerated as a member of the State Federation in the hope that it would reform from its Socialist tendencies. You can say that I will never tolerate being tried before a body of Socialists."[42] Spokesmen for the Assembly readily admitted that Socialists were members of their organization, but they denied that they dominated their policies. John Nugent was able to beat back his opposition.

He summoned a special convention in Charleston and appointed a committee, which cleared him of all charges. On the other hand, Nugent's prestige had been seriously undermined. His resignation soon after the convention adjourned vindicated in many workers' minds the position the Socialists had taken.[43]

The Nugent incident had barely died down when West Virginia began to feel the effects of the 1907 depression. In the Mountain State, the so-called "Banker's Panic" was anything but the short economic setback that it is sometimes pictured.[44] By 1908, newspapers around the state noted that home building was at a standstill and that small businesses were going under daily. The rising rate of unemployment was soon placing a severe strain on the welfare capacities of many municipalities, and emergency measures became commonplace. Charleston's city council appropriated $1,000 dollars to feed the destitute because "there never was a time in Charleston when so much destitution existed. Children cannot be sent to school because they have no shoes or stockings to wear," and, "families are living in homes without head because of the lack of fuel."[45] Wheeling relief committees were organized to help alleviate similar conditions. "It is a common occurrence," complained *The Wheeling Intelligencer*, "to see children of the city running about with no shoes or stockings on their feet. Their father's not having been employed for several months being unable to provide for their wants; families have been found to have no fuel nor anything to eat in their homes, and people are actually starving."[46] Similarly, in Huntington, the city's poor fund ran out and the situation was desperate with "children of a hundred families are crying for food and the city cannot fill their mouths. The truant officer demands that the waifs be sent to school, but they have no shoes to keep their tender little feet from the cold, frosty sidewalks."[47]

The worker's predicament was also serious in the mining camps. The operators tried to keep their mines going even in the crisis because of the difficulty of reassembling a labor force; however, many of those that stayed open were able to run at only about one-tenth of their capacity.⁴⁸ Many living miners complained of having only a day or two of work a month through much of 1908. Cleveland Toney, a life-long resident of the mining community of Dothan in Fayette County recalled,

> I'd get up every morning at five o'clock to see if the whistle would blow but that would sometimes happen only once or twice a month. At that rate, a man might make five or six dollars a month and out of that they'd take fifty cents for the doctor and fifteen cents for hospital insurance. A man just didn't have anything left for months on end.⁴⁹

Even in places where work was steadier, the miners could afford little more than the barest necessities, and the ingenuity of their wives was taxed to provide a decent table. The United Mine Workers in West Virginia recognized this difficulty and was forced to temporarily reduce its initiation fee from $10 to $1 in order to keep up its membership.⁵⁰

The Socialists were frequently able to win converts by capitalizing on the frame of mind of those who suffered from the effects of the Panic. Frank Snyder, editor of *The Labor Argus*, believed that many more workers were seriously questioning the value of capitalism. This was understandable when all one had to do was "Think of the present panic which has thrown thousands of men on the streets looking for jobs! Think of the starving men, women, and children; the increase of suicides, of robberies, banks closing their doors, bankruptcies, et cetera. Snyder believed that a large number of workers were ready to . . . drop all past affiliations and our personal ideas of the past, and open our minds."⁵¹ Fred Smith, a miner and schoolteacher in Fayette County, remembered that he and several of his friends did just that when Samuel C. Cross, an ex-Republican state legislator, turned Socialist, waged a successful recruiting drive around Dothan and Mossey in 1908.⁵² Along the same line was the experience of George W. Harper, a painter who was to become secretary of one of Charleston's Socialist locals. "I was always a Republican but I got so disgusted about the Panic that the next time around I just voted Democrat." As he left the polls on Charleston's West Side, Harper encountered Joe Wiggins, George Rathburn, and Charlie Boswell. "They were passing out Socialist literature which I read and what it said made a whole lot of sense to me."[53] This receptiveness was noted by Socialist organizers. Alfred Lavinder felt that after 1908 it was easier to recruit miners for both socialism and unionism. "I got a lot of members for both," recalled Lavinder, "by pointing out that capitalism was on the way out. It was trying to hang on by charity and soup houses, and wage cuts but that wouldn't work. The only way a man could protect himself was to keep the union strong. I told them about how the Illinois miners didn't lose a penny in the Panic."[54]

The depression lasted well into 1909 and created several serious labor disputes. In Clarksburg, violence occurred when the Baltimore and Ohio Railroad brought in strikebreakers because they claimed that financial conditions made it impossible to meet the wage hikes demanded by their employees.[55] Labor also faced a setback in Wheeling where, in spite of general support by union men of the area, the Amalgated Association of Iron, Steel, and Tin workers failed in their attempt to organize the city's plate mills.[56] Similarly in a much publicized case, the Hitchman Coal Company in northern West Virginia obtained an injunction in the Federal Court of Judge Dayton that prevented John Mitchell and T. L. Lewis from organizing the company's 1,000 miners.[57] Only in the Kanawha coal fields were the workers able to successfully withstand a challenge to their union positions.

In December of 1908, the operators of the unionized mines on Paint Creek demanded a modification of the joint agreements that they had negotiated the previous spring. The operators claimed the economic slowdown made it impossible for them to compete and admonished the United Mine Workers to make a special effort at organizing the New River, Cabin Creek, Island Creek sections of the state.[58] Fourteen coal operators on Paint Creek followed up their ultimatum with notices of wage reductions. This produced a strike by 2,000 miners determined to protect their joint agreement.[59] A week later, partly through the good offices of Governor Dawson, the strike was settled when the Paint Creek Colliery and Standard Splint Coal Companies granted the check-off or payroll deductions for union dues in exchange for payment on the basis of a long ton.[60]

Peace in the Kanawha coal fields was short-lived as the spring of 1909 marked the outbreak of the so-called "Long Ton Strike." A large number of mine operators resented the Pain Creek modification, claiming that the competition of the Paint Creek and non-union operations in the rest of the state were most damaging in light of the continued depressed condition of the industry. In April, many operators posted notices that in the future their companies would pay on the basis of the long ton.[61] A brief but general mine strike followed, which was finally settled when the Paint Creek operators agreed to return to the 1908 agreement.[62]

Socialist leadership used the Long Ton Strike to hammer home some lessons on the futility of allowing the means of production to remain in the hands of the capitalist. Harold Houston explained part of the problem to a large meeting at Mount Carbon, a coal town near Montgomery. Recent events demonstrated that the mine operators could not be trusted to keep their agreements. After all, Houston reminded, had not the Paint Creek people who started the trouble been party to the 1908 agreements? Furthermore, it was obvious that other operators used the confusion of the Paint Creek modification to break the union. For example, the Ronda and Dry Branch mines on Cabin Creek had tried to force a long ton, monthly pay, and discontinuance of check-off on their employees. Others were so quick to join in such tactics that it looks "very much like a put-up job."[63] Sam Morrison, a Socialist organizer from Miami on Cabin Creek, added another point. The Long Ton Strike showed how incapable the capitalists were of managing industrial capacities. There might be some sense to retaining them if they could produce and still give the workers a decent income, but it is not in their nature to do it. For instance, even though the grievance on Cabin Creek has been resolved, there is still no steady work because there has not been enough orders for coal. Morrison believed that recognition of these facts was dawning upon labor everywhere. Each new wage reduction and attempt at lengthening hours was only hastening the day when workers would act together industrially and politically.[64]

There was some real justification in the Socialists feeling that class-conscious political tendencies were growing stronger. The Panic had not only brought more converts officially into the Socialist party but had also strengthened the idea of independent political action among the West Virginia union men. All through late 1907 and early 1908, there were preparations for independent political action in upcoming elections. In the Wheeling area, members of glassworkers, stogie-makers, and miner's unions spearheaded the drive.[65] The Ohio Valley Trades and Labor Assembly were persuaded to form a United Labor Party to elect to the state legislature men who were genuinely pledged to labor and independent of the regular parties.[66] Just across the Ohio River, the members of the Belmont County Trades and Labor Assembly had voted over three to one to sponsor their own candidates in municipal and state elections.[67] In Kanawha County there was also more support for a labor party, especially after Ed Soulsby, a union miner, and L. A. "Pop" Frazier, a Charleston printer, failed to win nominations in the Republican County Convention. And finally, there were threats of labor political action in the eastern end of the state where alleged interference by the Elkins Coal Company had been instrumental in defeating Samuel Montgomery's bid for re-nomination to the State Senate.[68]

In contrast to their unsuccessful attempts in 1906 at promoting an independent labor ticket, the Socialists and their allies were better able to defeat obstructionist tactics by those who disagreed with them. The techniques used by the opponents of the various United Labor Parties were similar. It was argued that the workers would simply be wasting their votes because they were not yet strong enough to really elect anyone. Such a political course would merely take votes away from good men who would be found on either the Republican or Democratic ticket.[69] The opponents also hoped the question of financing labor parties would dampen enthusiasm. A reporter for the *Wheeling Intelligencer* analyzed their strategy perfectly when he reported that Llewlyn Lewis of Martin's Ferry frightened the delegates to the Belmont County Labor Party Convention "into a blue funk" with the high costs of their movement. Lewis, who was president of the Ohio State Federation, suggested that well over $2,000 would be needed at once so each delegate ought to be assessed from $5 to $10 dollars. Socialists leaders like Mike Snyder of the miners, and Andrew Crunelle, of the Flint Glass Workers, argued that they could elect their own men to office with financing that could be covered by a twenty-cent assessment on all union men. The radicals prevailed, but only after Lewis was ruled out of order when he tried to establish a very complicated nomination procedure, and a $40 filing fee for candidates.[70] In Wheeling, the Political Committee of the Ohio Valley Trades and Labor Assembly, led by Albert Bauer, Valentine Reuther, J. T. Hecker, and other radicals, waged a successful fight against similar arguments.[71]

The attempt of the A.F. of L. leadership to deliver the labor to the Democratic Party also ran into difficulty in West Virginia. A letter from Samuel Gompers to the Belmont Trades Assembly, urging support for Democratic candidates and asking for campaign contributions, was rejected for a variety of reasons. Both Republican and non-partisan union men were angered by the departure from what they considered the traditional A.F. of L. political position. The Socialists and United Labor Party backers added their voices to the dissent and borrowed a page from their opponent's book by claiming that the Assembly needed all its funds for the United Labor Party.[72] A plea for support of Democratic candidates by Mr. Sam Denedry, an A.F. of L. organizer, also met a cool reception from Wheeling union men. After debating the matter for several meetings in October, 1908, Wheeling gave the A.F. of L. a perfunctory endorsement;

however, all their funds, the use of their meeting hall, and their newspaper support went to the United Labor Party.[73]

There was also strong opposition to Gompers's political position in the southern part of the state. Many union men in Kanawha County felt that the Democratic Party had no special claim on the worker's allegiance. As a matter of fact, they stated that some of the most stubborn non-union mine operators on Cabin Creek were Democrats. The *Labor Argus* reflected this feeling when it editorialized, "The Republican orator will abuse the Democrats for their hostility toward labor, and the Democratic orator will lambaste the Republicans, and the conscientious and thinking union men will know that both sets are telling the truth."[74] There was also opposition in the Huntington Trades and Labor Assembly spearheaded by the Socialists. The radicals argued that it was ridiculous for Gompers to seek endorsement for a political party that produced such anti-labor governors as Frank Stunenberg of Idaho, and Sparks of Nebraska. Moreover, William T. Curry, State Federation of Labor secretary-treasurer, and a Socialist member of the Huntington Central Labor Body, pointed out that Gompers was rather tardy in his attempt to mobilize labor's power in elections. The Socialists had been agitating and preaching the necessity of independent political action on the part of the workers for years. Actually, Curry contended, Gompers and the Executive Council of the A.F. of L. had recommended that the union stay out of partisan politics until the pressure from the discontent of the rank and file finally forced their hand.[75]

With the exception of Belmont County United Labor Party's strong showing, it is difficult to ascertain how successful the local parties were. The importance for the Socialists, however, was that the election demonstrated that for two years workers had been breaking from old political allegiances. Furthermore, the Socialists realized that in order to hold their new converts and attract other prospects, they would have to do more than point up the failures of the many capitalist institutions. Rather, they would have to educate the worker to the value of the Cooperative Commonwealth.

The West Virginia Socialists apparently understood that it would be no simple task to imbue the workers with radical ideology. A good deal of persistent education was necessary because the laboring class had for so long been indoctrinated by a capitalist-controlled social system. Harold Houston presented the problem clearly when he said, "at the present time, the majority of the workers are not conscious of their real interests, that is, they are not class-conscious. They still have the 'capitalist's mind,' that is, they hold ideas that the capitalists want them to hold."[76] Moreover, the Socialists sensed that creating class-conscious groups of workers would have to be done carefully and with concern for the cultural and psychological characteristics of the area. Though from time to time there were attempts at technical explanations of Marx, the Mountain State Socialists devoted most of their efforts to pragmatically selecting points they thought would be readily understood by prospective members.

The first problem was to convince the workers that the wage laborers were unkindly exploited under capitalism. This was accomplished by constant reference to the Labor Theory of Value. "Did you ever stop to think," asked the *Labor Argus* in a fairly typical editorial, "that all the necessities, all luxuries, and all wealth are products of your labor whether brain or brawn? You feed and clothe the world. You supply the luxuries and delicacies for the tables of the idle rich, while you and your families must exist on cheap, course food."[77] Only occasionally was there an explanation of why capitalism worked this way. Instead, the major emphasis was on the extent of the capitalist expropriation of surplus value, estimated at $18 billion a year or three-quarters of everything that was produced. This, in turn, explained the great contradictions in modern society: incalculable wealth and desperate poverty; commercial travelers and tramps; great colleges and large penitentiaries; calculated refinement and unmentionable squalor. The Socialists stressed that such contradictions gave the lie to the prevalent impression that there were no classes in the American Republic.[78]

The premise that labor created everything but was never fairly compensated had wide appeal. Interviews with several West Virginia Socialists reveal that this argument had been an important factor in bringing about their conversion. A good example was the case of Price Williams, who grew up in Moundsville. He recalled that as a very young man he was impressed by the soapbox speeches of an Italian huckster and amateur chemist by the name of Gambesi whose major point was that 5 percent of the people controlled 95 percent of the wealth.[79] Even non-Socialist mine workers remembered that they liked the radicals' idea of getting the full value of their labor. This was demonstrated in a debate at the United Mine Workers' 1912 Convention at Indianapolis. Delegate Williams, a Socialist from District 2, asked that the statement "an equitable share of the fruits of the labor" be struck from the union's Declaration of Principles. Williams reminded the convention that in 1909 the union had agreed to the principle that the miners were entitled to "the full social value of our product," and that position should be reaffirmed. Delegate Finney of District 5 objected. "The full value of our toil would mean, to my mind, that the man who employs us will receive no compensation for the money he has invested. We could not under any circumstances have a clause in the preamble of that kind. . . ." Delegate Hefferly doubtless spoke for many when he replied to Finney, "I take it there are no delegates here, nor are their constituents at home, that do not want the full product of their toil." But Van Bitner, also of District 5, showed how wide an appeal the Labor Theory of Value might be among non-Socialists. "I think that so far as the English is concerned there is not the least difference between the Amendment and the report of the committee. Equitable 'means just' and that is all that the United Mine Workers of America can ask for—that which is just and right."[80]

The West Virginia Socialists strove to convince the workers of the need for constant political and economic struggles with the capitalists. For only when the workers won control of the facilities of production and distribution could a truly just society be achieved.

The local Socialists did not rely exclusively upon Marx for a historic justification for this class struggle. Just as often they drew upon traditions more familiar to American workingmen. "We are aware," wrote a Parkersburg Socialist, "that our fight against capitalism is the same fight that Jesus fought. We know the Capitalist class of that day crucified Jesus because he preached the truth, and the capitalist class is crucifying the truth and justice as long as they have the power to do so."[81] The persistence of the class struggle had been recognized by no less a figure than Abraham Lincoln. In a speech in 1847, the great Emancipator had stated that, "Inasmuch as most good things are produced by labor, it follows that all such things of right belong to those whose labor has produced them. But it has so happened in all ages of the world that some have labored and others have, without labor, enjoyed a large proportion of the fruits. . . ." Moreover, it was argued that Lincoln was keenly in tune with Socialist ideals. Not only had he believed that the prime object of any government was to secure for the workers the full product of their toil, but he had encouraged the worldwide movement of solidarity of the working class by a letter of support to a committee of the First International in London. And finally, the Socialists were always quick to remind the workers that by winning the class struggle, they were freeing not only their own class but all classes in modern society.[82]

Creating a Socialist Culture

The class struggle that would end in the eventual victory over the capitalists invariably raised the question of the sanctity of private property. The West Virginia Socialist Party was well aware of the historic importance of the concept of property to the American worker. Therefore, a good deal of discussion centered on what property would be left to individuals once the central goal of Cooperative Commonwealth had been achieved and the major tools of production, distribution, and communications were owned by all the people.⁸³ Interviews and examination of local party press reveal a very wide range of opinion on the subject; however, it is possible to discern a rough consensus.

The local Socialists agreed with the *Appeal to Reason* that the movement was not a plot to take away all property and divide it up among the multitude. As Samuel Cross put it, "Socialism teaches no such rascality . . . which would be as silly as dividing up a postage stamp, or a lamp post in a highway."⁸⁴ Naturally there would be a better distribution of wealth as the worker would finally get more of what was rightly his and there would be more aid to those who "couldn't make it on their own."⁸⁵ It was true, however, that a slightly different definition of private property would prevail under the Cooperative Commonwealth. A man would own anything that he could take with him, like his horse, his buggy, or his books. In addition, every man would have a house that was his and his family's as long as they used it, and they could beautify it to suit their own tastes. While some might criticize the latter, the Socialists argued rather persuasively that a home would be more secure than under the present system when the coal company or the mortgage banker could take your dwelling practically at will.⁸⁶ In short, there would be far more private property under socialism and "your title to your home would be like your wife. You did not buy her and you cannot sell her and nobody can lawfully take her away from you."⁸⁷

In an essentially rural state like West Virginia, the question of land ownership became a matter of real concern to the local Socialists. This was especially true of these early years of rapid growth when the party hoped to attract farmer support. The Socialists understood the fears of the farmers who had been told by the capitalists' press that the radicals would take away their farms and drop them on the roadside while all agricultural land was collectivized. The truth was that no farmer who was putting his land to productive use had anything to fear. As it would turn out, the farmer would also have more private property and opportunity under socialism. Cheap land was passing away; therefore, access to existing acreage that was not being utilized should become an unalienable right. Furthermore, the farmer would be able to realize a greater profit for his work since the Cooperative Commonwealth would provide machinery, model farms, and special agricultural schools. His costs would be cut by the use of state-approved, low-interest loan, public-owned storage, transportation, and marketing facilities. And finally, it might even come to pass that the spirit of cooperation would eventually create in the farmers the desire to work on communal land. If so, advised the Socialists, "that bridge can be easily crossed when we come to it."[88]

West Virginia Socialist platform and publications went to great length to show that there was no basic conflict between socialism and Christianity. Jesus Christ was often portrayed as the first Socialist who came into the world to establish a social order based on unselfish cooperation. It was the money interests of that day that had been behind His crucifixion. Despite the efforts of other dedicated disciples down through history, the Christian church remained in the hands of the corruptors—Christ's original teaching. Therefore, what Socialists often rejected was the institutional church or, as they would say, "not Christianity but Churchianity."[89] Herndon Link, a secretary of his local at Ronceverte, explained this attitude in verse. A "wanderer" through life asks Father Time to interpret a vision:

> "He cleared his throat, he shook his head and
> then the old man laughed,
> He said the crafts were churches, the members were the crews,
> The preachers were the captains and all they had to do,
> was cater to the big ship (capitalism), and among other things
> had to dance to the music when the
> Captain pulled the strings."[90]

By replacing capitalism, the Cooperative Commonwealth would redeem the promises of Christ. For socialism was not only an economic revolt of the working class, but also the "most stupendous moral revolt the earth has ever known."[91]

Available evidence suggests that a great many converts were made by this approach. Victor Reuther recalled that his father "felt constantly challenged to apply religious ethics to the world of economics and politics."[92] Reverend Fred Smith remembers his conversion to socialism as "accepting doctrines that were compatible with the highest moral principles."[93] John Brown, a carpenter and ironically enough, the grandson of John Brown of Harper's Ferry, was sent by the national party into West Virginia in 1910. He claimed that he accepted the Creed of the Bible, "inasmuch as ye have done it to one of the least of my brothers, ye have done it unto me."[94] This is not to suggest that all West Virginia Socialists were good Christians. For example, Wyatt Thompson, editor of the *Huntington Socialist and Labor Star*, claimed that many of the real leaders of the West Virginia Party were free thinkers like himself. However, Thompson pointed out, "There were a lot of comrades who associated socialism with Christianity. Well, we certainly didn't do anything to discourage them. As a matter of fact, you might even say we encouraged them."[95]

In addition to portraying themselves as being on the Lord's side, the West Virginia Socialists emphasized that they were the only political organization that exemplified America's original ideals. This claim was consistent with the party's national platform, which boasted that the Socialists were "defenders and preservers of the idea of liberty and self government, in which the nation was born."[96] The radicals' particular interpretation of American history was used to strengthen their position. According to this view, America's institutions were founded in freedom by colonists who fled oppressive European societies. The Revolution and Declaration of Independence represented important steps in such democratic growth. But the movement had been thwarted in 1787 when the privileged classes drew up the Constitution while the "Proletarian fighters of the Revolution had gone back to the farmers and workshops." From that time on, money powers began to corrupt the country's heritage of freedom. State and national legislatures became mere agencies of the protected interests. Major political parties invariably came under their control. Modern political organizations were good cases in point. The Democratic Party, which had formerly been controlled by the slave-owning aristocracy, was now jointly in the hands of the child-slave plutocracy and the bosses of the "criminal elements of our slums." As for the Republican, its original high ideals were soon perverted by the influence of the "predatory criminals of the palace."[97] Only the Socialist Party was democratically organized and controlled and consequently fit to redeem the principles of the Revolutionary Fathers.

The Socialists promised to transform America into a genuine political democracy. They would begin by abolishing the Constitution of the states and nation and replace them with a framework more in keeping with the ideals of direct democracy. Basic legislative power would be vested in one, house bodies elected by citizens who would possess universal suffrage. The bills passed by these bodies would be the law of the land until rejected by a referendum vote of the people. In addition, a president without a veto and all judges would be elected, and would serve no longer than four years. These and all other public officials would be subjected to recall by the vote of the citizens.[98]

The West Virginia Socialists also believed that a real functional democracy required a vigorous local government. Therefore, all the cities and districts of each state ought to have absolute self-government. The cities could thus establish their own utilities, laundries, slaughterhouses, bathhouses, and even build houses for their citizens.[99] It might seem logical that the Socialists would be supporters of a more scientific form of city government in order to implement their program. But as Samuel Hays has shown, the working class was often opposed to many of those progressive reforms that were designed to produce efficiency in municipal affairs.[100]

The Wheeling labor radicals shared with most of their fellow workingmen a suspicion of the efforts of that city's Municipal Reform League to create a new commission form of government. The Ohio Valley Trades and Labor Assembly claimed that the Municipal Reform League was not a group of public-spirited citizens trying to improve city service and end corruption. Instead the League was an organization that obeys in "slavish submission to the will of the giant steel trust looking toward the wiping out of the influence of labor in the entire Wheeling district."[101] Charleston workingmen were equally critical of attempts to replace the old ward system with city councilmen elected at large on a bipartisan basis. Such an arrangement was seen as a subtle attempt by the "Whiskey Ring" and political bosses to thwart the growing political power of the working class. Besides, a democratic society did not need a "gang of newfangled idea experts."[102] In fact, most of the planning in a Socialist-run city would be done by voluntary committees of interested citizens.[103] This may seem a naïve attitude for the radicals to take, especially in light of their acknowledgment of its growing complexity and interdependence of society. However, it roughly paralleled the idea of industrial democracy by many West Virginia Socialists. By this plan, workers' committees in basic industries would make important production decisions.[104]

The Socialists also promised to redeem the natural heritage of America. There would be broad programs of reforestation and land reclamation. Moreover, the public domain would be extended to all potential water-power sites, quarries, and oil reserves. Thus, the Socialist state of the future would not only be a more beautiful place to live, but public management of resources would provide timber at cost, better farmland, and very cheap power.[105]

In general, the Mountain State Socialists were able to strike an appealing balance between immediate reform and the overriding goal of the Cooperative Commonwealth. Party principles made it clear, of course, that no reforms would really work as long as the means of production and distribution remained in the hands of the capitalists.[106] At the same time, state and city platforms offered the widest variety of reform programs from free textbooks for public schools, progressive income tax, boards of health, down to rather prosaic local items like streetlights for the workingmen's districts in Charleston.[107]

The local radicals were occasionally equivocal in their application of Socialist principles. The West Virginia party's stand on equality for the Negro was a case in point. The local Socialists claimed they desired to unite all workers regardless of "nationality, color, or creed."[108] Drives were sometimes proposed to attract Negro members into the West Virginia party. However, even the local Socialists most interested in these efforts urged that Negroes form separate local branches.[109] This attitude may only be a further indication of the radicals' understanding of the deep-seated prejudices of their fellow workingmen. Examples of this prejudice appear even in official union business. In a striking case, the carpenters of Huntington conducted a full inquiry to determine who had dealt them the great indignity of placing them behind a Negro contingent in a Labor Day parade.[110]

The West Virginia Socialists realized the need for the widest possible publicity for their doctrines. Through sacrifices of time and money, they had begun to achieve their goal. Funds were raised to sponsor regular Socialist Lyceum lecturers. Publicity committees of local branches circulated a large number of pamphlets and other socialist tracts.[111] Many radicals used their own funds to purchase bundles of the *Appeal to Reason,* which they hoped would interest the workers. This technique was paying off as more than five thousand West Virginians were subscribing to the *Appeal to Reason* by 1909.[112] In addition, the local Socialists managed to create the beginnings of their own press. In Charleston the radicals apparently pooled their savings and purchased *The Labor Argus,* which was owned and edited by Frank Snyder and his brother Alvin. Most of the money for this move was provided by the new Socialist editor Charles Boswell, who had come into Charleston from Virginia and had opened a small furniture business. The West Virginia radicals also had an important voice in Walter Hilton, the editor of the *Wheeling Majority.* Although the *Majority* was backed by the Amalgamated Association of Iron, Steel, and Tin workers, financing removed a problem and much of the success was due to Hilton's dedication.[113] By 1910, the labor press upon which most West Virginia workingmen relied was Socialist-owned or dominated.

The Mountain State Socialist Party could take great satisfaction in its growth from 1905 to 1911. From not more than a half dozen early chapters, it had grown to an organization of some fifty-three local branches with more being organized every day.[114] Party growth was reflected in impressive gains at the polls. The vote for Debs in 1908 represented almost a 100 percent increase over 1904. Furthermore, by 1910, many state and congressional candidates in counties with well-established Socialist organizations were doing even better with increases ranging up to 400 percent.[115] In the minds of more workers unionism and socialism were becoming synonymous. As a miner from Elkridge in Fayette County expressed it in 1910, "There is a spirit of unionism now that I candidly didn't believe ever existed before at this place. The boys here will organize a Socialist local next Friday."[116]

The West Virginia Socialists had been skillful in capitalizing on the discontent that resulted from a growing concentration of industrial holdings and a panic in 1907. The Socialist Party is often criticized for its failure to understand the American workingman and his traditions. This interpretation argues that the Socialists wasted time and energy with theoretical appeals for a class-conscious movement to workers who did not think in class terms and were far more interested in a larger share of the fruits of an expanding capitalistic economy.[117] The activities and educational efforts of the West Virginia Socialists for the period covered by this chapter suggests that the local radicals were well aware of the nature of their prospective converts. It may be that the fairly moderate position of the national party during these years set the tone. On the other hand, the evidence suggests that the Mountain State Socialists were not afraid to discuss some of the broadest implications of their program. Moreover, they were able to do it in a way that was compatible with such long-standing concepts as private property, religious beliefs, and historic national purpose.

CHAPTER III
The Susceptibility of the West Virginia Working-Class Leadership to the Appeal of Socialism

A fuller understanding of the nature and limitations of the West Virginia Socialist appeal must go beyond an appreciation of the party's tactical and propaganda techniques. It is equally important to attempt to comprehend why some workers were more influenced than others by the Socialist approach. In order to determine if any particular set of social variables characterized the Socialists, a master list of working-class radicals was formulated. The list consisted of workers who had demonstrated leadership by being either candidates for important political offices or by holding positions in state Socialist organizations.[1] Life data was then obtained for some eighty figures from this list. For purposes of comparison, life data were also obtained for a control group selected from holders of important trade union or political offices.[2]

The information gathered on the local Socialists and the control group is subject to several limitations. In the first place, there is relatively little material on workingmen in county histories, *Who's Who*, or genealogical sources.[3] Therefore, the great bulk of the data for this study was gathered by interviews. In order to make the sample as valid as possible, only those individuals were included for whom information was provided by a close relative. In the second place, this study is weighted in favor of Kanawha and Fayette counties, where it was more feasible for the researcher to locate individuals who could supply the need information. On the other hand, at least twelve counties are represented to some degree in the sample. In addition, every effort was used to keep the study balanced between the more rural coal-mining communities and the state's urban industrial centers.

In some respects, the Socialist and non-Socialist working class leaders were fairly similar. In the first place, both groups were at least as heavily native in composition as the total working force of the state. Only about 8 percent of the Socialist and 10 percent of the control sample were of foreign birth. This compares with a 9 percent foreign-birth, employed West Virginia males, whose occupation as listed in the 1910 census would classify them as working class.[4] The nativity of those leaders in the samples who were miners is especially impressive. Among the coal operatives in West Virginia, thirty percent were of foreign birth; however, only eight percent of the miners in the control group were born outside of the United States. The Socialist miner leadership was almost as thoroughly native, with 90 percent born in this country. Furthermore, many important members of the socialist sample traced the families back to figures in early American history. Darius O. Boone was a direct descendant of Daniel Boone's brother.[5] Cleveland Toney claimed his earliest descendant had come to this country with LaFayette.[6] Wyatt Thompson maintained that the first ancestor in this country came to America as an indentured servant on the *Mayflower*.[7] All of this may be surprising in light of the frequent stereotype of the Socialist Party as consisting mostly of foreigners.

On the other hand, it is possible that the socialism of some of those who were first-generation natives of this country was closer to that of the small percentage of their comrades who were foreign-born. Adherence to socialism by such ethnic groups is often viewed as an attempt on their part to retain a cultural identity or as a defense mechanism against rejection by the dominant society.[8] Certainly, some case for the interpretation could be made for many working-class Socialists in West Virginia. Close relatives of some radicals recalled that foreign-language publications were read in their homes.[9] Finns in Weston and Clarksburg had organized their own Socialist branches. Wheeling had a Polish Socialist local.[10] George DelForge felt that some of the socialism among the Belgian glassworkers came as a result of contact made on frequent "fire out" (summer) trips to their homeland.[11] Warren Martin, a retired glassworker who had "married into the trade," recalled that the farmers around Star City did not always appreciate or understand the Belgians. "A lot of them (farmers) felt the glassworkers drank too much and generally had too much fun."[12] Although respondents often tried to diminish the radicalism of relatives, something of glassworkers' reaction to the treatment above may be found in Edward Shay's description of his father's involvement in the local Socialist branch in Star City. "I wouldn't say that my father and the Council were really Socialists," Shay explained, "their organization was just a political party that the glassworkers got up to get into office. After all, the farmers around here were the Democrats and the big dogs in Morgantown controlled the Republican."[13]

The response of the West Virginia Socialist leaders to the interest of various ethnic groups was somewhat ambivalent. On the one hand, the local party welcomed all the support they could get and talked typically about the unity and brotherhood of the working class. On the other hand, outside of those of German background, few of obvious foreign background rose to the top ranks in the state party organizations. Part of the reason may be illustrated by the case of the local Finnish and Polish branches. While these groups sometimes contributed to the work of state movement, they were linked to the National Socialist Party primarily through membership in the various foreign-language federations. Wyatt Thompson claimed that such foreign-language groups lacked real commitment to the local struggles of the party because they "were mostly social clubs and not really interested in our political and economic work."[14] Much the same attitude prevailed toward Italians whom mine operators often identified as Socialists. For instance, a blacklist sent to operators in the New River coal fields described as troublemakers such "Socialists and Anarchists" as Tomas Verano, John M. Marazie, and Louis Gugliotha.[15] On the other hand, radicals usually saw the Italians as tools used by the industrialists to hold down standards or to break strikes. A miner from Raleigh County put it this way:

It seemed to me like they was more afraid of losing their job than I was, they'd work in more danger. Whenever they'd shoot their cut of coal down, why they wouldn't stay out very long. If there was a car up there to be loaded, why they'd go up and load that car and I wouldn't have done it at all, not under no consideration. That will burn up your lungs, that hot powder smoke.[16]

A few respondents did recognize that some radicalism existed among the Italians, but that it was drawn from different sources than that of the natives. "There were some Talis that were radical," explained one former miner, "but we never understood what they believed and none were ever in any locals that I know of."[17]

The most significant ethnic difference in the leadership study was a greater incidence of persons with Germanic background in the Socialist sample. However, the 35 percent German incidence for the Socialists, as compared to only 20 percent for the control group, does not begin to give a full idea of the key role played by many of German stock in the West Virginia movement. In almost every area of the state with any substantial radical organization there was usually an important individual of German descent. In Greenbrier County, for example, the most active organizers were Herndon Link, a painter, and A. O. Pope, a railroad engineer. Two German engravers, Herman Gunter and Oscar Gneiser, were influential in the Morgantown area. As has been noted elsewhere, Wheeling's large German population provided such key figures as Albert Bauer, Raymond Bauer, Valentine Reuther, and Adrian Albert. The area south of Wheeling to Parkersburg provided party executives like Herman Rheindhardt, Dr. George Cline, and L. M. Kirkendahl, and, of course in Charleston there was George "Pappy" Gherkin. In addition, lists of local branches of the West Virginia past are full of names like Adolt, Snyder, Bock, Diefenback, Huber, Stuntz, and Herlinger.[18] Other party leaders apparently accepted this German element without question.

The Socialists and the control group share several other similarities. Their political and economic background appeared to be fairly close. In political affiliation the radicals' fathers were divided equally between Democrats and Republicans, where the control group had almost 10 percent more individuals from a Republican than Democratic tradition. Both leadership samples appear not to have had a lower occupational status than their parents. As indicated by Table I, the possible exception was the larger percentage of Socialists whose fathers were farmers. This more rural background certainly meant that many of the Socialists had to make an adjustment to a rather different way of life.

Table I: Father's Occupation

	Miners	Semi-skilled (urban)	Skilled (urban)	Farmers	Professional or White Collar
Socialist	15%	5%	30%	43%	5%
Control	20%	7%	35%	32%	4%

But whether being a miner or an industrial worker was considered a lower occupational status is debatable. Many of the farms were, at best, marginal economic units where the work was hard and existence often precarious. A fairly typical description of this type of farm was given by one respondent:

I was the oldest of eight children and we have always had to supplement the family income of our forty acre farm. We generally tended other people's farms. We'd get the first three crops for clearing a field and from then on we'd get two shocks of corn and the owner would get one. . . . As soon as I was old enough, I went to Huntington and worked the winter in a brass foundry and then back to farm in the spring to help the family out.[19]

And finally, the great majority of both leadership groups were also skilled craftsmen. However, it does appear that the Socialists reached down more often than the control group into the ranks of the semi-skilled and unskilled workers for leaders, as Table II indicates.

Table II: Occupation By Skill

	Skilled	Semi-skilled	Unskilled
Socialist	88%	8%	4%
Control	96%	4%	0%

There were important reasons why the skilled craftsman often responded very favorably to the Socialist appeal. In part, it was due to the fact that the local party frequently provided aid and leadership to the workers in their political and economic struggles. Considering some of the formidable forces arrayed against the unions, this was no mean contribution on the part of the radicals. At the same time, the Socialist vision of the future society struck a familiar note to many craftsmen. There was much in the trade union experience of iron molders, glassblowers, cigar-makers, machinists, painters, carpenters, potters, and other skilled tradesmen that made reasonable the idea of the workers taking over the means of production and operating them in the interests of all the people.[20]

Well into the first decade of the twentieth century, the skilled worker exercised a great deal of control over the process of production. The practices of the window glassworkers may be used as a case in point. The National Window Glass Workers Union consisted of four trades: blowers, gatherers, flatteners, and cutters. These skilled workers formulated, through their union, complex rules that carefully regulated the pace of production and determined the job jurisdiction of each trade. A few of the rules adopted by the National Window Glass Workers in 1908 demonstrated that this craft union still had considerable power.

No blower or gatherer shall work faster than at the rate of nine rollers per hour. . . . members will not be allowed to work with anyone not a member of the association. Poor D. S. (Double Strength) may be set for grinding at the rate of 250 feet per week per pot or place. . . . No blower shall dip out pots nor shall any gatherer carry out rollers. . . . No flattener shall be allowed to rub flattening stones. . . . Blowers and gatherers will not be allowed to tear down or daub up clute holes. . . .[21]

Moreover, it was the union members, not the managers, who parceled out the available work. For instance, the union rules provided that "Each manufacturer shall be compelled to employ a boss cutter; said boss cutter to be a member of the National Window Glass Workers, and he shall divide and distribute the orders among the cutters."[22]

The skilled glassworkers made decisions in other areas that today would certainly be considered the prerogative of management. The unionized craftsmen were a minority of labor forces in any glass plant. A host of semi-skilled and unskilled workers performed the many necessary lifting, shoveling, sweeping, loading, carrying, packing, and repairing jobs that abound in the factory. Unprotected by any union, many of these workers were hired, fired, and paid at the discretion of skilled craftsmen.

For instance, the blowers and flatteners were responsible for obtaining their own helpers, known as snappers and lehr tenders.[23] In addition, the window glassworkers were powerful enough to negotiate a method of payment that made their income almost independent of their employer. This was known as the sliding scale and it tied wage for piecework to the rise and fall of the selling price of glass.[24]

Other craftsmen in West Virginia had power similar to that held by the window workers. Interviews with machinists revealed that in the Chesapeake and Ohio shop in Huntington, the scale committee elected by the union men negotiated a piece scale wage rate with the management. The machinists represented a pool of skilled labor to which a member of the elected committee distributed jobs on the basis of trade and seniority.[25] In the pottery industry, jiggermen sometimes hired their own helpers. Finally, the coal miners elected their own committee to supervise the number of "turns" and allocation of materials needed at the coal face.[26]

With this kind of background, the skilled craftsmen needed no abstract justification for the working-class control of the modern industrial state. As David Montgomery has written, the I.W.W.'s supposedly radical idea of the labor union as a revolutionary force and the basic unit of the Cooperative Commonwealth was "Nothing new to the American workers in 1905. They had been commonplace already for 30 or 40 years and had arisen in the minds of the craftsmen themselves. . . . It was a simple, logical extension of their daily trade union practice."[27]

The data considered thus far has probably done very little to answer the question of why some workers were more inclined toward Socialism than others. It may be that a satisfactory answer to that question will come only with a deeper psychological analysis than can be achieved with the method employed in this research; however, the responses to the several variables investigated may suggest areas for future study that will yield fruitful results.

When he appeared before a United States Senate Committee investigating the Cabin Creek-Paint Creek strike, Silas Nance, the Socialist Marshall of Eskdale, claimed that only the more unintelligent miners and company men were not Socialists.[28] Interviews with relatives of West Virginia working-class radicals would suggest that claims like Nantz's ought not to be too easily passed off as mere prejudice. Comments like "studious," "great reader," "talk about anything to you," "best read person around here," "inventive," "loved mathematics," and "crazy about good literature" were often used to describe many in the Socialist sample.

More professional witnesses sometimes made similar descriptions. For example, Winthrop Lane, a nationally known journalist, covering District 17's push into the southern West Virginia coal fields felt that Fred Mooney "might have been a student under other circumstances."[29] Such claims were not unique with regard to the West Virginia movement. As Professor Charles Zuebellin of the University of Chicago put it, "most of the really intelligent people everywhere (were socialist). You may not believe that, but if you will take the pains to investigate, you will be convinced."[30]

Unfortunately, too little research has gone into any comparative measure of the Socialist's intelligence. There is some meager evidence to suggest that some Socialist or pro-Socialist groups were a bit more intelligent than other political groupings. This belief is based first on a 1924 study by Henry T. Moore, who found that Dartmouth College students supporting La Follette were in the upper third of their class while those who supported Coolidge and Davis were considerably lower. Second, and perhaps more relevant to this study, was the fact that such Socialist working-class communities as Reading and Bridgeport stood well upon E. L. Thorndike's index of community "goodness" or high mental and moral qualities of the inhabitants.[31] As evident by the table below, a much stronger case can be made for greater intelligence or, at least, more education for the West Virginia radicals. The statistics for the Socialist sample show that 51 percent of this survey had an education that was probably superior to that normally expected of workingmen during the early decades of the twentieth century. Table III (following page) indicates that the Socialist education level was significantly higher than that of the control group.

Another indication of the greater intellectual proclivity of the Socialist sample appeared too often to be ignored. Fourteen percent of the radical workingmen had taught school as compared to a little less than 4 percent for the control sample. This phenomenon did not go unnoticed by non-Socialist contemporaries. "It was the school teacher element around here that started the movement" was the way Corbet Toney characterized the Socialist organization at Dothan and Mossey in Fayette County.[32] "I didn't know who all the radicals in West Charleston were," explained E. L. Bradley, "but one of them was a school teacher."[33] As a matter of fact, this description could have applied to several of the workingmen Socialists of Charleston like Tom Swinburn, George Rathburn, or his cousin, George Glass. The same could have been said of key organizers in other places in the state such as, Dennis Argabright of Hilltop, Meade Shafer of Welford, Warren Rumbaugh of Winifrede, Joseph Snider of Fairmont, Isam Beasley of Mill Creek, and D. O. Boone of Anthony, to mention only a few. Moreover, the number of radicals who were teachers was almost evenly divided between Socialist coal miners and those who were urban workingmen.

Table III: Educational Background

Years in School	Socialists	Control
Under 3 years	4%	12%
3 to 6 years (Free School)	45%	56%
6 to 12 years	41%	25%
Attended college or college graduate	10%	4%

Socialism appeared to meet some important special needs for radical West Virginia working-class leaders. For many, socialism was the answer to a search for a more complete intellectual pattern. Ulysses Cantley was a District Seventeen official and a Socialist organizer. His brother remembered the occasion of his brother's conversion, "He'd been away and we got a letter from him saying that he had finally found the answer to the problems that had bothered him for a long time."[34] Putting it a bit differently, Wyatt Thompson explained, "Once you understood the Socialist viewpoint, you were able to see things more clearly."[35] For others, socialism answered the need to be a broadly informed person and to be on the inside of things. "The thing I liked about Boswell, Rathbaurn, and the boys around the old *Labor Argus*," explained George Harper, "was that they knew what was going on everywhere. I've even known them to predict the future."[36]

This does not mean that, even though their educational level was lower, the control group did not share the Socialist desire for self-improvement. Though interview data is more difficult to obtain on these points, a picture emerges of a number of both groups taking many correspondence courses. This, along with more general reading, would have meant many hours of after-work time for men who had already put in a ten- or twelve- hour day. However, the range of interests of the Socialist group seems to have been greater. Relatives and friends were invariably impressed with the extent of the libraries possessed by the radicals. Even the small parts of these collections that remain indicate the range of interests of some of the Socialists. For example, there are only a few shelves of Herndon Link's library at Ronceverte. Nevertheless, there are books on spiritualism like Maurice Meterlinck's *The Light Beyond*; Fanny Paget's *How I Know the Dead Are Alive*; an anthropology like Fostia's *Prehistoric Races of the United States*; or Wilhelm "Bo" Ische's *The Evolution of Man*; a collection of novels by Victor Hugo and Jack London; books on pictorial and line composition and an assortment of American history works.[37] The remnants of other Socialists' libraries were similar to Link's with additional works on geology, mathematics, and Biblical criticism sharing the shelves with more standard works on socialism, economics, and politics.[38]

Another important difference between the Socialist sample and the control group was in religious orientation. At first, this difference was not so apparent since 50 percent or better of both groups fit into what may be considered a normal religious pattern. That is to say, 50 percent of the radicals and 54 percent of the control group fit into a religious spectrum that ranged from Baptist and Methodist to Presbyterian, Lutheran, Episcopal, and Catholic. In addition, significant numbers in both groups were not active in any established church. Some workers accounted for this lack of interest by pointing out the long hours of taxing work, which allowed little time for church.[39]

The statistical comparison of the radicals and control groups below suggests that the Socialists were more often found in both extreme positions of the religious spectrum. It comes as no surprise that many of the Socialists were recognized by friends and relatives as "free thinkers."

Table IV: Religious Attitudes and Preferences of Socialist and Non-Socialist Labor Leaders

	Socialist	Non-Socialist
Non-church members	16%	30%
Professed Atheists, Agnostics, and other "free thinkers"	9%	3%
Catholics, Episcopals, Lutherans, and Presbyterians	17%	16%
Baptists, Methodists	33%	38%
Pentecostal churches	25%	13%

For instance, it was well known in Wheeling labor circles that Walter Hilton was an authority on Unitarianism. He was the only layman invited to speak at a conference on the subject at Harvard University.[40] In the Field's Creek area of Kanawha County, "Rob" Morris, later elected constable on the Socialists ticket, was "hated by many because he was such an infidel."[41] In Huntington, several party members' religious positions were regarded as similar to

J. M. Near, who wrote, "I have been a member of the Socialist Party for eight years and an agnostic for thirty years before."[42]

A much more impressive religious characteristic of the Socialists was the high incidence of individuals in the radical sample who could be classified as Pentecostal. As Table IV indicates, the Socialist sample contained almost twice as many persons in these churches as the control group. A wide variety of sects, such as Seventh Day Adventists, Missionary Baptists, and Holiness, made up the Pentecostal group; however, the largest single sect was the Campbellites. Charles Holstein, who grew up at Coalburg in the Cabin Creek district, recalled that his father's Campbellite friends often met at each other's homes and practiced defending their religious and political positions. "Some would take one side of an issue and some would take the other. They might debate church questions one night and socialism another. Many an evening it was hard for me to tell where their religious debate left off and socialism began."[43] Henry Grounds, a district mine official and secretary of the Socialist local at Boomer, was described by his nephew as "The man who stood out in my mind because he really practiced his religion. He was a Campbellite and the nearest thing to what I'd call a really good man.[44]

Howard Quint has suggested that recent historians have overstated the importance of the social gospel movement on American Protestantism. Instead, Quint has pointed out, it is the basic conservatism of all American denominations that ought to be reemphasized. For it is their conservatism that have made this country's religious institutions bulwarks of the status quo and a formidable force blocking the spread of radical social and economic doctrine.[45] However, many of the denominations to which working-class radicals in the sample belonged were not necessarily an inhibiting force.

There was much in the Pentecostal tradition that could be called upon to justify and sustain radical social action.[46] For those in these religious groups, the special role of the working class in historical process often seemed based more on a Christian perfectionism than on Marx. "The true church says to the working class," wrote a Holiness church member, "teach the lesson of righteousness and capital will follow."[47] Wealth was viewed as being far from the reward given by God to his Christian stewards claimed by the gospel of wealth justification for laissez-faire capitalism. Members of Pentecostal churches did not need Socialist agitators to tell them of the immorality of the rich. Their preacher often made that clear. For instance, Reverend Hendershott, whose church attracted many Huntington Socialists, condemned the wild parties held by the "first families" of the city. "It is freely charged on the street," Hendershott reported on one of these affairs, "that the daughter of a certain Republican of national renown had the nipples of her breasts enameled blue to add to the gaiety of the occasion."[48] The Pentecostal radical often saw a testing of his faith in the trouble that befell him as a result of industrial conflict. When Charles "Coon" Jarrell was arrested and sent to the penitentiary at Moundsville for his strike activities, he was not surprised, for "it was only history repeating itself, for when Joseph was sold into Egypt, his brothers meant to do him harm but God meant it for good." This tribulation, Jarrell believe, was God's way of getting his children to see the light, for the jail experience made a man a "solid union man and a full fledged Socialist."[49] Socialism also tapped a millennialism spirit that found its strongest and more immediate strain in the Pentecostal sects. A radical from Fayette County wrote, "I had many visions from God. I visited hell and heaven through the power of God. . . . God spoke to me last winter and said if Socialism were adopted by all the world everybody would go to heaven on horses of fire and chariots just like Enoch."[50]

It may be going too far to suggest that the majority of the Socialist sample was more essentially spiritual than the control group. On the other hand, it is interesting to note how frequently relative to their counterparts in the control group the non-church goers in the Socialist sample were identified by relatives as basically religious personalities. George "Fleet" Parsons was one of the most active

Socialist organizers in Kanawha County. His son recalled that their home was so crowded that his mother often slept with the girls while his father shared the boys' bed. Like most miners, Parsons rose before daylight. However, Parsons's son remembered that his father got up even earlier than anyone else and read the Bible by firelight. "Yet he never professed a religion in his life and thought preachers were phonies," recalled his son.[51] Similar descriptions were made of other radicals. C. B. Chewning allegedly did not attend church, but was "strong on church principles."[52] Isom Beasley didn't "care for church but knew his Bible by heart."[53] Carl Shane belonged to no religious institution, but "always talked about his mother reading nothing but religious books to him and he could still tell you everything about them."[54]

It is important to remember that the sociological data used in this analysis cannot completely explain the susceptibility of the working class to socialism. Some idea of the complexity of the phenomenon was obvious from incidental impressions derived from the interviews. For example, it is likely that many individuals in the radical sample were chronically rebellious and antagonistic personalities. Comments like "nothing ever suited him," "you'd say black and he'd say white," or "I've seen him argue for a thing one day and take just the opposite view the next," were used in regard to several of the radicals. Wyatt Thompson candidly explained that his own susceptibility might have been due to the fact that "I guess for some reason I was always a rebel."[55] To others the party meant an opportunity for more satisfying careers. When asked about the danger of being a full-time organizer for the party, one radical responded, "Well, it was a heck of a lot better than being in the mines. I never did like that work much anyway." And a former party member from Charleston explained, "several of the boys joined the party for what they could get out of it, they knew they couldn't get anywhere otherwise."[56] It seems likely that these individuals and others whose grievances were more objective should be grouped together in the way they viewed socialism. For these radicals the Socialist Party represented a vehicle for deviating from the prevailing social patterns of their communities.

On the other hand, the most impressive result of this study was the high incidence of those radical workingmen who could interpret socialism as being in conformity with goals and ideals of many existing institutions. One further point serves as illustration. In every industrial community, whether a coal community or a mill town, one was likely to find a rather large number of fraternal organizations to which workingmen belonged. Although this type of data was the most difficult to obtain, enough workers' affiliations could be discovered to indicate that the radicals belonged to as many fraternal societies as the control group. However, the Socialists were found more often in organizations like the Order of the Redmen, Elks, or Eagles whose membership and ideals were more democratic. This appears to be especially true of the Redmen, which traces its origin to Revolutionary War Sons of Liberty in Maryland. For their part, the control group was more often found to be Knights of Pythias or Masons.[57]

Table V: Participation of Socialists in Fraternal Organizations

	Masons	I.O.O.F.	K.O.F.P.	Elks, Moose, Eagles	Redmen
Socialist	10%	10%	10%	25%	45%
Non-Socialist	36%	16%	22%	18%	8%

*Based on only 25% of sample

The evidence produced by this study permits a tentative description of working-class leaders who were attracted to socialism. They were more native and more rural in origin than their non-radical contemporaries. Although the local Socialists did not appear to be engaged in occupations of a lower status than that of their parents, the way of life and problems many of them discovered in the evolving industrial setting had a deep impact. Part of a letter from A. O. Pope of Ronceverte to *The Appeal of Reason* seems typical. "I did not realize," Pope wrote of the workers' difficulties, "such a condition existed until I got out among men who are dependent upon day labor for a living."[58] The great social sensitivity frequently displayed by the local Socialists may be related, in part, to the fact that they were better educated and possessed a broader range of interests than their more conservative peers. At the same time, the local radicals seem to have taken religious teachings more seriously than other workers. In some cases, this caused them to rebel against the institutional church while, at the same time, demonstrating its techniques in their own lives. In other cases, the radicals became more deeply committed to their particular denomination. For the most part, this tendency was most frequent among those who belonged to one of the radical Protestant sects that were common to working-class communities. The general characteristics of the majority of the Socialist sample would indicate that the range of radical appeal was potentially greater than might be expected.

CHAPTER IV
"We Had The Revolution": The West Virginia Socialist Party At Its Peak: 1912–1915

The Socialist Party of West Virginia achieved its greatest successes between 1912 and 1915. On both the political and industrial fronts it made significant progress. These victories were not unmixed blessings for they forced upon the party some formidable internal and external problems. Solutions to these difficulties were necessary to the continued viability of the West Virginia radical organization and influence.

In the spring of 1912, the Mountain State Socialists obtained endorsement for their party from the West Virginia Federation of Labor. In May, the representatives to the state's Central Labor Body met in Wheeling. On the second day of the convention, Herbert J. Ninness, a moulder and the secretary of one of Wheeling's Socialist organizations, moved that the *Wheeling Majority* be made the official newspaper of the Federation. Apparently encouraged by the delegates' approval of Ninness's motion, Harry J. Murphy, a member of Local 13 of the Operative Potters of Cameron in neighboring Marshall County, proposed that the State Federation officially urge the workingmen of West Virginia to vote for the state and national candidates of the Socialist Party in the next election. This resolution was defeated. However, by May 15, the radicals were ready to try once more.[1]

It was the report of the State Federation's Legislative Committee that provided the Socialists with more leverage. Andrew Niehas, a potter and Socialist from Wheeling, explained for the committee that the makeup and attitudes of the state legislature were such that about the best the delegates could hope for was the passage of a workmen's compensation law. Niehas added that it had been impossible to obtain a strong employers' liability act. A rising personality in the State Federation of Labor and a recent convert to socialism, Harry P. Corcoran, of the Wheeling Stogie Workers, explained that union men should not be surprised at the report, and then sank the hook by warning, "as long as 75 to 80 percent of the members of the legislature represent the capitalists, we haven't as much chance as a 'snowball in hell' of getting desired legislation."[2] At that point, Valentine Reuther, the Socialist President of Wheeling's Brewery Driver's Union, suggested that the only solution was the solidarity of the working class. Therefore, he proposed that all unions be admonished to join the State Federation. Furthermore, all organizations of that body should urge their members to affiliate with the "working class political party—the party that stands squarely upon the class struggle." Though Reuther's motion had not mentioned the party by name, he had clearly defined it as the only political organization that had for its objective, "the control of the government by the workers, the abolishing of the exploitation of the workers through the capitalists system, and the giving of the unions the full social value of their toil." Certainly, there was no doubt of the meaning of Reuther's motion in the minds of those who waged a futile fight against it and insisted that their voices be recorded as opposing.[3]

The Mine Wars Begin

Coincidentally, May of 1912 also marked the beginning of events that would precipitate the great Cabin Creek-Paint Creek Coal Strike, and presented the Socialist Party of West Virginia with some of its greatest challenges. The trouble in the Kanawha coal fields began on May 2 when the miners on Paint Creek struck because their employers had refused to consent with the remainder of the Kanawha County operators in granting one-half of the pay increase agreed to by the United Mine Workers and the operators of the central competitive fields at their recent meeting in Cleveland.[4]

The Paint Creek operators claimed that they could not afford what amounted to a two and one-half cents a ton increase because they lost money the previous year. Depending upon whose figures one wishes to believe, there is evidence that the coal business in southern West Virginia was beginning to realize more of a profit after a relatively hand-to-mouth existence and that the operators hoped to make the most of the brighter picture. Furthermore, the Paint Creek operators felt that it was especially unfair for them to acquiesce in any wage increase when just over the mountain their competition on Cabin Creek ran at a greater profit on non-union labor.[5]

It is clear that the United Mine Workers of America saw the importance of this strike. Local issues not withstanding, a largely unorganized West Virginia was an important threat to the progress of the national union. The Mountain State miners' share of total national production had increased from 8.4% in 1900 to 12.5% by 1912.[6] Consequently, it was vital that the miners' organization not suffer another setback like it received in 1904 when Cabin Creek was lost during a dispute over check-off.[7] Union officials realized that they had to hold Paint Creek operators in line and make strenuous efforts to organize more of the Kanawha and New River mine districts in order to guarantee their union's future in West Virginia. Therefore, it was not long before union organizers were spreading the strike to the unorganized Cabin Creek and New River areas.[8]

During the early days of the strike, the strategy of the Paint Creek operators was to keep their operations going. They hired men who allegedly were to make needed repairs on tipples and other above-ground facilities. At the same time, notices were posted advising the miners that economic conditions did not warrant a wage increase and offering work at the scale of wages prior to March 31, 1912. Workers who would not accept this offer were told to vacate their company houses at once.[9] The miners ignored the eviction notices and attempted to prevent the tipple work, which they felt was thinly disguised strike-breaking activity. The operators, in turn, brought in substantial numbers of Baldwin-Felts guards to protect their property, and to proceed with evictions. Anticipating a bitter struggle, the operators also imported a large number of high-powered rifles and some machine guns. At Mucklow, about five miles from the mouth of Paint Creek, an iron fort was erected and armed with a machine gun. In the face of such overwhelming force, the miners retreated into safer union strongholds, incorporated towns, or to tent villages established on private property not controlled by the coal companies. The most famous of the latter was Holly Grove near the mouth of Paint Creek.[10]

Violence had been characteristic of West Virginia coal strikes. But the bloodshed that accompanied the Paint Creek-Cabin Creek strike during the summer of 1912 took on the symptoms of a real civil war. Miners began procuring forty-five to seventy Springfield rifles and ammunition from Charleston. Each side blamed the other for the sporadic attacks that took place. In late July, the miners, organized into squads and companies with handkerchiefs tied to their arms, conducted operations against Mucklow with real military precision. Only the arrival of mine guard reinforcements prevented the town from being overrun.[11] A similar full-scale battle took place at Dry Branch on Cabin Creek while smaller skirmishes broke out elsewhere. Regular law enforcement officials had difficulty keeping any kind of order. Charles Crawford, the constable on Cabin Creek, was fired upon by snipers when he tried to ascertain the facts about the Dry Branch incident, and as a result he wrote that he "went back to my home at Miami and never went back to my office until the strike was settled." The increasing violence and pleas for law enforcement by officials brought the first of two declarations of martial law by Governor William Glasscock and contingents of state militia to restore order.[12]

These and subsequent events were made to order for the Socialists to assert their leadership. They took upon themselves many of the most dangerous tasks, some of which the regular mine worker leadership were not anxious to assume. When Frank Keeney discovered that the United Mine Workers headquarters in Charleston could provide no one to help him in his efforts to organize Cabin Creek, he turned to the Socialists. It was "Mother" Jones who was courageous enough to go with Keeney to the incorporated community of Eskdale and there bluff machine-gun-armed mine guards into allowing her to hold a mass meeting. This meeting was such a success that the Cabin Creek miners joined the struggle and Eskdale became a center of militant strike activity.[13]

"Mother," as she was affectionately called, became one of the central figures of the strike. She had been an organizer in the labor movement for almost forty years, a task that she began shortly after the tragedy of losing her husband and children in a southern yellow fever epidemic, and her possessions in the Chicago fire.[14] Her radicalism was well known. Inflammatory speeches earned her a jail sentence in Clarksburg, West Virginia, during the 1902 coal strike. She participated in the formation of the I.W.W. in 1905 and had come into the Kanawha Valley fresh from the Cripple Creek strike. A week after the Eskdale incident, "Mother" Jones led 6,000 striking miners to the state capitol building to pressure Governor Glasscock into removing the hated mine guards. Some of her ability to inspire was apparent as she harangued the miner with:

This fight will not stop until the last damn guard is disarmed. Talk about a few guards getting bullets in their skulls, the whole damned lot of them ought to get bullets in their skulls . . . can't you see how to do the business? If they proclaim martial law, bury your guns. You can tell the governor that, if you see him. . . .[15]

Local radicals often took the lead in supplying the miners with weapons and directing their use. At Eskdale, Socialists E. E. Cunningham and Silas Nance organized a chapter of the American Rifle Association in order to obtain government surplus Krag-Jorgenson rifles at low prices.[16] Additional Springfield rifles, ammunition, and explosives were brought up the north side of the Kanawha River to the Italian mining community of Boomer and then ferried across at night to the strike zone. Wyatt Thompson left his Socialist paper in Huntington long enough to pitch in. As he recalled:

> My humble duty was the delivery of high powered rifle ammunition secured for the miners by their good friend, O. J. Morrison, to the battlers within the martial law zone. I had just delivered [sic] a couple of suitcases full to the south side of the river . . . and was stepping into the Johnboat to be rowed back to the north bank, when the soldiers turned a spotlight on us from the high river bank. . . . I had my back to them and I also had on a belt with holster and revolver, I eased the gun from the holster and flipped it into the river, and I don't think they ever did believe the story I told them of wearing that holster to carry tools in.[17]

Other Socialists like George "Fleet" Parsons, John Brown, Ulysses S. Cantley, Walter Deal, O. W. Williams, and Charles Boswell were active in organizing for the defense of towns, marshalling points, and leading armed patrols.[18] Many local radicals also contributed to the growing militancy of the miners by urging direct action. For example, two days after "Mother" Jones spoke at Eskdale, Harold Houston explained his attitude to an enthusiastic audience at the Holly Grove tent community. "I have become in recent years almost what they call 'Haywoodite'. Some of the friends in the state say I must be removed from office because I believe in direct action. Gentlemen, I believe in action that gets results, and as Bill Haywood says, 'The more direct, the better.'" Such extreme measures were justified in part by the conditions in the mining community. Again, Houston explained, "I try to be temperate, but it is very hard. I intended to talk mild until I came up this valley. And if it has that sort of effect on me, what must it have upon you who have to live in it."[19]

At the same time, the more militant Socialists endeavored to create an awareness among the strikers that their struggle might have much greater significance. Houston urged the miners to follow the strategy Bill Haywood had outlined for the textile workers at Lowell, Massachusetts. Their demand for higher wages should be repeated until the miners get possession of the mines.[20] "Mother" Jones wanted the strikers to see their struggle in West Virginia as part of the industrial and economic war that was going on all over the United States. These conflicts, she maintained, were building up to a revolution in which the workers would demand their rights and take them by force.[21] Moreover, the action of the operators and the miners' retaliation might well indicate that the ".... active conflict between the fully developed forces of Capital and the Army of Organized labor" would begin in West Virginia.[22] There was much that transpired which lent credibility to the radical Socialists' analysis.

The behavior of the state militia could be cited as proof that the government of West Virginia was a mere tool of capitalist interests. At first, the great majority of miners welcomed the soldiers and were pleased when steps were taken by the military to disarm all parties in the district, and several mine guards were sent to Charleston to await trial. The remainder of the "Baldwin Thugs" were allegedly ordered to leave the district.[23] Soon, however, the situation began to change as the military was used to evict some miners from their homes, and to prevent *The Labor Argus* and other radical literature from circulating in the strike zone. Even more serious was the fact that militiamen were soon escorting strikebreakers into the district, thus allowing many operators to resume nearly normal production. The latter occurred during the interim between martial law periods when the governor, in a step to guarantee the peace, had allowed national guardsmen to work as private police.[24]

According to the Socialists, the about-face by the army was direct proof of the power of wealth over government. It had become obvious to the coal barons that a strong feeling of friendship existed between the soldiers and the miners. To change this situation, influence was used to open militia enrollment to all sorts of "saloon bums, pimps, tin horn gamblers, and Baldwin Guards." Thus, the militiamen who had remained were nothing but the scab hirelings of the operators.[25]

Additional evidence of the power of the special interests of West

Virginia came from the failure of state officials to work out arbitration of this strike as well as future industrial conflicts. Governor Glasscock tried to bring the contending parties together in September. The United Mine Workers agreed, but the operators refused to attend.[26] Equally frustrating were the failures of a meeting sponsored by State Senator Sam Montgomery to bring together coal operators, miners, and representatives of civil, commercial, and industrial organizations to formulate arbitration legislation. Glasscock, in true progressive fashion, blamed the "bipartisan invisible government," which continually frustrated constructive industrial efforts.[27] The Socialists agreed and explained that the invisible government was, in fact, Clarence W. Watson, the president of Consolidation Coal Company of Fairmont. His was the corrupting influence that has enabled the operators to maintain the guard system and brought the State of West Virginia to the edge of civil war. The radicals' way to correct the state's backward attitude on industrial matters was to elect Socialists to office.[28]

Pockets of Socialism: The 1912 Election

The publicity surrounding the events of the strike in the coal fields lifted the spirits and prospects of the West Virginia party members for the election of 1912. In Kanawha and Fayette counties this enthusiasm was noticeable early in the summer. In June and July the Socialist parties of both counties held large nominating conventions. Kanawha County's meeting was held on June first. It was chaired by Harold Houston and Ulysses S. Cantley, a District 17 United Mine Worker official and Socialist Party organizer. The *Charleston Gazette* bestowed one of its rare compliments on the Socialist Party by noting that the convention was "especially well attended for a third party."[29]

As the tempo of the strike picked up, the Kanawha County Socialists increased their political efforts. Mass meetings were held all over the strike zone. One of the most popular speakers was

T. L. "Doc" Tincher, a Chesapeake and Ohio Railroad engineer turned dentist. His theme was that West Virginia coal fields were little Russias ruled over by men like "Czar Cabell" whose power rested on those modern Cossacks, the Baldwin-Felts guards.[30] Vigorous efforts were made to ensure that the striking miners were correctly registered. On October 20, two or three thousand union men attended a speech by "Mother" Jones in which she emphasized that their long-standing grievances would be remedied only by voting a straight Socialist ticket.[31] The next day was declared "Socialist Day" and large groups of miners were taken to the County Court House to correct their addresses.[32]

Similar tactics were followed in other parts of the state. In nearby Charleston, a mass meeting was arranged for Eugene V. Debs at Lee and Dickinson streets. John Brown and Dallas R. Tickle, the party's City Councilman joined Debs in outlining the trouble in the mining areas.[33] At Salem in Harrison County, the party's candidates were led to their rally by a brass band of Belgian window glassworkers.[34] The Socialists in the Morgantown area organized a meeting at Star City, which, incidentally, had elected a Socialist administration in 1911. Mayor William Shay sponsored the tireless "Mother" Jones, who lectured on the strike situation.[35] In September, pre-election rallies were held all over Marshall and Ohio counties in the northern panhandle. One of the Wheeling meetings was a very large affair held at the Fair Grounds. The main speakers were J. Kier Hardie, Max Hayes, and Duncan McDonald. The latter two were United Mine Workers officials. They were followed by local Socialist candidates like Harry P. Corcoran, a vice president of the National Stogie Makers League, who was running for the House of Delegates, and Walter Hilton who was seeking to be governor.[36] In practically all the counties where any kind of Socialist organization existed, the party fielded more complete slates of candidates than ever before.[37]

The results of the election of 1912 were most gratifying to the West Virginia Socialist Party. It was true that the 5.7 percent vote for Debs was only approximately the national average (5.9 percent).

On the other hand, the Socialists had polled over fifteen thousand votes. This was double their vote of 1910 and a 302 percent increase over 1908, the greatest percentage of increase in the nation.[38] A large part of this vote came from the mine fields. Of the ten most productive coal counties, six had Socialist voting percentages well above the state's average.[39] Within the local Socialist Party, candidates were elected in the magisterial districts of Cabin Creek in Kanawha County and Falls in Fayette County. These victories were usually credited to a growing class consciousness that was produced by evictions, hardships endured in tent colonies, and the use of state militia or mine guards.[40]

By using the relatively complete returns available for Fayette County, some cautious generalization may be suggested about the coal field precincts that demonstrated strong Socialist tendencies.[41] In the first place, several points of radical strength were in the small, incorporated, or independent communities where there were miners who owned their homes or farms and traveled short distances to work in nearby coal operations. One such community was one of the first in the county to have its own Socialist local.[42] It may well be that it was in just such villages that radical miners found an especially receptive climate of opinion. As Herbert Gutman has suggested, in communities like these a large part of the working population still clung to agrarian or at least older sets of values.[43] For example, the *Charleston Gazette* describes the precinct of Mossy, which the Socialists went on to carry in 1912, as having been "a farming community, and is now mining. The coal mines there having been opened but a year or so ago, and are owned by Pittsburgh capitalists. It is said to be an ideal mining settlement."[44] Another stronghold of socialism was the nearby community of Dothan, where miners and farmers worked at coal banks in Carlisle, Oakland, Whipple, and Lick Fork.[45] Similar situations prevailed in such widely scattered Fayette communities as Lansing, Victor, Kincaid, Gatewood, and Hilltop. Miners from Red Star voted in the latter. Both Hilltop and Red Star were independent communities that had early Socialist locals. The son of a Socialist, who became mayor of Hilltop on a Citizens ticket in 1911, characterized his community as a "farm town and always more independent than the towns around it."[46] To many in such communities socialism held the hope for a more natural and humane order. One miner's wife wrote in part:

> In the days when we were well off, not many years ago,
> The men wore homemade trousers made of tow,
> The most of us were farmers and we had enough to eat,
> We raised all kinds of vegetables, and hogs to make our meat.
> We were well off, so well off them times we now regret;
> But when Socialism gets in power, we may be well off yet.
> In the days so well remembered, most of us owned our land,
> But to others not so fortunate, we would lend a helping hand.
> We would let him have a place to live, perhaps a rocky spot,
> And never cared much whether we collected our rent or not.
> We were well off, so well off times we now regret,
> But when Socialism gets in power, we may be well off yet.
> And now we are so hard up for the want of clothes and food,
> And we have to pray for water and burn coal instead of wood,
> Our boys works like bank mules, a living now to make,
> They work from sun rise till sun down as if life was at stake
> Now we are so hard up, we never can forget;
> But when Socialism gets in power we may be well off yet.[47]

Another group of Socialist precincts were composed of communities that were more typically coal camps. These would include such places as Hawks Next, part of Ansted along New River, most of the camps along Armstrong Creek, which flows into the Kanawha, and all of the Falls district, which is in close proximity to Kanawha County.[48] Most of the coal and coke production of Fayette County were developed by English capitalists. For example, Ansted was named for an English geologist, David T. Ansted, who convinced several fellow countrymen to put money into the development of the miners of the area.⁴⁹ A similar situation prevailed in the Armstrong Creek area where the mines were opened by G. H. Powell, who headed the Mount Carbon Coal Company.⁵⁰ However, the factor that such communities had in common with the strong Socialist voting precincts mentioned previously was the relative freedom for radicals to agitate.

The variety of attitudes toward union agitation and the amount of control that should be exercised by the operators were often surprising. Some Fayette operators like Justin Collins, Sam Dixon, and James Scott were rigidly anti-union. On the other hand, Patty Rend, William McKell, and T. C. Powell were much more tolerant. For example, retired miners frequently point to Rend's mines as those where the employees were always the most reluctant to strike. Similarly, in the early attempts by the United Mine Workers to organize Fayette County, the McKell's properties were among the few places where meetings could be held.⁵¹

Mine operators who were determined to prevent radical agitation and to control elections often achieved their goal. "King" Sam Dixon, the largest mine operator and Republican leader in Fayette County, was always alert to the danger from Socialists and dealt with them in a heavy-handed manner. In one striking example, some eight or ten delegates, "mainly German Socialists," from one of the Dixon operations came to their superintendent and demanded a check-weighman because they felt they were being cheated. Although this was their right under West Virginia law, the boss told the committee to move out and vacate their houses. The miners struck the next day, but Dixon authorized the use of Baldwin-Felts detectives to break the strike and "kick out all Socialist agitators."⁵² With one exception, voting precincts in Dixon-controlled mining camps had the lowest percentage of 1912 Socialist votes in Fayette County.⁵³

Mount Hope, the headquarters of Sam Dixon's New River Coal Company, presents an interesting contrast with the nearby community of Oak Hill. John Kenneth Turner, the *Appeal to Reason* correspondent to the West Virginia Mine War, was made aware of this situation when he and L. C. Rogers were preparing to leave Oak Hill, a "free town on a ridge." "This is the safest town in the district," remarked one of a pair of union miners who were seeing them off, "Now you ought to see Mount Hope! I live there, but I can't go home. . . . The mayor told me that no union man gets any protection in this town."[54]

In the urban industrial centers of West Virginia, the precincts with substantial Socialist votes demonstrate the type of worker to whom the Socialist Party appealed. In Charleston, it was the predominately white, Protestant tradespeople of the Third Ward that voted more heavily for the Socialist candidates. They were even strong enough to elect one of them to the City Council in 1911.[55] In Huntington, the party found success in the twenty-second through the twenty-seventh precincts where the employees of the Chesapeake and Ohio and Engine shops resided.[56] In Morgantown, the party obtained support from the glassworkers in the Second, Fifth, and Fourth Ward.[57] They also elected a Socialist councilman in April, 1912.[58] In Wheeling, the radicals drew well in practically all the downtown wards, but especially in Webster district, where many of the city's tobacco and steel plants were located. The population of Webster voting Socialist was a mixture of low-income native-born, some recent migrants, and a few Negroes.[59]

Although the Mountain State Socialists were able to attract votes from both major political parties, their opportunity and ability to convert Republican workingmen appears to have been greater. In the first place, the party's appeal was always strongest in the more urban or industrial counties that bordered Ohio and Pennsylvania. Eight out of ten of those counties with high percentages of Socialist votes had been primarily Republican.[60] In several urban areas the workingman precincts demonstrated this tendency. For example, in Huntington, those precincts with a high Socialist vote also had a very low regular Republican vote in 1912. On the other hand, those precincts with the highest regular Republican votes had the lowest Socialist vote.⁶¹ It is tempting to conclude that many Republican union men were more attracted to the Socialist Party or voted for the Progressives. On the other hand, many union men elsewhere were rather suspicious of progressive politicians. At least, such was the case of many members of the Ohio Valley Trades and Labor Assembly who were wary of the conference called by Governor Glasscock to draw up possible arbitration legislation for consideration by the next legislature. The Assembly had urged such a meeting, but when they saw the names of those attending, they feared it "was a political move, and in the interest of the Bull Moose Party."⁶²

An analysis of Fayette County's four magisterial districts in which mining was most extensive further illustrates the Socialist appeal. In the Falls district, which bordered Kanawha County, the Socialists drew about the same proportion of votes from each majority party. This may partially be explained by the large number of Italians in the community of Boomer who normally voted Democrat. In the three other magisterial districts of Fayetteville, Kanawha, and Mountain Cove, it was predominately Republican voters who switched to the Socialists.⁶³

The growing support for the West Virginia Socialist movement may be partially attributed to the fact that the national party waged one of its most vigorous campaigns in 1912. However, the local radicals believed that events of the Paint Creek-Cabin Creek struggle were more responsible. Not only had the strike brought the party converts and votes, but it had also inspired older members to greater exertion. One month after the strike the comrades in Huntington, led by Dana Harper, a brick-mason, and Edwin Firth, a potter, established their own newspaper, *The Socialist and Labor Star*.⁶⁴ Later in the summer, radicals in Clarksburg and Parkersburg had taken similar action.⁶⁵ Vigorous organizing campaigns were also launched in anticipation of a growing class consciousness.⁶⁶ Subsequent events in the strike area were to give even further encouragement to party members.

Martial Law, Violence, and Henry Hatfield

Shortly after the elections of 1912, martial law was reimposed upon the strike zone. Charles Crawford has written that the immediate cause for troops being called back into the district was the miners' aggressiveness in stopping the transportation of strike breakers. On November 15, bullets rained down from the hills upon a Chesapeake and Ohio train bringing men from New York. The next day, two or three hundred miners allegedly set up a blockade and forced every mining train to stop for inspection. In at least one case, the strikers detached two cars of transportation men from one of the trains and would not let them proceed.[67] On the other hand, the Socialists claimed that these events were but an excuse to "wipe out entirely the splendid spirit of solidarity that has manifested itself so much through the whole conflict."[68]

The Socialists felt that their strength politically and economically had caused grave concern among operators and their political henchmen. One Cabin Creek operator later testified that the influence of the radicals had, indeed, turned the strike into something different. As George Williams put it, "I went up the Creek and investigated myself, before we brought in transportation, and I saw it was not a question of fighting as I knew the fighting of unionism in the past, it was merely the Industrial Workers of the World introduced under the name of United Mine Workers.[69] Much of the same sentiment was expressed by a commission that Governor Glasscock had appointed to investigate the mining conditions in the strike zone. The members of the commission, P. J. Donahue, a Catholic bishop from Wheeling; Fred O. Blue, the state tax commissioner; and S. L. Walker, a captain of the State Militia, condemned the guard system, the employer's blacklist, high store prices, and unfair docking practices. However, they were so greatly disturbed over the aggressive organizational tactics of the strikers that, according to Fred Mooney, "they lost sight of the industrial struggle entirely and spend most of its time chasing the bogey of socialism."[70] The action of elected officials and the companies of militia sent in during the new martial law period lent real credence to the Socialists' position. Several days before the militia was officially authorized to return to the strike zone, several important Socialists were arrested and brought before a military tribunal sitting at Pratt, West Virginia. Those strikers and agitators who were judged guilty were sentenced to terms of from four to seven and one half years.[71] To legalize this action, the martial law proclamation was made retroactive with "offenses against the civil law prior to the proclamation of November 15, 1912, shall be regarded as offenses under military law." Furthermore, the military tribunal was given wide latitude in passing sentences by being empowered to "…impose such sentences either lighter or heavier than those imposed under the civil law, as in their judgment the offender may merit." By this authority, Silas Nance, the Socialist marshall of Eskdale, was given five years for interfering with a former militia man, Captain A. C. Wood, an ex-private policeman who was arresting a man without a warrant.[72] Although the incident took place a full eight days before martial law was declared, Nance was sentenced to five years in the state penitentiary at Moundsville. A similar sentence was given to Dan "Few Clothes" Chain, a Negro Socialist, who was found guilty of obstructing a train.[73] With the situation apparently under control, the National Guard was withdrawn leaving, according to the radicals, machine guns and other arms in the hands of the mine guards.[74] But the Socialists were far from beaten.

By early January, Socialist agitation in and out of the strike zone had grown. "All the Powers of Plutocracy Fails to Break the Miners' Strike," trumpeted *The Labor Argus*. The recent perversion of the law and constitutional guarantees demonstrated the desperate state of the coal operators, continued the radical Charleston paper. The coal barons had wanted "Mother" Jones and other union leaders deported. However, they were afraid of public reaction so they got "Willie" Glasscock to call in the militia or the "department of murder" to do this dirty work.[75] The decisions of the military courts violated the Constitution of the United States and the decision of the Supreme Court in *Ex parte Milligan*. They also violated the West Virginia Constitution, which allowed the governor to declare martial law at the request of some local official. The law also provided that the military power shall be subordinate to the civil power and that a private citizen cannot be tried for any offense that is recognized in civil courts.[76] Despite this, the West Virginia Supreme Court ruled that conditions were so bad that the military courts were legal even though the civil courts in the area were open.[77] The Socialists were quick to point out that this perversion of the law merely bore out the classical Marxist principle that government was just a committee that managed the affairs of the capitalist class.[78] By way of contrast, the Socialists put forward the fairness of their own elected officials as examples of the even-handed justice to be anticipated when workers controlled the state. George Parsons reported to *The Labor Argus* that on January 14, when a non-union man was brought before Brandt Scott, the newly elected Socialist justice of the peace, the man was given the lightest possible sentence. On the other hand, the next day two union miners were brought in for causing a disturbance and beating up a non-union man. Squire Scott threw the book at them by slapping a $25 fine on each and then giving them a stern lecture. Such was the justice that could "be obtained by the way you cast your ballot."[79]

In their efforts to bring the facts of what had happened in the coal fields and to marshall aid for the embattled strikers, the West Virginia Socialists found sympathy everywhere. The Huntington Trades and Labor Assembly sent $100 to the strikers and sponsored a huge rally to arouse public opinion in their city. In addition, the Huntington union men invited Valentine Reuther to speak to them about the strike situation and endorsed his talk with a permanent strike fund.[80] Charles Boswell, John Brown, and others held a very successful meeting in the northern part of the state in such cities as Clarksburg and Wheeling.[81] "Mother" Jones, accompanied John Brown, arranged mass meetings in Cincinnati,

Cleveland, New York, Washington, D.C., and some other large cities.[82] Aid from the workingmen of many of these places buoyed the spirit of the strikers and helped them withstand the bloodiest period of the industrial conflict.

The actions of the coal operators of the strike area in February 1913 indicated that they did see that their position was precarious. Without the presence of the militia, they had great difficulty bringing in strikebreakers and keeping them at the mines. In part, this was due to the fact that the men who were recruited in Chicago and New York were often deceived. There is ample evidence that many men were brought to the strike zone in closed and guarded cars and kept in relative isolation lest they discovered a strike was in progress. Frank Keller, who had migrated from Moscow, Russia, only seven years before, was brought to Decota on Cabin Creek. When he and his companions found out it was a scab job, "We ran most of the way to Eskdale about seven miles. I think we broke all records going down that mountain. My shoes were alright when I started, had broken through when I came to Eskdale." It was a shattering experience for Keller, who admitted, "I am a nervous wreck and my leg pains me where the guard struck me. I don't know how I am going to get back to New York."[83] Actually, Keller and the other men, who had escaped on their own or did so because of the pressure put on by the strikers, were frequently guided out of the region and, where possible, given temporary jobs or transportation money to go home.[84]

On February 7, the coal operators attempted to open and make secure the rail access to their mines. A special engine and baggage car had been prepared by the Chesapeake and Ohio Railroad with a one-half-inch boilerplate for armor and portholes on each side. The miners dubbed this "Bull Moose," as it was commanded by an alleged Progressive Republican Sheriff Bonner Hill and twenty-five deputies. With lights out, this train poured both rifle and machine-gun fire into the miners' tent village at Holly Grove. Miraculously, only one miner, Sesco Estep, was killed while trying to get his daughter to safety. However, several others were wounded, including Mrs. John Hall, who was shot through both legs.[85]

In retaliation, the strikers moved their families to the relative protection of Hansford at the mouth of Paint Creek. There, arms and men were gathered for an attack on Mucklow, where it was rumored Gatling guns were being prepared to wipe out the miners and their families. At about eleven o'clock in the morning on February 12, seventy-five strikers were met by a contingent of mine guards and in the subsequent battle, twelve miners and four guards were killed. The miners, however, had won the day and had driven the guards back.[86]

Governor Glasscock once more declared martial law and dispatched two companies of national guardsmen, who began to make wholesale arrests. There can be little doubt that the political and military authorities regarded the silencing of Socialists as their major objective. In the martial law zone, the arrest of radicals like Alfred and George W. Lavinder, the Scott Brothers, U. S. Cantley, John W. Brown, and George "Fleet" Parsons was a fairly easy matter. For those outside the immediate jurisdiction of the military court, it was necessary to obtain warrants from a justice of that magisterial district and make the arrest. For example, "Mother" Jones was one of a thirty-five-member committee appointed to visit the governor. As a delegation from this group approached the east wing of the Capitol building, "Mother" Jones was taken from her two companions, Fred Mooney and Walter Diehl, pushed into an automobile by Dan Cunningham, a notorious mine guard, and driven to the so-called "bull pen" at Pratt to await trial. Warrants from Squire Deering's court were also used to pick up Charles H. Boswell, the editor of *The Labor Argus,* plus two United Mine Workers organizers, Paul Paulsen and Charles Batley. In all, 150 to 200 suspects appeared before a five-man military court presided over by Judge Advocate Colonel George S. Wallace of Huntington.[87]

The Socialists believed that this military commission had orders to put the radical strike leaders away where they could do no further harm.[88] Harold Houston and A. M. Belcher, the United Mine Workers' attorneys, refused to recognize the jurisdiction of the military court and applied to the United State Circuit Court for a writ of *habeas corpus* to obtain a release of the prisoners. When fifty-three of the prisoners were assembled at the Pratt Odd Fellows' Hall, "Mother" Jones, John Brown, Boswell, Batley, Parsons, and Paulsen refused to make a plea or acknowledge the authority of the military tribunal. The Circuit Court did issue a restraining order, but the Republican sheriff, Bonner Hill, refused to serve it. According to John Brown, the leaders were then segregated from the rest of the strikers. The latter were broken down by being "…sweated and subjected to the third degree with the horrors of the penitentiary depicted on one side and the hope of being acquitted on the other." These prisoners subsequently signed a paper that they felt the court would be fair and entered a plea of "not guilty." Armed with these affidavits, the lawyers for the military and operators were able to get the District Court to uphold the trial report of the military commission. Yet through all of this, as the Socialists pointed out, West Virginia law authorities had done nothing to the murderers in the Bull Moose Special.[89]

Soon after his inauguration, Governor Henry D. Hatfield, a medical doctor and descendant of the famous feuding Hatfields of southern West Virginia, made a personal investigation of the strike with an eye toward bringing about a settlement. Hatfield had apparently promised in campaign speeches a better deal for the United Mine Workers.[90] The governor did begin to release a number of the prisoners convicted by the military court, provided they would take no future part in the strike. He also effected the withdrawal of some of the soldiers from the area. Furthermore, it appears likely that Hatfield encouraged the proposal for a basic settlement, which President White, national president of the United Mine Workers of America, made on March 26, 1913. White asked for semi-monthly pay, the right of an elected check-weighman, a 2,000-pound ton, a joint commission of five representatives from the operators and the union to fix all wage rates by taking into account the competitive conditions, and the rehiring of all miners without discrimination for union membership.[91]

The coal operators refused to settle on the basis of White's proposals and Governor Hatfield was forced to make even more concessions. He suggested that the miners be given the right to organize, a nine-hour day, semi-monthly pay, no discrimination against union men, and the right of the worker to buy where he wished. The operators agreed with these terms with a reminder that the right to have a check-weighman had never been denied and that nondiscrimination meant the right of the men to purchase where they pleased.[92] The United Mine Workers' officials called a convention to consider the governor's proposals.

According to the Socialists' view, this convention showed the collusion that existed between Hatfield and much of the union hierarchy. The radicals maintained that about 90 percent of the delegates and two of the officials were against the settlement. However, the delegates were persuaded by a variety of devices. First of all, claimed the Socialists, the "pay roll" (union officials) worked the delegates like ward-healing politicians by plying them with drinks and promises. Next, the pro-settlement forces allegedly convinced Harold Houston that acceptance of the governor's proposals was the best thing for the miners and their union. Houston "weakened" and agreed to advocate acceptance if the operators would define no discrimination as meaning that all strikers would get their jobs back.[93] The coal operators would not agree to this principle and Hatfield either could not or would not do anything about it. As he told the delegates on April 27, "I feel that it would be presumptuous on my part and overstepping any power given me, to suggest to the employee whom he should employ. . ." And when the delegates showed reluctance to go along, the governor delivered his famous ultimatum that the strikers would either accept the terms offered in thirty-six hours or they would be deported from the district.[94]

The Socialists labeled the Hatfield settlement a sellout and agitated vigorously against its implementation. They argued that the rank-and-file coal miners were against it because it did not touch upon the basic demands of strikers. The three objectives of the struggle had been the abolition of the guard system, recognition of the union, and they payment of the Kanawha scale of wages, which would have meant a wage increase of from 50 to 75 percent.[95] Many Socialists outside the strike zone were as astounded as Walter Hilton at the hollowness of the proposed settlement. The right of the miners to have a check-weighman and to buy wherever they wished was already guaranteed by state law. As for a nine-hour day, Hilton pointed out that over 400,000 workers in this country had already achieved an eight-hour day.[96] Such weak provisions seemed even more ludicrous to the Socialists because they felt that the strike had been all but won. Wyatt Thompson emphasized that the miners had endured unspeakable hardships only to have their victory stolen by some traitorous union officials and a "stand-pat" Republican governor who had masqueraded as the laboring-man's friend.[97] Charles Boswell agreed and admonished the miners, "Trust no man who does not belong to your own political party—the Socialist Party—and keep an eye on him."[98]

Governor Hatfield had warned against continued agitation. His ultimatum to the strikers had indicated that he would not tolerate any action prolonging the hostility whether it come from "inside or outside the strike zone."[99] Furthermore, Hatfield knew the source of militant strike leadership. Shortly before making his settlement proposals, he had written to Walter Jones, a Socialist lawyer and lecturer from Clarksburg,

> You belong to that class of character assassins who have been aiding and abetting in the conditions that exist in the strike region more than any other element of people . . . I want you to thoroughly understand that law and order will be preserved in West Virginia as long as I am governor, and if it is necessary to "jug" such characters as you and keep you there, it will be done.[100]

Hatfield made good his threats and the power of his office came down hard on the Socialists. Late in April, militia units commanded by General Elliot and Major Tom Davis raided *The Labor Argus* and arrested Fred (Fritz) Merrick, who was suspected of being a temporary editor. The Socialists also accused Hatfield and his coal operator allies of being behind the mine guards who threw bricks at George W. Gillispie and other speakers at a protest meeting sponsored by the Huntington Trades and Labor Assembly. These same guards shot into the crowd before being chased away.[101] At any rate, there was no doubt that it was typewritten orders from the governor that authorized the sacking of the *Huntington Socialist and Labor Star*. On May 10, militiamen and deputies from Cabell County wrecked the *Star's* plant, scattered type over a wide area, and arrested the paper's five Socialist owners. Later, the militia surrounded the homes of their prisoners and, without warrants, made a search for more evidence.[102] Many of the Socialist officeholders in the strike zone were pulled in. This included constables, justices of the peace, Rome Mitchell, Robert Morris, and Brandt Scott whose books were also confiscated.[103] Orders were issued to arrest other radical organizers and agitators who might be considered important. Lawrence "Peggy" Dwyer was brought in while Harold Houston escaped only by fleeing the state.[104]

While Governor Hatfield may have ended the coal strike, his action actually seemed to increase the political and economic importance of West Virginia to the National Socialist movement. The *Appeal to Reason* had explained to its readers that ". . . no part of the United States is so pregnant with possibilities as that great mining state in the East." The Kansas publication believed that West Virginia could well be the first state in the union to be captured politically by the party. To achieve their goal, each subscriber (always collectively referred to as "the Appeal Army") was asked to contribute $1 to flood West Virginia with propaganda. A $2,000 fund was raised at once.[105] The national officials of the Socialist Party agreed with the *Appeal to Reason's* assessment of the West Virginia situation. J. L. Engdahl promised that the National Executive Committee would launch America's greatest working-class educational campaign in the Mountain State. The groundwork for their effort had already been laid among the miners since the vast majority of union miners were already voting Socialist. All that was needed, Engdahl contended, was a real grounding in the party principles. The National Executive Committee sent some funds to help put the *Huntington Star* back on its feel and set in motion a program that would bring in such effective organizers as George Goebel, Anna Maley, and Fred Strickland to help bring about a Socialist victory.[106] Furthermore, a special committee composed of Adolph Germer, Victor Berger, and Eugene V. Debs was assigned to investigate the West Virginia situation and render whatever aid they could to their imprisoned comrades.[107]

Local Socialists were also convinced that the political and economic organization of the West Virginia laboring men could be greatly accelerated. In the mine districts, the interest in and strength of socialism was growing almost too rapidly. In the New River fields embracing Fayette, Raleigh, and Wyoming counties, miners had elected a Socialist, L. C. Rogers, of Oak Hill, as the president of District 29 of the United Mine Workers of America.[108] Mass meetings sponsored by the Ohio Valley and Huntington Trades and Labor Assembly to support the strikers drew unusually large crowds.[109] Interviews with living Socialists confirm the high spirit and hope for real progress that party members felt had resulted from the strike situation. All of them agreed with H. Lee Rodes, one of the earliest members of the local at Gatewood, who recalled, "You wouldn't believe how much less trouble we had getting people to see the light after the 1912 strike . . . the coal barons, Baldwin Felts, and tin horns (militia) made Socialists faster than the best organization we ever had could."[110] On the other hand, many of the leaders of the West Virginia party recognized that the new opportunities also presented some internal problems.

Edward H. Kintzer, the state secretary of the party, admitted that the Socialists in West Virginia had an unparalleled opportunity, but were not really prepared to capitalize on it. Kintzer had come from Pennsylvania to Clarksburg as a bookkeeper and later manager of a glass factory. The key to Socialist success, according to Kintzer, was the strong local organization. Those who looked to the radicals for strike support and leadership or who cast their ballot for Socialist Party candidates now had to become real dues-paying members of a "live wire" local. Kintzer complained that although the party had increased its voting strength, the organization showed little improvement over 1908. In a way, this situation was understandable because a great deal of energy and funds had been expended on the industrial war. But now, Kintzer maintained, the job was to create new locals, strengthen those that were weak, and revive the dead ones.[111]

Of Socialists, Miners, Wobblies, and Militants

Another important question was the problem of correct strategy. This matter was thrown into perspective by the National Socialist Investigating Committee's work in West Virginia. On May 17, 1913, Eugene Debs and Adolph Germer arrived in Charleston and were joined in a short time by Victor Berger. The committee spent several days in conference with United Mine Workers officials. Accompanied by Thomas Haggerty of District 17, they went to see Governor Hatfield.[112] Debs felt this meeting was highly beneficial in that the governor was persuaded that he had made serious mistakes in the closing of the *Star* and *Argus* and arbitrarily arresting the Socialist leaders in the mining regions. Governor Hatfield allegedly promised restitution for the damage to the radical press and the release of all Socialist prisoners. The committee was also persuaded that the governor now saw the Socialist movement in an entirely new light and had given his word that representatives from the party and United Mine Workers would be absolutely free to organize politically and economically among the workers of West Virginia. The governor even assigned one of his personal assistants to conduct the Socialist committee through the strike zone.[113] Furthermore, Debs believed that he and his colleagues had, "barring a very few who are bent upon arraying them against each other," created a better understanding between United Mine Workers officials and the Socialist Party.[114]

The actions and report of the National Committee aroused a storm of opposition among the more radical West Virginia Socialists. It was felt that the national office had not been early enough concerned about the West Virginia situation and had been shocked into finally giving some help.[115] Moreover, the National Executive Committee bound their representatives to cooperate with the officials of the United Mine Workers. Thus, Tom Haggerty and Joe Vasey, both "bitter anti-Socialist," were able to pour their version of events into the committee members' ears. This had happened, Wyatt Thompson maintained, despite the fact that he and Fred Merrick had warned Debs of just such a possibility when the latter visited them in the Kanawha County Jail.[116] The local branch in Huntington to which Thompson belonged was quick to point out that the National Investigating Committee had actually endorsed the action taken against the Socialists by a capitalist government. The branch's local secretary, Edwin Firth, wanted to know why.[117] The answer, according to Fritz Merrick, was that the committee's commitment to political action prevented them from offending influential leaders of craft unions.[118]

Debs's defense of the action of the National Investigating Committee was vigorous and came close to validating Merrick's criticism. Debs was worried that the more militant Socialists would spoil what looked like good chances for winning both the United Mine Workers and the State of West Virginia for socialism.[119] James Weinstein has discovered that Debs felt that the United Mine Workers was gradually becoming a truly revolutionary industrial union.[120] However, care and timing were important before they could be led to the Socialist Party. As late as 1912, Debs was cautioning Adolph Germer with regard to proper strategy at the United Mine Workers Convention,

If the Socialists attempted as reported to commit the convention to the Socialist Party, they made a tactical mistake. If it could be done by acclamation, it would still be a mistake. Working class political action is what they should be committed to and no party in particular at this stage.[121]

Anything that would divide a struggling union like the United Mine Workers in West Virginia was dangerous. It was with this in mind that Debs wrote in rebuttal to the criticisms of Thompson, Boswell, Merrick, and others.

The whole trouble is that some Chicago IWWites, in spirit at least, are seeking to disrupt and drive out the United Mine Workers to make room for the IWW and its program of sabotage, and strike at the ballot box with an axe.[122]

The more militant Socialists in West Virginia denied that they were members of the Industrial Workers of the World, but the Huntington Socialist newspaper generally gave encouragement to those who espoused a philosophy akin to that of the Wobblies. Its editor, Wyatt Thompson, was the intellectual leader of the West Virginia left wing. In what was quite a stretch of the truth, he responded to Debs that he had never seen a real live I.W.W.ite. Thompson sensed that the I.W.W.'s greatest problem was that they drifted in and out of communities and seldom stayed long enough to build a solid local organization.[123] On the other hand, the Wobblies were usually around when the workers' fight was the most difficult. Many of their ideas were excellent. For example, the emphasis upon direct action, including sabotage and the general strike, suggested an excellent strategy to combat a very powerful and diverse industrial complex. Besides, such techniques were usually the best way to create class solidarity. As Thompson put it, "the general strike is simply putting into effect the old labor motto, 'an injury to one is an injury to all.'" Equally important was the I.W.W.'s leadership in criticizing the craft form of labor organization and their attempt to build the industrial unions that would be the training ground where workers learned how to operate a future Socialist state.[124] This was exactly what the West Virginia miners ought to do, Thompson maintained. They should be initiated "into the mysteries of Twentieth Century fighting tactics, including a thorough working knowledge of that powerful weapon—industrial unionism—one big union in which the rank and file decide all questions for themselves."[125]

The left wing of the Mountain State Socialists believed that the I.W.W.'s tendency to minimize political action was a mistake. This study has already shown that the militant Socialists of West Virginia were committed to political action. In addition to the common party assumption that elections served an educative function and were a good indicator of the growth of class consciousness, political participation was often justified with arguments that reinforced the primary of economic action. West Virginia militants stressed that although aggressive industrial unionism may wring some concessions from the capitalists, political power was necessary to insure that these gains would be enforced. Moreover, the workers could never really obtain industrial control as long as the government provided troops to the capitalists to prevent it. Thus, the only way to insure that economic action would be successful, as well as peaceful, was to use political power to neutralize the military and for the workers themselves to be armed.[126]

More conservative Socialists in West Virginia agreed with their radical comrades that the Hatfield settlement was a sellout and that there would probably be further trouble in the coal fields.[127] On the other hand, they supported Debs's contention that this was not the time to do anything that would divide the ranks of labor. Through the pages of *The Wheeling Majority* the conservative Socialist position was established. Walter Hilton acknowledged that his newspaper had ardently advocated political action, but not because politics alone would be sufficient to create the Cooperative Commonwealth. On the contrary, the economic organization of the working class was perhaps even more important.[128] But it was for precisely that reason that the conservative Socialists were opposed to what they understood was the philosophy of the I.W.W.

On several occasions, Wheeling Socialists carried on debates with representatives of the Industrial Workers of the World. Most of the Wheeling radicals were skilled tradesmen who had spent many years in building the labor organizations of the upper Ohio River Valley. One of these Socialists, W. A. Peters, a painter and decorator, responded in April 1913 to I.W.W. speech made by F. C. Green, a book salesman. Peters claimed that it was foolish for Mr. Green to take up the cry of labor solidarity when the Industrial Workers of the World were doing more to disrupt the labor movement than anyone else. In an editorial, Walter Hilton elaborated the point. The present unions had taken hard work to build and, unlike Wobbly groups, were bringing the workers many important gains. To urge a union member to give up this hope would be to fly in the face of the basic instinct for survival. It would be like asking a man who was clinging to a lifeboat to let go as real rescue would be his at some indefinite time in the future. Besides, Hilton continued, if those who want a better society leave the existing unions, these organizations and their treasuries would be taken over by the most corruptible type of officials who would turn their unions into mere "scab herding agencies."[129]

Almost a year later the Ohio Valley Trades and Labor Assembly and the Belmont County Trades Assembly condemned the activities of Joseph Ettor, who was a prominent Wobbly. Ettor and his comrades were organizing among the mine workers near Bellaire, Ohio, and preaching the doctrine of the general strike. Ettor defended his actions as the shortest path to the revolution for which all Socialists were striving. However, he realized that this would be hard for the Wheeling tradesmen to understand because they had a vested interest in a system that placed their various crafts in a favorable position. As far as Ettor was concerned, all that the Socialists in Wheeling would ever do for the revolution was pass decorous resolutions.[130]

Joseph Ettor's remark raised the ire of Walton Hilton. The editor claimed that the I.W.W. was a collection of "every freak and bug" in the labor movement. Industrial unionism, Hilton admitted, had to come, but it would not be through any short-cut techniques. The general strike wouldn't work for the miners or anyone else as long as great numbers of craftsmen remained unorganized or there were large groups of unemployed men willing to work under any circumstances. The revolution would only come, Hilton stressed, by the hard work of organizing the workers as thoroughly as possible. This could be done best by building on the existing unions. Federations would be formed that would gather dozens of trades into a united front that would win as the union men of Wheeling had been doing and not lose as the I.W.W. had done in Akron and elsewhere.[131]

From the latter part of 1913 through early 1914, several vigorous organizing campaigns were carried on by West Virginia trade unionists. The Huntington and Wheeling central labor bodies were making special efforts to bring more workers into the unions and more unions into their Trades Assemblies. In the coal fields, United Mine Workers officials were planning a drive on the New River, Fairmont, Pocahontas, and Norfolk and Western fields.[132] All these movements gave the West Virginia Socialists opportunities to urge their particular organizational strategies.

In the strike areas the Socialists capitalized on the obvious dissatisfaction that persisted over the Hatfield settlement. By the summer of 1913, there were many expressions of discontent in the Kanawha district. Miners were complaining that the operators were not hiring strike leaders back; that several places were not paying on the basis of a short ton; that mine guards had not been removed; and that the union was not being recognized.[133] Wyatt Thompson claimed in his newspaper that not one miner in a hundred had anything but the sharpest criticism of the "so-called settlement."[134] A similar situation prevailed in the New River district, where the United Mine officials had managed to extend the provisions of the Hatfield Agreement to District 29. However, this agreement was repudiated by the miners in a convention at Beckley in Raleigh County, where they threatened a strike unless they were given the original demands of the Paint Creek-Cabin Creek Strike.[135]

The Socialists urged the miners to remake their union on a real revolutionary basis. By this, the Socialists meant that the miners' union had to be more than industrial in form. It also had to function democratically. To accomplish this, it would be necessary to throw out the present leadership, which had proved its craft nature by being party to the Hatfield Agreement.[136] It is difficult to determine if the rank and file understood this long-range goal. What is certain is that they understood that their leaders had let them down. As Fred Mooney wrote in his autobiography, "I was bitterly opposed to the terms of the settlement agreed to in the Cabin Creek Strike and had criticized officers of the Union for what seemed to me to be a partial surrender of the miners' demands."[137] On June 1, 1913, a meeting of locals 2508, 1209, and 2353 of District 17, chaired by Rome Mitchell, passed a formal resolution to International President John P. White. It asked that Thomas Haggerty and Joe Vasey be recalled from West Virginia.[138] The new officers of District 29 apparently felt much the same way. When Zeb Campbell, a Socialist vice president of the district, asked his president if Tom Haggerty was trying to sell out District 29, L. C. Rogers replied, "I am going back to try to save what I can." Before long strikes were breaking out again all over the two districts. At Boomer, a large number of the Italian strikers went from mine to mine behind a red flag, urging workers to join the strike.[139]

The regular leadership of District 17 realized the growing threat to the progress they felt the union was making under their guidance and they responded with defensive action. Since most of the labor press in the state was Socialist, the regular leadership established the *Miner's Herald* from the facilities of Luther C. Montgomery's *Montgomery News*. This "official organ" deplored the wildcat strikes as dangerous violations of their contracts. These admonitions were accompanied by mass meetings in which the officers tried to convince the miners that they should live up to their agreements. Tom Cairns, the president of the district, told these crowds that whatever they might feel about the agreement, if the organization lived up to it, the operators would see that it pays to deal with the union. A frequent guest speaker at such meetings was Quinn Morton, a Paint Creek operator, who was now preaching good business relationships to the miners.[140]

While mine union officials were helped by a few operators, the actions of other owners hurt. In September 1913, operators from the major southern West Virginia coal fields gathered in Huntington. The outcome of this meeting was the creation of an Operator's Protective Association whose members contributed ten cents from each ton of coal mined to a central fund. It was hoped that $1 million could be raised to help elect conservatives to office and protect private property "from destruction by the Socialists, otherwise known as the United Mine Workers of America... (such) demagogues and agitators are a menace to business and we will drive the radicals out."[141]

Sam Montgomery, whose progressive attempts to enlighten management had been frustrated more than once, could scarcely believe the incredible stupidity of the operators. He explained to them that in one morning's meeting they had issued a challenge that Eugene Debs, Victor Berger, and the leaders of the National Socialist Party would not be slow to accept. Montgomery also pointed out that the operator's fund made their previous charges against the union look foolish. Not long ago, they had been accusing the United Mine Workers of being the tool of out-of-state operators and now the operators were saying it was a front for the Socialists. Worst of all, Montgomery continued, the operators had placed conservative union leaders in the position where it would be more difficult to disagree with the Socialists without being linked to the capitalists. In fact, many would be drawn into the radicals' arms. Montgomery emphasized his point with, "If in this fight I should be compelled to take a position between the Socialists and the coal operators, I would join the Socialists."[142]

Early in 1914, the leadership of United Mine Workers District 17 decided that the threat from the radicals was so serious that more drastic action was needed. One of the officials urged, "It is time to take the bull by the horns and give these disorganizers and disrupters the same dose that they have gotten in Illinois, Iowa, and Kansas; namely, expulsion." *The Labor Argus* was accused of being captured by the Baldwin-Felts Agency and Harold Houston was relieved as a union legal counsel.[143] The specials targets of the purge were such young radicals as Frank Keeney, Fred Mooney, W. F. Ray, and Walter Deal. Fred Mooney claimed that he and the other rebels were "shadowed" and attacked in the pages of the *Miner's Herald*. Just before the district convention in 1914, formal charges were brought against these four men. President Cairns sent Clarence Griffith, a vice president and himself a moderate Socialist, to try Mooney at Cannelton. Seeing how much support Mooney had, Griffith allegedly tore up the charges and threw them from the Montgomery Bridge into the Kanawha River. The charges and trials against the others had about as much success.[144]

The revolt of the Socialists in District 17 came at the union convention in April of 1914. The radicals were determined to reform their organization. The first step came with the motion by Fred Mooney that the District Scale Committee be elected from the floor rather than appointed by the chairman. Although the motion passed, a real deadlock occurred when the Socialists and their allies tried to get the right people on the committee. Mooney, the Lusk brothers, Bess Linville, and Charles Boswell met at George Gherkins's home in Charleston and planned their strategy. It was decided to bring to the attention of the convention a letter found by one of Charles Lusk's children in the wastebasket at the company store at Longacre. The letter from a Mr. Knox of the Kanawha and Hocking Coal Company to S. C. Gaeley, the general manager at Longacre, created pandemonium among the delegates. It read, in part,

Had a talk with Cairnes and Haggerty. They think a suspension can be avoided. Have complete understanding with them and know about what to expect. Of course, a convention will be called and a scale committee appointed, after which the convention will adjourn. Expect smooth sailing if the radicals can be controlled.

The Socialists succeeded in getting a committee appointed to authenticate the letter. However, Ben Morris, the International Executive board member from District 17, frustrated the committee's work by tipping off Mr. Knox. The radicals forced an end to the convention with a resolution that if check-off was not assured, the district would strike. Relations between the Socialist miners and their leaders deteriorated to the point that the miners of Cabin Creek area pulled out of the district and created District 30.[145]

Socialism in Other Industries

The spring and summer of 1913 was also a busy time for the Socialists in the Wheeling area. They spearheaded an organizational drive by the Ohio Valley Trades and Labor Assembly. The Wheeling central body had, of course, always been vigorous in promoting membership in its affiliated unions. On this occasion, however, the assembly's goals were much more ambitious. Possibly because of the competitive threat of I.W.W. in the area, Walter Hilton, Albert Bauer, Herbert Ninness, and other Socialists were pushing the idea of a more vigorous organizing of industry on a federated craft basis.[146] In April 1913, Walter Hilton persuaded the delegates of the Trades and Labor Assembly to urge their respective unions to formally endorse their campaign and assess each member twenty-five cents per month to finance it.[147] Once the craft unions were so organized, negotiations with various industries could be made for all the unions represented among the firm's employees. As Walter Hilton described it, "We consider that industrial union agreements entered into by one craft without regard to other crafts equally affected to be dangerous and weakening to all the workers of Wheeling. . ."[148]

The second goal of the Ohio Valley Trades and Labor Assembly was even more ambitious. It was hoped that the organizational drive could be extended to include all unorganized workers, even those who were considered unskilled or semi-skilled. Walter Hilton was the real force behind the movement. In his newspaper he warned his fellow tradesmen that the complete organization of their crafts would not be nearly enough. The development of machines was making the craft less important and the unionization of the unskilled and semi-skilled a necessity.[149]

Hilton's belief in the great need to thoroughly organize all the workers around a particular plant had been strengthened by his participation in a recent strike at the tin plants owned by the Phillips Sheet and Tin Plate Company. The strike, which began in early July of 1913, was the result of drive by the Amalgamated Association of Iron, Steel, and Tin Workers to unionize the company's Pope Mill and Steubenville, Ohio. Furthermore, it had been agreed by the unionized tin workers' lodges at Wheeling and Follansbee that they would push organization of the Phillips' Company plants at Weirton and Clarksburg, West Virginia.[150] The strike was bitterly contested, with the company guards herding in strikebreakers, firing rifles in the direction of mill workers' homes, and gunning down several strike leaders from a moving automobile in Steubenville. The company tried desperately to give the impression its plants were still open by creating lots of black smoke, clanging tools, driving around equipment. However, it took an injunction from Judge Saterat Columbus to end the strike at Steubenville. At Clarksburg, where Walter Hilton and Edward Kintzer had been helping Dick Selvey establish a union, the company simply set up a rival committee of unskilled and anti-union men, dealt with them, and resumed production on an open-shop basis.[151]

The organizational campaign of the Wheeling labor bodies made some noticeable progress. More than twenty unions pledged their full support early in the campaign. Among these were bus drivers, firemen, painters, leather workers, potters, machinists, bakers, molders, carpenters, butchers, and printers.[152] Some unions vowed that they would only work on jobs that employed union craftsmen. By December 1913, the Trades and Labor Assembly's organizing campaign had raised almost $400. It had sponsored a mammoth rally to which over fifteen national unions sent an officer or representative and a Federal Trade Union had been created, with Walter B. Hilton as its first president.[153]

On the other hand, Hilton and Ninness discovered that extending their organizational campaign to cover the unskilled was plagued with many difficulties. In the first place, they had felt from the interest manifested in their rally on November 30, 1913, that many trades would bring the unskilled workers into their union even though in some inferior categories. Occasionally this worked. For example, the electrical workers extended an invitation to the unskilled workers on their jobs to fill out application forms for status in the union.[154] Just as often, however, the Socialists ran into problems. The hod carriers, for instance, had been aided by a sympathy strike and Hilton felt they learned the benefit that solidarity could bring. However, when he tried to get them to accept common laborers into their union, they balked because they "cannot hereafter do the work of the laborers when their own work is slack, without infringing upon the rights of the common laborers."[155] The expansion program must also have alienated some of the building trades section of the Belmont County Assembly. These trade members complained to John L. Lewis. Mr. Lewis, as an organizer for the A. F. of L., had been in Wheeling before trying to work out the differences between the cigar makers and stogie workers. Using the same tactics as he had in 1907, Lewis pointed out that of the 1,623 central bodies in the United States, the Ohio Valley Trades and Labor Assembly was the only one not affiliated with the A. F. of L. Lewis threatened to create a new central body unless the stogie-makers resigned from the Wheeling Assembly. Therefore, when he saw that the Wheeling tradesmen were firm in support of the "stogies," Lewis formed the Tri-City Trades and Labor

Assembly. Although this action did not stop Hilton's organizational campaign, it apparently hampered it, since much energy had to be expended to keep the loyalty of the member organizations to the Ohio Valley Trade and Labor Assembly.[156]

Hilton and his colleagues also ran into apathy on the part of many unskilled and semi-skilled workers. These workers apparently did not always deem it advantageous to belong to any union, much less one dominated by a craft elite. For example, Miss Bond and Miss Dawson, who had been trying to organize unskilled women at some Wheeling plants, complained that they arranged several meetings with leaders, ". . . but in no case did the meetings materialize."[157] It may well be that the unskilled workers did not completely trust the craft union men to live up to their agreements. This had been the experience of some packers when they struck earlier against Wheeling's Imperial Glass Company. The packers were led to believe that the American Flint Glass Workers Union would support their strike and offered them membership; however, bowing to pressure from the A. F. of L., the Flint support was withdrawn and promise of membership postponed to some future time.[158] At about the same time, a similar incident occurred among the unskilled employees at the Banner Glass Factory in South Charleston. Fearing the competitive threat of the machines in the young American Window Glass Company, the Banner and several other hand plants decided they could nip their new rivals in the bud by working through the traditional "fire out" period in the summer. Unfortunately, this action would have violated the last negotiated contract; therefore, the union president, Joe Neenan, promised the unskilled employees union membership if they would strike to bring the glassworkers back in line. The strike was successful, but Neenan's promise of union membership for the laborers was never kept.[159]

This discussion of West Virginia Socialist union strategy is not meant to suggest that the party was, at this point, torn asunder by philosophical controversy. Nor were these ideological-strategical differences easily divided into a north–south sectionalism. Much of the top leadership in Wheeling was fairly conservative. For example, when Harry Schwartz, a stogie-maker, pushed the I.W.W. approach in a meeting of one of Wheeling's local Socialist branches, he was vigorously rebutted by A. L. Bauer, E. J. Weekly, N. J. Hare, Walter Hilton, and W. A. Peters, practically the top leadership of Wheeling Socialists.[160] On the other hand, Harry Leeds of Wheeling, John C. Higgins of Star City, and Edward Kintzer of Clarksburg were northern West Virginians and quite radical.[161] Similarly, there were many moderate Socialists in the southern part of the state. *The Huntington Socialist Star* pointed out that a great debate was raging in Kanawha County over mass industrial action or working through craft organizations. One of the most active organizers, George "Fleet" Parsons, always spoke in such moderate terms as, "I do not believe in taking by force, but by the slow process of law, through better legislation or the outcome of wiser ballots."[162] Duff Scott believed that he and many other miners did not like Bill Haywood's constant ". . . Cuttin' back on the capitalists in a violent way."[163] John Brown also disavowed the IWWites as he wrote from the Harrison County Jail to W. A. Peters of Wheeling, "I know of but two Haywoods in this county and I am not one of them."[164] Certainly, West Virginia had a strong left wing and was one of the few states to vote against recalling Bill Haywood. The vote of 157 to 154 may give some indication of how relatively close the division was in the party.[165] At any rate, differences over strategy had not prevented party members from cooperating in the Socialist-inspired drives of 1913 and 1914 to unionize more of West Virginia's labor force, nor did they prevent unity in achieving other objectives.

In most matters, the actions of Socialist locals all over the Mountain State were very similar. Whether they believed in revolutionary, mass industrial action or not, they applied themselves to the solution of the workers' everyday problems. The Huntington Socialists were as active in their Central Labor Body's attempt to force a bond election for the creation of a municipally owned waterworks as their Wheeling comrades were in making sure that a $300,000 bond issue would be earmarked for a water-filtration plant.[166] All

Socialist organizations did their best to promote economic organization through the establishment of cooperative stores. These enterprises were launched at such diverse locations as Wheeling, Star City, Fairmont, Red Star, Chelyan, and Huntington.[167] Regardless of ideology the West Virginia Socialists were making strenuous efforts to organize new and strengthen old party locals. And finally, most West Virginia radicals entered enthusiastically the election campaigns of 1914 on the assumption that they might yet win political control of West Virginia.[168]

The Fruits of Revolution: The 1914 Election

The results of the election of 1914 fell far short of the Socialists' high expectations. They were able to re-elect their district officers in Cabin Creek but the state-wide vote dropped from 5.7 percent in 1912 to a little over 4 percent. Most of this drop occurred in the northwestern portion of West Virginia. The greatest loss came in Ohio County where the party's vote was off some 5 percent. This loss may have been attributed to the ability of Eugene Debs to run much stronger in that area than the local party candidates. On the strength of this Ohio County vote, Debs had polled nearly 1,200 more votes than state and local candidates in 1912. Allowing for this Debs appeal, the West Virginia radicals had just about maintained the vote they received in 1912.[169]

Many reasons may account for the failure of the Socialists to substantially increase their vote in 1914. Several groups of voters whose support might well have made a significant difference for the party's fortune were not converted. First of all, there was the farm vote. The West Virginia radicals understood that the state was basically rural, and in order to grow, more of the farmers would have to be won. Organizers attempted to do just that. The Reverend Del Upton worked hard in rural Mason County; R. L. Dayton, the Socialist mayor of Hendricks, promised a victory in Tucker County; and the most active organizer in West Virginia,

George "Fleet" Parsons, made a special effort among the farmers in Fayette County.[170] George Glass and others worked vigorously in the farm area of Kanawha County because they realized that their lowest number of votes had come from these rural sections.[171] Moreover, these organizers used persuasive arguments. They pointed out to the tenant and small farmer that they actually worked longer hours and lived in conditions that a coal miner would not tolerate. For the more substantial farmer, the Socialists solved the problem of why only $500 to $600 dollars a year could be realized on a capital investment of $10,000 to $20,000 dollars. Their answer was that the farmer was exploited by steel and other trusts when he bought railroads, and jobbers when he sold.[172]

Despite their efforts, the Socialist vote in the farm region remained small. Ironically, a great number of the West Virginia Socialist Party owned farms or had left the farms as young men. Such top-level or early party people as Darius Boone of Anthony, Benjamin Hunt of Gatewood, and Raymond Bauer of Wheeling were farmers. Charles Boswell of the *Argus* had come from a Virginia tobacco farm and returned there in later years. Moreover, some men like Matt Shaffer and Julius W. Hill had been active grangers. Hill traced his ancestors to the earliest settlers of Nicholas and Kanawha counties. As a young man he had become a Grange officer and eventually a Socialist. He often spoke to his fellow agrarians about the importance of their following his example.[173] A rural background did not, however, always mean that the local radicals were effective in winning farmers to the cause. George Glass sensed the problem: "We did pretty good in getting the boys who had little farms and walked as far as six or eight miles to work part time in a mine, but there was one-section of Kelly's Creek, a big settlement that stayed in their old ways. They farmed, seldom went off the creek, and were hard-shell Baptists."[174] Mrs. Glass's observations is borne out again in Fayette County where the Socialist vote was smallest in magisterial districts, and where the old pattern of small farms was relatively undisturbed.[175]

The national leadership of the Socialist Party felt that West Virginia was an excellent place to join black and white workers on a class basis. If this alliance could be achieved in the Mountain State, ran the argument, it would signal the launching of a great southern drive by the party.[176] When state secretary, Harold Houston, recognized the potential of Negro membership, he asked for back organizers.[177] It seems, however, that only the more left-wing Huntington organization did anything along this line. Allegedly, a Socialist Negro organizer had been brought in and a local branch had been established.[178] In addition, there is some evidence that there were a few Negro radicals in the coal fields.[179]

Analysis of some predominantly Negro voting precincts in Huntington and Charleston, however, show a well below-average Socialist vote. The coal fields of Fayette and McDowell counties had the largest Negro populations, McDowell's Socialist vote in 1914 was only about 1 percent. Although Fayette's radical vote was one of the highest in the state, there seems to be little or no correlation between, for example, the existence of Negro schools and high Socialist voting in those precincts.[180]

The basic reason for Negro apathy toward the Socialist Party may be partly explained by the fact that the black man did not see that the racial attitudes of this party showed much improvement over those of the Republicans. Most pleas for black votes in West Virginia held little hope for social equality between the Negro and his radical peers. "We do not want the amalgamation of the races, nor do you," explained the *Huntington Star*. "We want you (however) to have the full product of your toil."[181] The editor of the *Pioneer Press*, a Negro newspaper from Martinsburg, discussed the reluctance of the black man to follow the Socialist Party. Although the Socialist preached solidarity, he seldom really practiced it, felt the editor. In fact, many of the party's leaders revealed that attitude clearly by favoring the exclusion of Orientals and other non-white groups. "All of which means that the Fatherhood of God, the progress of mankind, onward and upward forever is really not the creed of the American Socialist Party."[182]

One of the major reasons for the failure of the West Virginia Socialists to expand their political power was that the major party politicians, along with conservative labor leaders, began to take the radicals much more seriously. The previously mentioned Operation Protective Association and its defense fund were only part of a counter-offensive by business and industrial leaders and their political allies. Richard Hadsell, in his study of Justus Collins, has suggested that by late 1913 the non-union coal operators in southern West Virginia were more determined than ever to keep out radicals and union agitators. Furthermore, these operators had at their disposal a Baldwin-Felts Detective Agency that had been well seasoned by the great mine strikers of West Virginia and Colorado. Since the "Wertz" bill passed by the 1913 State Legislature, which was supposed to outlaw mine guards carried no penalty, the agency's police system and espionage force were busier than ever.[183] For instance, in March 1913 Felts wrote one of his agents to take a job as a union organizer to uncover "quite a few railroad men in and around Thurmond who are Socialists. . ."[184] A similar situation prevailed in the Fairmont fields where Bob and Frank Shuttlesworth, special agents of the Consolidation Coal Company, shot John Brown in the stomach.[185] The same type of company thugs were suspected of beating J. Verve Johnson, a well-known Harrison County Socialist, and J. H. Snider, his Marion County host.[186]

Political power was being used to make Socialist campaigning more difficult. Clarksburg and Fairmont passed laws that forbade public addresses without the special permission of the mayor or police chief. When Anna Maley tried to announce to a Fairmont crowd that no permit for a Socialist rally could be obtained, she was arrested, charged with holding an unauthorized meeting, and thrown into jail. Fred Strickland was arrested in Clarksburg when he spoke from the courthouse steps after the major refused to give him permission for his meeting. A similar fate befell several other speakers and organizers, the most famous being the rather long jail term received by Miss Fanny Sellins.[187] To apply such pressure required even more effort by business leaders in order to secure sympathetic public officials. As one of Justus Collins's superintendents wrote in regard to McDowell County, "As long as we have the county officials with us here in McDowell, we will have no trouble. In other counties, not so happily situated, we may have trouble in getting the right kind of results."[188]

Industrialists were receiving greater support from the laboring men who were worried by Socialists' growing strength. In Huntington, for example, the powerful Carpenter's Union 302 became very upset when the radicals were elected to the highest office in the Trade and Labor Assembly. The carpenters temporarily withdrew their delegates from the Central Labor Body. Wyatt Thompson explained that it was the industrial unionism of the Socialists that disturbed the carpenters, who "fought us back in every way; in the assembly and in the elections."[189] A similar reaction took place among the more conservative Huntington machinists. Sometime in 1914, the Socialists in the Chesapeake and Ohio shop, led by J. O. Payton, challenged the established local unions' hierarchy under Tom Preston. The radicals demanded an election and claimed that they were the legitimate representatives of the rank and file. It was only the intervention of the Grand Lodge of the Machinists that kept Tom Preston and his group in power.[190] It is difficult to document how influential these conservative carpenters and machinists were in preventing an expansion of the Huntington Socialist vote in 1914. In some mine areas, however, the case can be more clearly made.

The Republican Party in Fayette County was in serious trouble by 1914. On the one hand, there was the growing strength of a reform Fusion Party, led by William McKell. Launched in 1910, this combination of independent Republicans and progressive Democrats appeared to be a real threat to take over the county.[191] On the other hand, there was the increased popularity of the Socialists. Moreover, the Republicans faced these challenges stripped by the 1912 West Virginia Prohibition Amendment of one of their most important sources of patronage. It was this predicament that caused the Fayette County Republican Organization to make common cause with the local United Mine Workers leadership, which was also being challenged by radical-led dissidents. The party fielded by this alliance in 1914 was known as the Independent Labor Party.[192]

A list of the most active campaigners of the Independent Labor Party included most of the conservative United Mine Workers leadership. Making speeches all over the county were locally prominent figures of District 17, such as its president, Tom Cairnes, along with Ben Morris, Pat Gatens, and Bert Hastings, the incumbent mayor of Montgomery. From District 29 there were L. C. Rogers, the newly elected president, R. D. White, James Gilmore, R. B. Cobb, and others. Joining the effort from time to time were national mine worker organizers Tom Haggerty, Joe Vasey, W. A. Rogers, Frank Ramage, Andy Watkins, and even John P. White, the national president.[193]

The Independent Labor Party's campaign was well organized. It was launched at Mt. Hope by no less a figure than Governor Henry D. Hatfield. A campaign caravan went from community to community in a half-dozen automobiles. To their audiences the Labor Party speakers made some lavish promises, which included public highways through all mining camps; payment on a 2,000-pound ton; uniform pay scales for all types of work; social centers in all schoolhouses; a six-day week with an eight-hour day; and checkweighman if desired. Negro speakers were assigned to the campaign caravan and attempts were made to attract Socialist votes. Mr. Jones Gott, a "devoted Socialist" from Iowa, was secured to urge the more radical miners that they had an opportunity in this election to create a broadly based workingman's party.[194] Socialists who worked against the Independent Labor Party were purged by L. C. Rogers, who had recently resigned as a Socialist and gone over to the regular U.M.W. faction.[195]

The Socialists and the Fusionists cooperated in fighting the Independent Labor Party. The Socialist Party Press warned their member miners of the dangers of the Labor Party. As Harold Houston wrote, "Fayette and Raleigh Counties are overrun by these political buccaneers who are setting up decoy labor parties."[196] Local radicals often obtained resolutions from their chapters condemning L. C. Rogers, demanding his resignation, and urging miners to vote for the Socialists. Fusionist leaders circulated a petition signed by 1,000 workers, which repudiated the Independent Labor Party as a cheap tool of the corrupt operators and their "Whiskey Ring" allies.[197]

The election of 1914 in Fayette County was a victory for the Democratic-Fusion ticket. There were no less than six different parties on the ballot; however, the Democrats, Progressives, and Independent Republicans all ran the same candidates for the state House of Delegates and local county offices. Therefore, the reform Fusion groups elected a congressman and most state officials. On the other hand, the Republican-sponsored Independent Labor ticket did appear to hold the line against any great expansion of the Socialist vote. This was especially true of the important Fayetteville magisterial district, where the Labor Party obtained 13 percent of the vote. The strongest Socialist precinct of Lowe, Mossy, and Gatewood were able to withstand the Labor Party challenge. However, in the five remaining strong Socialist voting precincts, the Republican-backed party was more effective.[198]

Socialism at High Tide

Despite their failure to achieve a spectacular election victory, the West Virginia Socialists had gained much. They had established a widespread and thriving press, consisting of the *Charleston Labor Argus*, the *Huntington Socialists and Labor Star*, *The Parkersburg Socialist*, *The Clarksburg Socialist*, *The Beckley Labor Pilot*, *The Wheeling Majority*, and a West Virginia comrade edited *The Plain Dealer* in Cameron. Party members' influence in labor bodies was very significant. Socialist candidates had been officially endorsed by the State Federation of Labor, the Ohio Valley Trades and Labor Assembly, and the

Huntington Trades and Labor Assembly. Socialists held the major offices in the Huntington Trades Assembly from 1912 to 1915 when they represented that body at both the West Virginia and the American Federation of Labor conventions.[199] Furthermore, when George Gillespie was sent to Rochester, New York, to represent his fellow tradesmen from Huntington, he was instructed to vote against the anti-Socialist faction led by John Lennon.[200]

The Socialists had also helped West Virginia workers gain economic self-control by establishing cooperatives. These stores, organized by party members, were located over a wide geographic area in places like Wheeling, Huntington, Hilltop, Star City, Chelyan, Powellton, and Miami.[201] Moreover, the party had elected their members to an estimated fifty public offices, including five complete city governments and mayors in three others.[202] All of these concrete accomplishments only seem small when measured against the high expectations of the party. Such expectations were as true of those West Virginia Socialists who emphasized the priority of political action as those who urged the general strike. However, there is little doubt that the left wing was more than a little disappointed. As Wyatt Thompson put it, "Hell's bells, we had the Revolution in that '13, '14 thing and were just plain cheated out of it."[203]

CHAPTER V
The Decline of the West Virginia Socialist Party: 1915–1920

The West Virginia Socialists had to deal with the same crisis that confronted their comrades everywhere during the period from 1915 to 1920. The First World War and the Russian Revolution created such severe strains that only the strongest Socialist organizations could survive. Unfortunately, the West Virginia radicals were to meet this challenge in an already weakened condition.

Crippling Laws and Union Factionalism

The turning point in the political fortunes of the Mountain State Socialists appeared to be the passage of a primary election law by the 1915 State Legislature. The Socialists felt that this bill, which passed easily as a reform measure, was aimed directly at them. The law, as the *Argus Star* stated, "knocks the Socialist organization into a cocked hat."[1] Under this legislature a party could not be considered "established" unless it had gotten 5 percent of the vote in each congressional district in the last biennial election. This figure was just enough to prevent the Socialist Party from being considered. The only course left opened to the party was nominations by petition, which had to be signed by over 27,000 supporters. This was almost an impossible task. The primary law also threatened the discipline of the Socialist organization since it provided that party officials would be selected in the primary election rather than at the convention. Heretofore, in order to be an official in the party, one had to pay dues, subscribe to the party pledge, and obey the party constitution.

The Socialists also considered the new law to be class legislation of the rankest sort. It required filing fees that were so exorbitant that few workingmen could afford to run. It took $500 to file for the United States Senate, $300 for a congressional or state office, $25 for county, and $10 for local office. Finally, the law required one to register as a Socialist to vote for the party's candidates in the primary. Since voter registration books were open to anyone, a fine blacklist for employers was readily provided.[2]

Many Socialists were determined that their party should not acknowledge the legitimacy of the primary law by fielding candidates in coming elections. Some radicals had become deeply disappointed by the party's failures to achieve more results for the efforts devoted to politics. "We had worked hard and had influence with the workers," complained George Harper, "but unless we could elect our people by a whopping majority, they'd count them out."[3] The more militant Socialists also had philosophical reasons for opposing further political action. Several felt that election success would draw into the party opportunistic elements that would diminish the party's revolutionary fervor. As one of them had warned, "Better a thousand times that we should go down in defeat with the red flag flying at the mast, than we should creep into office shorn of every vestige of principle."[4] Others like Wyatt Thompson and Charles Boswell used the primary law as a justification for the Socialists devoting themselves to creating a truly radical union that would pursue direct action. They made plain their position as they editorialized in May 1915:

The present policies of Craft Unionism are the same thing as a blind bridle on a horse; just something to keep them from seeing clearly . . . since we no longer have a chance to legislate our masters off our backs . . . now that working classes of West Virginia have been disfranchised, "direct action" is the only possible way left to protest against the capitalist system of political corruption and robber. . . .[5]

Such arguments were part of the reason that several county Socialist nominating committees did not place candidates in the field.

For instance, Clarence Griffith presided over a bitter and protracted debate in the Kanawha County Socialist convention, which met at the Court House in Charleston on July 2. This debate ended with the decision not to field candidates.[6]

It seems probable that a large number of West Virginia Socialists still believed that real progress could be made only by political methods or, at least, by a balance between political and industrial action. Edwin Firth hoped that pressure on the state government for repeal of the law could be exerted by the State Federation of Labor; therefore, he sponsored a measure to that effect at the 1916 convention.[7] Edward Kintzer, the former secretary of the party, tried to obtain a promise from the West Virginia Secretary of State Stuart B. Reed, that the nominees of a special convention the party had called for August would be certified. Stuart Reed referred the matter to the state's legal officer, Attorney General A. A. Lilly. The attorney general replied that the Socialists could nominate for state-wide office by convention or any method they choose, but the party would have to place them on the ballot by certificates unless it was decided that the party had gotten 10 percent of the vote in the last election.[8] A few weeks later, Stuart Reed ruled that the Socialist candidates recently nominated as presidential electors could be certified without petitions.[9]

Socialists in all parts of the Mountain State were encouraged by Stuart Reed's ruling. A state convention was held in Clarksburg, where Matthew W. Holt, a Weston dentist, was nominated for governor. At the same meeting, the state secretary of the party sent out a call for all Socialist branches to make nominations.[10] In Kanawha County those radicals who felt their July meeting had been steamrolled by some "hot heads" met and chose county candidates.[11] In Ohio and Marshall counties, candidates were selected and the services of Fred D. Hill, an Oklahoma Socialist, and U.M.W. organizers Florence Walters and Anna Maley were obtained to kick off the campaign.[12] All of this activity took place in the midst of a good bit of confusion in Socialist ranks.

The Socialists were not sure that their nominations for state and county offices would be certified by county officials. Robin Hudnal, the secretary of the Socialist Board of Education of Cabin Creek district, hoped that the state attorney general would explain how Kanawha County candidates would be placed on the official ballot. Attorney General Lilly felt that in the light of Secretary of State Reed's ruling, the Socialists ought to have been allowed to select their nominees at the time of the June primary. Since this had not been done, Attorney General Lilly was "at a loss to know how it would proceed."[13] A good deal of energy and money was also being expended by the radicals in trying to get favorable legal rulings from county officials on their candidates. For instance, in Ohio County, the clerk of the county court and the prosecuting attorney ruled that the party would be required to pay the fees under the new law. The Wheeling branch responded by starting a fund to appeal this decision.[14] In Huntington, Edwin Firth had earlier solicited funds from that city's workingmen to take the Socialists' case into the Cabell County courts.[15] In Kanawha County, Harold Houston had fought a case on the primary law to the County Court of Appeals. In the meantime, Houston felt the only safe course for the local organization was the circulation of petitions for their nominees.[16]

The confusion and division in West Virginia Socialist ranks made it difficult to hold their party together for the elections in 1916. This situation was not entirely the product of the primary law. For many left-wing Socialists, the passage of the election reform measure only confirmed in their minds the necessity of relying primarily on economic action to bring about the Cooperative Commonwealth. Recent events in the United Mine Workers' organizations in southern West Virginia encouraged this position. The Socialist-led revolt from District 17 appeared to be producing the type of industrial unionism the left-wingers believed was necessary to match the power of the corporation.

The actual break in miners organization came when the radicals, led by Frank Keeney and Fred Mooney, accused Thomas

Haggerty and Tom Cairns of the misuse of union money. Not only were the officers criticized for using union funds in the interest of Republican candidates in Fayette County, but also in bringing about the election of sympathetic officials in 17 and 29. These acts had thwarted the will of the majority and plunged the districts deeply into debt. To cover this up, Haggerty had appointed Everette Stover, "a strike breaker and worker of black hands," as auditor of District 17 at a large salary. This step apparently did not help, as the dissidents at United Mine Workers' locals of Cannelton, Longacre, and Marting (which together claimed to represent over 50 percent of the union miners of the district) organized an auditing committee of their own and uncovered a debt of $5,000.[17]

The dissident miners in District 17 moved to ride their organization of the allegedly corrupt officials. The Socialist-dominated mine union local at Mucklow on Paint Creek sent G. W. Garret to canvass the district for support of a petition asking for the recall of Thomas Haggerty, the national organizer. Thirty-one locals pledged their support to the effort. The rebels also moved to oust Tom Cairns from the presidency of District 17 at their annual convention at Montgomery. Cairns skillfully outmaneuvered his opposition by packing the convention with delegates from strictly paper locals, which had allegedly been established on the fringes of the Fairmont Fields.[18]

The revolt among the mine workers soon spread to District 29. The cry of fraud and corruption boiled up in the district convention, which was held at Mount Hope in Fayette County. Adding to this discontent were numerous complaints about the poor wage rates negotiated in the last contract.[19] However, unlike District 17, the miners in convention at Mount Hope suspended their president, L. C. Rogers, and asked the national organization to investigate the situation. At the same time, many of these New River miners apparently joined with the dissidents of the Kanawha fields in forming a new organization, District 30.[20]

The leaders of District 30 claimed they did not wish to leave the United Mine Workers organization. However, events soon brought about a split with the parent organization. The officers of District 30, Frank Keeney, J. L. Workman, and Lawrence "Peggy" Dwyer, sought recognition from the miners' national organization. They complained that the regular officers had changed the policy of the districts. Instead of an industrial organization that was fighting to increase wages and improve conditions generally, the union was in danger of becoming a business organization that existed only to collect dues and keep the mine corporations happy.[21] The responses from the national office were deeply disappointing. A special investigating committee, headed by Frank J. Hayes and consisting of William Harrison, Robert W. Gaffney, M. D. Nash, and D. A. Frampton, held mass meetings, examined books, took testimony, and completely exonerated the election of Tom Haggerty and L. C. Rogers.[22] Furthermore, President White rejected the petitions of the fifty-two local unions in District 17 requesting the recall of Thomas Haggerty. John White's reply in June 1915 was that the regular leadership in the district had made substantial progress for the union. The United Mine Workers now had a real chance to organize West Virginia. Besides, White continued, any unwarranted interference on his part would threaten a long-standing principle of local autonomy that was so important to the United Mine Workers of America.[23]

District 30 decided to take the case before the next convention of United Mine Workers. President White hoped to prevent a floor fight and sent "Mother" Jones to arrange for a preconvention meeting with the rebels.[24] Frank Keeney, Bruttinati, John Workman, and "Peggy" Dwyer were chosen to present their case for District 30. Also present at the early meeting were "Mother" Jones and Vice President Hayes. President White claimed that harmony at the convention was of utmost importance in order that the union's prospects for a wage increase would not be jeopardized by letting the operators see the union divided. The District 30 representatives agreed provided that all the regular officials and Thomas Haggerty be removed from office and that the national committee would take over the West Virginia districts until a supervised election could be held. L. C. Rogers and Tom Cairns supposedly agreed to the plan, but a committee appointed to investigate the situation failed to outline to Keeney what action it would take. Feeling betrayed, Keeney and his delegates returned to West Virginia.[25] This did not end the matter as Adolph Germer and Duncan MacDonald carried on the fight against White and his cohorts. A decisive split was only averted by a dramatic appeal for unity by "Mother" Jones.[26]

Back in West Virginia, Frank Keeney informed President White he might avert a permanent rupture by wiring District 30 no later than February 2 of the national committee's intent to keep its agreement. When no reply came, several hundred delegates representing perhaps 4,000 miners met at Eskdale on Cabin Creek and established the West Virginia Mine Workers Organization.[27]

The new mine organization, with little or no financial resources, took steps to establish themselves by immediately negotiating contract with operators on Cabin Creek and Big Coal River. After demonstrating to the Cabin Creek operators that they had the largest following in those areas, the Maverick mining group was able to work out an agreement in which their members were to be paid as great an advance as was received in any organized field in West Virginia or the four competitive states. Moreover, this contract was apparently better than that worked out by the regular leadership. The West Virginia Mine Workers secured a raise on the rate of pay for pillar work and for mines with low coal. Lawrence Dwyer pointed out that while the regular leadership had negotiated a three cents a ton increase, no mention had been made of yardage payment for which the miners had previously received $1. In addition, a miner from Minden in Fayette County added that in the contract obtained by regular leadership, the rate for removing slate was actually reduced from eight to five cents.[28]

The West Virginia Mine Workers Organization felt that the method of negotiating their contract was as important as its provisions. The avowed goal of the leaders of the secession movement of a "revolutionary industrial union" could be built only on the principle of a functioning democracy. Therefore, the scale committee was elected from the floor of the Eskdale Convention. Once these representatives had hammered out a contract with the operators, they were required to take it to each local union where all miners in good standing were allowed to vote on the provisions. If a contract failed to please a majority of the locals, the scale committee had to try to iron out the men's objections with the operators.[29] This procedure was exactly the same method used by the Mountain State Socialists in selecting their candidates for political campaigns.[30]

In his autobiography, Fred Mooney suggested that the West Virginia Mine Workers Organization was "in for a drubbing."[31] The rebels anticipated such retaliation because they believed that the regular leadership could not allow the rank-and-file union man in the rest of the districts to see how contracts ought to be made. The United Mine Workers hoped that many of the dissidents could be persuaded to return by pleas from some of the radicals who had not followed Keeney and the others. For example, John Brown was recruited to try to win men in the Coal River area. "Mother" Jones, who felt the battle to reform the union must be from within, was sent to Eskdale to propose peace meetings, but she allegedly went away convinced of the justice of the rebels' cause.[32] Having failed in the art of friendly persuasion, the regular United Mine Workers leadership took more drastic action. Several operators in the New River area were induced to fire miners friendly to the West Virginia Mine Workers Organization. Agents were recruited to physically harass the rebels. For instance, miners at Kayford Number Nine at the head of Cabin Creek complained that they could not live up to their contract for fear of being shot. And finally, Tom Haggerty and Tom Cairns brought injunction proceedings against the West Virginia Mine Workers Organization.[33]

Despite the strong opposition of the United Mine Workers, the West Virginia Mine Workers Organization scored a victory. Basically, the national officers of the United Mine Workers agreed to the terms Frank Keeney had proposed to prevent the split. District 29 and 17 were taken over and their officers suspended until an election could be held. National board members, Charles Batley and George Hargrove, were to supervise the districts, and Harold Houston was apparently appointed interim president for District 17. The West Virginia Mine Organization was apparently disbanded when its officers campaigned for control of the regular mine organization. In the following election, Frank Keeney and Lawrence "Peggy" Dwyer were elected president and vice president of the combined District 29 and 17.[34]

The victories in the mine fields convinced the militant Socialists that they were following the correct course in concentrating on "direct action." *The Argus Star* exalted, "The men who seceded from District Seventeen United Mine Workers of America last summer are the real representatives of revolutionary unionism . . . ." If the example could be repeated and enlarged, the Socialist state would at last be on its way to reality.[35] Eugene Debs agreed with that analysis. In a letter to Charles Boswell, Debs admitted that at one time he believed the United Mine Workers of America was so near to being on the correct revolutionary course that it might have led the way to the creation of a "general industrial organization." But now, Debs went on, "The revolutionary minority was completely overwhelmed by the maudlin sentiment that insisted on 'harmony' in the face of the gravest charges of extravagance and corruption against the national officers . . . ." Debs believed the promise of the United Mine Workers could yet be redeemed by the West Virginia Rebels. The local militants were also encouraged by the examples of Socialists in other parts of the world. For example, Belgian workingmen had provided an excellent example of how a general strike could even guarantee political rights. The same thing could happen in West Virginia. In the meantime, the militants pledged themselves to fight against any attempt by local Socialists to engage in a political campaign and to prevent any fusion with Democrats and Republicans.[36]

The 1916 Election

The major political parties in West Virginia realized that they had a golden opportunity to make inroads in the Socialist ranks. In the primary election of 1916, many radicals felt free to support one of the Republican candidates for governor. The forces promoting Attorney General A. A. Lilly did get some Socialist support for him.[37] Unfortunately, the attorney general's pro-business attitude as prosecuting attorney of Raleigh County limited his appeal.[38] Therefore, the Lilly forces allegedly adopted a different strategy. Documents signed by Socialists attacking Hatfield and his support of Lilly's rival were circulated. At the same time, Lilly money was supposed to have been used to try to get Socialists to nominate local tickets.[39]

The other Republican hopeful was Supreme Court Judge Ira Robinson. The judge was greatly admired in labor circles for his dissenting opinion in the 1913 martial law cases. The labor support that Robinson received in his successful bid for nomination and campaign in the general election was impressive. Many important United Mine Workers organizers and officials such as J. C. Hurt, Tom Haggerty, Luke Lanham, Den Davis, Everette Stover, and L. C. Rogers endorsed the judge.[40]

In addition, pro-Robinson forces secured endorsement for his candidacy from the Ohio Valley Trades and Labor Assembly, and made inroads in other city assemblies.[41] Important Socialists across the state joined the efforts to elect Robinson. From Wheeling, Harry F. Corcoran campaigned for Robinson in the northern part of the state.[42] In Harrison County, D. A. Duthie, a secretary of a Socialist local, and Edward Kintzer were trying to get as many of their comrades as possible to support the judge. And in Kanawha County Harold Houston had endorsed Robinson as the most logical candidate for the working class.[43]

It seems likely that the bulk of the West Virginia Socialists interested in supporting a practical alternative to their own candidates were ready to support the Democratic Party. In part, this interest reflected the growing appeal that the Wilson Administration had for the workingmen. Legislation passed or pending in such areas as eight-hour days, fiscal reform, non-partisan tariff commission, child labor, and workman's compensation were credited to Democratic leadership. Moreover, President Wilson's promise to keep the United States out of the European war was warmly received.[44] On the other hand, much of the Democratic Party's appeal was more local in origin. For instance, in northern West Virginia, a young Democratic congressman, Matthew M. Neely, had raised his party's stock among the workingmen by leading a fight to impeach federal Judge Alston G. Dayton whose injunctions had stymied so many union drives. There is also evidence that some reform Democrats like George I. Neal in Cabell County were working hard to win the labor vote.[45] In addition, whether justified or not, the Republican Party was blamed by workingmen for measures like the primary bill and "Johnson's Pistol Toting Bill," which discriminated against the laboring man.[46]

Democrats from various parts of West Virginia advised their candidate for governor, John J. Cornwell, of the growing interest in the party that Socialists were showing. For example, in Fayette County, W. J. Hall, of the radical stronghold of Mount Carbon, advised Cornwell that there were 1,100 Socialists in Kanawha magisterial district that would follow the Democrats if only a little time and money were spent there.[47] From Greenbrier County, Cornwell was informed that it looked as though the Socialists and Prohibitionist would switch their votes to Democratic candidates.[48] In the Socialist-controlled towns of Hendricks, Tucker County, a radical by the name of McNeeley was sure he could get the bulk of the Socialists to vote Democratic even though many of them had been Republican.[49] And finally, Cornwell was told that if he expected to carry Ohio County, it would be imperative to attract Socialists.[50]

John Cornwell responded cautiously but positively to appeals that he court the radical labor vote. The service of several Socialists was obtained to help Cornwell's campaign. To work for their cause in Harrison County, the Democrats secured W. W. Keeney, a painter by trade. Keeney was originally a Democrat and a miner from McDowell County. He had converted first to the Prohibition Party, later became a Hatfield Republican, and finally a Socialist.

Keeney had plunged into Socialist speech-making and organizing in Mingo and Harrison counties.[51] He now hoped for a Cornwell victory and believed that with the help of comrade R. R. Willet, the efforts by Edward Kintzer and Duthie, the Republicans could be blocked.[52] Keeney also aided Cornwell in recruiting other Socialists like George "Fleet" Parsons to work in the southern part of the state.[53] Furthermore, Cornwell's appeal was enhanced by the fact that well-known radicals like "Mother" Jones and John Brown were campaigning for Woodrow Wilson and Ned Chilton for the United States Senate.[54]

The great expectations they had for capturing radical support were evident in the Democrats' response to the prospect of a Socialist ticket. Unlike his Republican counterpart who was apparently encouraging a separate Socialist ticket, Cornwell did all he could to discourage one. The Democratic leader in Fayette County, W. W. Osenton, had contacted M. B. Coulter, one of the most active Socialists in the New River area. Similarly, Democratic money from Fairmont was allegedly used to prevent the placing of the Socialist Party on the Kanawha County ballot. Coulter was to do all that he could to prevent the Socialists in Fayette County from naming a ticket. At least so testified a Loudon magisterial district radical who claimed that he refused the money but knew for sure of others who accepted.[55] At any rate, Cornwell's campaign strategy seemed to be paying off. Fairly typical were the inquiries by two miners from MacDonald in Fayette County:

We are miners and have been Socialist in politics, but we were impressed with your talk at Mount Hope and would like to take the liberty of asking you some questions which if answered by you, as we feel they will be, we are convinced we can secure for you several votes from the Socialists.[56]

The Socialist Campaign of 1916 was very ineffectual. The wildest sort of rumors and recriminations caused discouragement of several of the local organizations. In Huntington, for example, many loyal party members carried on a running feud with comrades who wanted to back "some reasonable alternative."[57] In Kanawha County, Harold Houston was accused first of trying to prevent a Socialist ticket and then of using Republican money to sponsor a radical slate. The latter action resulted in Houston being sued by Clarence Griffith, chairman of the Kanawha County Socialist Organization, for an unauthorized use of the party name.[58] The Socialist local at Gatewood, Fayette County, warned their members that expulsion awaited any party man who ran on or supported another ticket.[59] Interviews with living workingmen, Socialist and non-Socialist, indicate that many of them sensed that 1916 was something of a turning point. Fairly characteristic was Homer L. Rodes's comments that, "I don't think the party was the same from the time when Gene Debs didn't run. . . . There was some mix-up about the boys running here."[60] In fact, the Fayette County record books show that the Socialist Party had no candidates for local offices. It was the first time that had happened since the formation of the party in that county in 1903.[61] This same pattern seems to hold for most of the state. It appears that even for the House of Delegates races not more than a half-dozen counties indicated Socialist candidates were running. This compares with nineteen or more counties in which Socialist candidates were fielded in 1914.[62]

The vote of the West Virginia Socialists fell dramatically in 1916. The party's share of the vote for national and state-wide offices was down from a little over 4 percent in 1914 to a little over 2 percent. The decline appears to have been quite general.[63] In the more urban-industrial Socialist strongholds, the party experienced some serious losses. The extent of this decline may be gained by an analysis of representative precincts in Harrison County where glass, tin, iron, and steel, and other factory workers were concentrated.[64]

The Mountain State Socialists suffered their greatest losses in 1916 in the mining areas. Fayette County's radical vote fell from 11 percent in 1914 to 3 percent in 1916, while in Kanawha County it dropped from 18 percent to 3 percent.[65] Some Socialist strongholds in these counties demonstrated an even more dramatic loss. Mt. Carbon, which the party carried in 1914 with 52 percent of the vote, had delivered only 12 percent in 1916. Similarly, nearby Elkbridge, skidded from 57 to 6 percent with other precincts in Fayette County showing comparable decline.[66] In Cabin Creek district of Kanawha County, the party vote fell from 47 percent to 11 percent. Socialist candidates in 1915 had polled as high as 1,950 votes whereas in 1916, Lincoln Holstein and other aspirants had been able to attract only between 300 and 400 votes.[67] Predominantly coal-mining districts of high Socialist voting pattern in Harrison County further demonstrate this trend.[68]

Many political observers felt that the bulk of the disaffected West Virginia Socialists voted for Democratic candidates. It was this shift that may have been the margin needed to elect John Cornwell as the first Democratic governor of the state in twenty years. Cornwell's victory was by the slim margin of 2,775 votes.[69] "The failure of the Socialists to vote their own ticket and their pretty solid line-up in the ranks of Democrats," analyzed the *Charleston Post*, "was enough . . . to account for the plurality of Mr. Cornwell in the State."[70] Quite a few of these voters came from Cabin Creek district, where the party lost some 1,417 votes, the great majority of which went Democratic.[71] A more detailed picture of the swing to Cornwell and his party is provided by Fayette County. For instance, the four most important coal-producing magisterial districts were overwhelmingly Republican in 1906. However, in 1916 they were all carried by the Democrats. Moreover, the high Socialist voting precincts within these districts show some of the most dramatic shifts away from the Republicans.[72]

City precincts with a strong Socialist voting pattern appear to have followed generally the trend of their comrades in the coal districts. Soon after the election of 1916, the *Wheeling Majority* was sure as Charleston newspapers that "about half of the Socialist sympathizers appeared to have voted for Wilson."[73] However, some samplings of votes in Ohio County indicate that the urban Socialists often switched their support to Republican candidates. It also appears that the losses incurred in these areas by the party were not as significant as those in mining precincts.[74] Much the same picture emerges from Harrison County by examining socialist strongholds among the glass, tin, and steel works of Clarksburg, Salem, Adamston, and Bridgeport.[75]

The failure of the West Virginia Socialist Party to wage a vigorous political campaign in 1916 was damaging for several reasons. In the first place it was a reflection of the frustration and division in party ranks. Many of the more militant local radicals saw in the passage of the Primary Election Law confirmation of the futility of pursuing political action. At the same time the creation of the West Virginia Miners Organization symbolized to the militants the type of industrial union action that offered the best hope of bringing about the future Socialist state. This exclusive concentration on economic action was not only discouraging to those radicals who helped bring about change through the political process, but also created a way for the Democratic Party to make inroads into local Socialist ranks. Just as significant was the fact that the West Virginia party was weakened at the very time when it needed all of its strength to deal with the impact of the events surrounding the First World War.

The Perils of Peace and War

At first, the atmosphere created by the war in Europe provided the local radicals with an issue of peace that might reunite and strengthen their party. Mountain State Socialists had traditionally opposed anything that smacked of militarism by state or national government. Increasing the size of the regular army or National Guard, creation of state constabulary, or even the promotion of the Boy Scouts of America, were often taken as examples of the capitalists' use of the martial spirit to protect their ill-gotten property from the exploited workers everywhere.[76] Thus, the Socialists led the West Virginia State Federation of Labor in condemnation of American forays into Mexico that were in the interests of a few capitalists who had obtained questionable concessions.[77]

When war broke out in Europe, West Virginia Socialists eagerly supported American neutrality. To the West Virginia radicals, the war was the predictable result of the maturing productive capacities of European nations facing an ever narrowing world market. The workers of all nations were friends and should not be sacrificed in the interests of those who were exploiting them. Therefore, the Socialists in America must lead their fellow workers in making sure the administration did not alter its present course.[78] In the summer of 1914, the Huntington Socialist Organization sponsored a "Red Week" and secured the cooperation of the Huntington Trades and Labor Assembly in the week's high point, an anti-war rally. At the same time, the Socialist Local at Gatewood in Fayette County was warning that although President Wilson was opposed to the war, he was also cooperating with the capitalists in their rush to supply the belligerent nations. This latter action was not only un-neutral, but was also raising food prices. The only safe course, claimed the Gatewood comrades, was an embargo.[79]

As pressure for American involvement in the European war increased, the attempts by West Virginia Socialists to keep the country neutral found strong support among their fellow workers. For example, December 6, 1915, was set aside by the preparedness forces in Wheeling as a day to display the American flag as a symbol of support for the war effort of the Allies. In response, the Wheeling Socialists were successful in getting the Ohio Valley

Trades and Labor Assembly to request that its members display the words "Peace and Goodwill toward Men" as a counter-demonstration to the preparedness forces. In addition, the Assembly sent a strong resolution to President Wilson, urging that America follow a course of peace and not the path to war.[80] In Huntington, Socialists petitioned President Wilson, hoping to prevent the torpedoed vessels of belligerents from being used to inflame public opinion. Huntington Socialists publicized their resolution to President Wilson, which stated that they did not regard the death of Americans on the *Lusitania* as a cause for talk of war against Germany. These "adventurous American passengers" had ample warning and traveled on the ill-fated vessel at risk of their own lives and the peace of the United States.[81] Walter Hilton used the editorial pages of his newspaper to explain what would happen if war came. Hilton warned that it would be the painters, carpenters, bricklayers, tinners, and mill workers who filled the ranks, then the trenches, hospitals, and finally the cemeteries. War agitators had been active, only two years and Wheeling was already beginning to feel the effect. Pressure was being subtly exerted on the press and public officials, who were increasingly taking on an attitude similar to a local police judge who reprimanded a foreigner for speaking disrespectfully of the United States.[82] Other central labor bodies evidenced attitudes similar to the Wheeling workingmen. The Kanawha Valley Central Labor Union feared that modern warhawks would lead America into affairs that did not concern them. The Charleston area workingmen urged that there be no declaration of war until the working class, who had to bear the burden of the struggle, had an opportunity of expressing their opinion by a national referendum.[83] And when Jacob Boes proposed that the Belmont Trades and Labor Assembly endorse the A.F. of L's position that the United States should not be drawn into the war with preparedness fever, his motion passed with only four dissenting votes.[84]

America's eventual entrance into the First World War brought an angry reaction from many West Virginia Socialists. Charlie

Walters, a United Mine Workers official, recalled coming to District 17 headquarters in Charleston not long after war was declared. He found that President Frank Keeney had been drinking and was in a nasty mood. "I hope that any troops that this government sends overseas to fight this rotten war are killed. That is the only thing this country will understand."[85] The Reverend Fred Smith, formerly of Dothan in Fayette County, remembered that John Brown told a group of miners that "if he was taken into the army and told by an officer to shoot some Henry Dubb, I'd shoot him (the officer) instead."[86] In Huntington, Edwin Firth, the acting state secretary of the party, asked, "Are you (workers) going to lay your heads on the chopping block of a capitalist war? Let the capitalists fight their wars. . . ." In Kanawha County, the Socialists circulated leaflets against American entrance into the war. This upset Governor Cornwell, who complained of the public speeches by radical lawyer, Harold Houston, who had stated, "Wilson had jumped the poor Kaiser" with no real justification and that the workers should not take up arms against Germany where the laboring man was better off than in America.[87] Furthermore, George Gillespie, from Huntington, and Dr. Matthew Holt represented the West Virginia Socialists at the party's national convention in Saint Louis. Dr. Holt delivered one of the main addresses at the Planter's Hotel. He deplored American participation in the war and told the delegates that he and his wife had sent their son to South America to avoid being sacrificed in this immoral war.[88]

On the other hand, some Socialists gave more immediate, if reluctant, support to the war effort. The *Wheeling Majority*, which was usually a pretty fair barometer of the general attitude of the laboring man of the panhandle area, explained its sudden switch from its former peace stand. A democratic society, editorialized Walter Hilton, can work only when the minority is willing to bow to the will of the majority. Therefore, all Americans were obliged to support the war effort even if they disagreed with it. However, this did not mean that the workingman should not be aware of what a momentous step this nation was taking. With this commitment to a European struggle, America might be turning from a democracy minding its own business to an oligarchy involved in directing other people's affairs. It is difficult to say if the majority of laboring men agreed completely with Hilton's position. At any rate, the Ohio Valley Trades and Labor Assembly pledged its loyalty and support to the United States government while Jacob Boes led the Belmont Trades and Labor Assembly in a similar course.[89]

Throughout 1918, the enthusiasm of many more Socialists for the war effort increased. In part, the change came through the government's propaganda efforts, which were aimed at securing the cooperation of the workingman. Especially effective in this regard was the work of the American Alliance for Labor and Democracy, which was sponsored by the National Civic Federation, and George Creel's Committee on Public Information. The Alliance published the views of pro-war Socialists like Charles Edward Russell, John Spargo, W. J. Ghent, and A. M. Simons. These radicals, representing all shades of opinion within the party, stressed that by cooperating with Wilson in the war effort, democratic ideals could be spread to the rest of the world and significant steps toward domestic socialism would be taken at home with the government intervention in the economy.[90] *The Wheeling Majority* began to run articles by the Alliance and picked up the theme of the pro-war Socialists. Articles on the strides being made in government and local ownership by Dr. Harry Laidler, Carl D. Thompson, and spokesmen of the Public Ownership League of America became a regular feature of the paper.[91] Such articles fell on fertile ground since The *Appeal to Reason*, which circulated widely over West Virginia, had been saying much the same thing for a year or more. Interviews with some West Virginia radicals indicate that they agreed with the Appeal's view that "We shouldn't approve the war but this may be a time of vital social reconstruction and we should take advantage of it."[92]

The gains made by labor through the operations of other wartime agencies also increased workingmen's support of the Wilson

Administration. The powers of the War Labor Board and the Labor Department were used frequently to bring employers into line in disputes with workingmen. When the small Wheeling ironworks of the J. E. Moss Company refused to recognize the desire of its men to organize a union, a labor department representative soon brought the company around. W. E. Liller, of the Labor Department, was similarly helpful when the stripper girls of Wheeling's stogie plants were seeking a wage increase. The Labor Department man helped Charles Huggins and Mat Greer of the Ohio Valley Trades and Labor Assembly prepare the stogie girls' case before the War Labor Board. They soon obtained a satisfactory raise from the stogie manufacturers.[93] Machinists in West Virginia credited the War Labor Board with their achievement of an eight-hour workday.[94] It was felt in labor circles that such encouragement had definitely increased the number of union men and women in West Virginia. For example, the Ohio Valley Trades and Labor Assembly and the Belmont County Ohio Central Labor Body indicated that their membership was up by several thousand members.[95]

Government support also increased the size of the West Virginia United Mine Workers Union by helping to sustain their organizational drive of 1918. Under the aggressive leadership of Frank Keeney, Fred Mooney, "Peggy" Dwyer, and others, the miners had been working to unionize the Fairmont coal fields. The work had been difficult until Clarence Watson, whose family interests controlled the miners of Marion County, withdrew his opposition. This was done, according to Fred Mooney, because John Cornwell and the Democratic Party leadership realized that the shift of radical mine workers in Kanawha County had made possible his election as governor. Therefore, Cornwell laid the groundwork for an agreement with union leaders, giving Clarence Watson the promise of political support in his bid for the United States Senate in return for freedom to organize the Fairmont fields.[96] When the mine workers turned their attention to the unorganized area of New River and the Winding Gulf districts, they were stymied until they were aided by the

War Labor Board. Two of the board's directors were John P. White and Rembrant Peale of the United Mine Workers.[97] Justin Collins, superintendent, had warned earlier that such government backing was in the offing. He had written, "I take it that Frank A. Hayes and others are going to make good their threat of either making a new contract on the basis such as they want to endeavor to shut down the mines . . . the fact that Hayes is so persistent indicated that he is sure of his backing from Washington."[98]

One of the most important factors to either create or solidify radical support for the war was the momentous change in Russia. West Virginia Socialists of all persuasions were enthusiastic about the Russian Revolution and subsequent Bolshevik takeover. Walter Hilton was amazed but pleased by the events in Russia. It was hard for the Wheeling editor to believe the first news of the revolution because Russia was "so backward industrially," but Hilton felt anything might be possible in wartime. The Bolshevik coup was even more startling, but Hilton urged American radicals not to fear the overthrow of Karensky. "We have been taught that such developments ought to go through stages . . . but it is not so impossible for Russia to leap the gap." Moreover, there was an obvious lesson for America in these events, Hilton explained. When conditions were as bad as they were in Russia, people would not wait patiently for the tedious process of elections, statutes, and court decisions, but would take matters into their own hands.[99] Houston Young, a former Republican secretary of state, remembered coming upon "the red Socialist" lawyer, Harold Houston, shortly after the word of the Bolshevik revolution got to West Virginia. "We were on our way to the Charleston Elks Club," Young recalled, "Houston was ecstatic and threw his arms apart and said, 'This is the most glorious day in the history of the world, the Bolshevists have taken over in Russia.' I could never figure out how a guy like that had ever gotten into the Elks."[100] These and other West Virginia Socialists felt a special need to defend the fledgling Bolshevik government, and to marshal public opinion to that end. Speeches supporting the Bolsheviks were made before comrades and to the public on street corners. Some of these followed the theme of John Brown that Germany was spreading misinformation about the Russians in hopes of sowing the seeds of distrust in the United States.[101] Furthermore, several Socialist locals in West Virginia and Belmont County, Ohio, made a special effort to circulate pro-Bolshevik literature.[102]

Signs of the new attitude toward the war by conservative and radical Mountain State workingmen were obvious at the time of the government's Liberty Bond drive. "Mother" Jones appeared before the State Federation of Labor asking the delegates in the spring convention of 1918 to "back the president with bonds." Much to the delight of the delegates, she added that the wealth of the capitalists ought to be conscripted along with the bodies of the workingmen. At the same proceedings, C. Frank Keeney urged that maximum production efforts be employed to carry on the war.[103] Keeney further demonstrated his changed attitude toward mobilization by serving as the grand marshall of a three-mile-long parade that launched Charleston's bond drive. One of the main speakers at the rally following that parade was Harold Houston. The Socialist lawyer explained to throngs of people the change of heart on the party of many radicals, "In the early stages of the war, we were disposed to criticize the president but now we believe that President Wilson is one of the greatest men the country has produced. He is one of the greatest exponents of democracy and human freedom the world has even known."[104] In Wheeling, the Ohio Valley Trades and Labor Assembly outdid all other community groups with bond drives, escorting inductees to railroad departing, and patriotic parades. From all over the state came similar news of unions that had large radical membership like Flint glass, window glass, machinists, and miners boasting of the large sacrifice of men and money they had made to the war.[105]

By the time of the fourth Liberty loan more West Virginia radicals were willing to listen to calls from pro-war Socialists for abandonment of the party's anti-war stand taken in St. Louis. Walter

Hilton used Debs as an example of what was happening to those who felt that new circumstances required that the party adjust its position. As Hilton pointed out, it was "hard for those who have preached for years that all wars were European and capitalistic . . . to realize that this war is international and democratic and that American participation was logical and inevitable." Hilton felt that now there was no reason for any further doubts. Germany's determination to crush Socialist countries like Russia and Finland ought to be all the indication that West Virginia Socialists needed. So now, Hilton urged, "the workers of the Wheeling District rise to this solemn duty, and without flamboyant flag-flapping that have so often served but to clothes insincerity, have joined with their brothers everywhere."[106]

Bolsheviks and Mountaineers: The Red Scare in West Virginia

Paradoxically, the support for the Bolsheviks, which finally united the West Virginia Socialists in the war effort, was to hinder their hopes for a comeback in the postwar period. In the first place, many Mountain State radicals were having second thoughts about the Bolsheviks as models for the Socialist state of the future. This attitude was often reflected in the attacks on the Russians beginning in 1919 by many nationally prominent, "pro-war socialists." American Alliance for Labor Democracy sponsored writers "Algie" Simons, W. J. Ghent, Charles Edward Russell, J. G. Phelps Stokes, and Chester M. Wright, which made the most telling points. Simons explained that his interviews with the deposed Kerensky revealed the ferociousness and excessive brutality of the Bolsheviks. Chester Wright, a former editor of the *New York Call*, struck a more responsive chord in the West Virginia radical tradition when he labeled the Bolsheviks undemocratic. In a series of articles in the *Wheeling Majority*, Wright pointed out that real progress toward socialism could only come democratically while Bolshevism was just the opposite. It was dictatorship by Lenin and his followers, all of whom laughed at democracy. Wright understood that there were those Socialists who would defend Lenin's kind of despotism by arguing that it would be better to allow some injustice to the capitalists through a dictatorship of a proletariat than to continue to have the kind of mass injustice perpetrated by the old governing class. Wright reminded those who took that position that ". . . a despotism of any kind is a despotism." Wright, Ghent, Russell, Simmons, and the others pointed to the English socialism as a more appropriate model for American workers.[107]

The extent of the local disenchantment with the Bolsheviks' methods is difficult to determine. However, there is no question that it was dividing the party in West Virginia as well as nationally. George Glass remembered that in the Charleston area he and several others were persuaded that a quick revolution such as had occurred in Russia would not happen in the United States.[108] On the other hand, George Harper, another secretary of a local branch in another section of the same city, agreed with "Mother" Jones, whom he recalled had told a rally, "I want to see a shorter work day and more pay and I want to see the workers run the county and if that's Bolshevism, then I am a Bolshevik."[109] In the Wheeling area the situation was similar. While many Ohio County party members agreed with the general position outlined by the American Alliance for Labor and Democracy, there were also those like Raymond Bauer, who was still excited about the Bolshevik takeover and saw it in religious terms, with capitalists justly paying for their past sins. Besides, Bauer pointed out in another place, the workers should wait and see what the end result of the communist state would be.[110] Moreover, several local Socialist branches for both the northern and southern sections of West Virginia condemned the National Executive Committee's expulsion of the Ohio and Michigan state organizations from the party. The locals demanded national referendum of all Socialists to see if this undemocratic action would stand.[111]

Across the Ohio River in Belmont County, the picture was similar. Even though the Ohio Socialist Party became one of the supporters of the more revolutionary techniques of the communists, there were those who spoke out against that tendency.[112] For example, Fred White, of the Martin's Ferry local branch, was quoted in the *Wheeling News* to the effect that he and his comrades could not agree with the actions of the Bolsheviks. The Belmont County Socialist Executive Committee put pressure on the Martin's Ferry local branch to obtain a retraction. The local responded by entertaining a motion to the effect that the article did not represent the true feelings of their branch; however, enough comrades apparently felt that White spoke their sentiments to defeat the motion twice.[113]

West Virginia Socialists also found that support for Bolshevism made it more difficult to operate in the postwar environment. In part, this was true because of an increase in government suppression of radical groups. The West Virginia Socialists had already received a taste of what that could mean. The federal government had prosecuted several prominent memberships for alleged violations of the wartime measures aimed at preventing disloyal speech and action. One was Gus. A. Gneiser, a state committeeman who was tried in February 1918 for his association with a Liberty defense fund.[114] While Gneiser was apparently not convinced, Paul Bosko of Morgantown and Dana Harper of Huntington were sentenced to Atlanta for obstructing the war effort.[115] Local officials and vigilantes also intimidated party members and the Socialist press. Walter Hilton complained that even though his paper was solidly behind the war and his staff had subscribed 100 percent to bond drives, the *Majority* and its editor had been burned in effigy. The most serious blow, however, was the mysterious burning of the plant of the combined *Argus Star*, thus silencing that important left-wing vehicle.[116]

After the formation of the Third International in March 1919, conservative Americans' fear of the spread of revolution or at least revolutionary principles to this country mounted. Known as the "Red Scare," this period was marked by an increase in official pressure on suspected radicals by national and local governments. The special target of these drives were foreign-born workers, who were often thought to be potentially the most dangerous.[117] In West Virginia federal undercover operators were busy ferreting out possible subversives. For instance, secret agent 37 reported to United States Marshall C. E. Smith at Fairmont that the Italians at the mining community of Wendell were talking of starting a revolution.[118] Agent number 35 in Harrison County reported that Gus Kocsis, a Hungarian miner, was urging his co-workers to strike until the capitalists class gave in and granted Socialists' demands in full. According to the government agent, Kocsis had on one occasion said that, "the American working class had just as much right to turn Bolsheviks as the Russians.... He said, of course, we will suffer at the beginning of the strike, but when the revolution broke out it will be 'goodbye capitalist.'"[119] Department of Justice agents found Monongalia and Taylor counties to be "particularly nasty," due to the establishment of several chartered locals of the Industrial Workers of the World as well as other pro-Bolshevik organizations.[120] Careful note was also made of the circulation of alien revolutionary propaganda. For example, Italians at Fairmont were receiving *Cronaca Sovversiva*, an anarchist publication, while Russian Wobblies at Randall near Star City were distributing thousands of radical pamphlets. The crackdown on these suspects came as part of the natural pick up and deportation of radicals by Attorney General A. Mitchell Palmer. Approximately 100 suspected Bolshevists and Wobblies were arrested in Marion, Monongalia, Taylor, and Harrison counties.[121]

Local politicians sensed the public temper and had warmed rather quickly to the "Red Scare." From the governor down came due warnings of impending revolution. John Cornwell told such industrial associations as the Williamson coal operators and National Paint and Varnish Convention that trouble could be expected from the Industrial Workers of the World and the Bolsheviks; however, the governor explained he was working closely with federal officials in the matter. A similar line was taken by state legislators who secured the passage of a Constabulary Bill. This measure, which established a police force of three companies with sixty men each, was urged in order to help keep West Virginia from becoming a dumping ground for Bolsheviks.[122] Moreover, labor claimed that many of the new law officers had been previously used by the state as secret agents searching for radical activity.[123] In addition, the 1919 Legislature passed a Red Flag Bill, which outlawed the displaying of the red flag of Bolshevism and the black flag of anarchism. It also provided that "It shall be unlawful for any person to speak, print, publish, or communicate by language, sign, picture, or otherwise any teachings, doctrines, or counsels in sympathy or in favor of the ideals, institutions, or forms of government hostile, inimical or antagonistic to those now or hereafter existing under the Constitution and laws of the state or the United States."[124]

The experience of West Virginia union men in the steel and coal strikes of 1919 made clear that connection with any kind of radicalism of the state had been mobilized as part of the drive by the National Committee for the Organization of the Iron and Steel Industry which had been created in 1918 by the A.F. of L.[125] The local strike leader, Jack "the Giant Killer" Peters, had done his job well enough that over 15,000 men came out on strike in the Wheeling area in support of the National Committee's demands for union recognition and better working conditions.[126] In additions, a planned march of 8,000 miners from Steubenville to Weirton was unnecessary since the West Virginia iron and steel men had done their own organizing.[127] However, the same technique of linking the union with radicalism used by steel management elsewhere in the county all but erased the early gains by the West Virginia Steel Workers. In Weirton, the scapegoats were Finnish Socialists, who were alleged by management to be Wobblies and Bolsheviks bent on starting a revolution. Contrary to the view that "the civil liberties of the strikers were fairly well respected in West Virginia," the Finnish Socialists were driven from town by a company detective-lend vigilante committee.[128] By the middle of October the steel mills of Weirton were operating at full capacity.[129]

Similar attempts to link the steel workers with radicals took place in the Steel Works of Bellaire and other plants around Wheeling. Part of this strategy was to divide the workers. Union men in Bellaire complained of management's placing of cards in their pay envelopes with Old Glory at the top and the red flag at the bottom and in between the word "which?"[130]

While the Steel Strike was sputtering out, the West Virginia miners were playing an important role in the national conflict in the Bituminous coal industry. The soft coal trouble centered around the fact that the United Mine Workers wanted to break the no-strike agreement they had with the war-time Fuel Administration. Though the agreement was not to expire until the end of March 1920, the mine workers felt it could not be maintained for two reasons. In the first place, it was alleged by the miners that recent purchasing actions of the director general of the railroads had encouraged the operators to increase the price of coal $1.50 above the officially fixed price. In the second place, the cost of living had risen much faster than wages, creating real hardships for many miners.[131] West Virginia's non-unionized Guyan and Logan coal fields were a critical area to solving these problems. For example, production in the Logan field alone had jumped some 95 percent between 1914 and 1921 as compared to a 23 percent increase in the rest of the state. While the unusual war demand continued, the high production in the Logan fields could be absorbed without too much trouble. However, with the coming of peace, these unorganized fields were gaining an advantage in the market by wage cuts.[132]

The Bituminous Strike of 1919 in West Virginia was marked by a series of violent exchanges between mines and operators that would continue into the early 1920s. While the miners in the northern part of the state were the striking unionized mines, District 17 was launching a drive into the "billion-dollar coal fields" of Logan and Mingo counties. This drive resulted in at least two armed marches; a spectacular shoot-out between Baldwin Felts men and town officials known as the "Matewan Massacre; A Sharples Massacre" between miners and Logan County deputies; and finally, the full-scale battle of Blair Mountain in which armed miners were finally subdued by federal troops and a squadron of bombers.[133] It seems questionable that any of the Mine Workers' leaders saw these events as a prelude to a general revolution. However, as in the case of the Steel Strike, management capitalized on the general anti-Red hysteria. Rather typical was the line taken by George Jones, a Guyan coal operator, before a committee appointed by Governor Cornwell to look into conditions in the southern coal fields. In justifying the use of deputy sheriffs paid by the operators, Jones maintained that he was only protecting his men who were opposed to labor organizations. "Unions are now controlled by radicals, Industrial Workers of the World and Bolshevist," Jones continued, "who are not in sympathy with American ideals and who are seeking to destroy industry." In the northern coal fields, when miners in several places refused to follow the instructions of their leaders and return to the mines, the operators in Fairmont blamed "foreign radicals." These radicals in widely scattered places like Grant Town in Marion, Wendell in Taylor, and Thomas in Tucker Counties were allegedly keeping the strike going and plotting revenge for recent arrests of aliens.[134] Even while he was complaining that mine union officials had betrayed him and were not cooperating with his efforts to seek a peaceful solution to the miners' grievances, Governor Cornwell was lending credence to the operators' claims by describing unions as Bolshevik-ridden.[135]

West Virginia labor spokesmen tried to defend themselves and their organizations against what they felt were unfair charges of radicalism. Governor Cornwell and other public officials were challenged to produce real members of the Industrial Workers of the World or Bolsheviks. Certainly it could not be maintained that Finns of Weirton were disloyal, explained the *Wheeling Majority*, for many of them were American citizens and some had served their county in the trenches of France. W. L. Cumberlidge, the secretary of the Ohio Valley Trades and Labor Assembly, Sam Montgomery, and others claimed that they knew better than the governor or any other politician the various facets of the labor movement in West Virginia and they had never associated with any radicals like the governor had described. As for the mine workers, Frank Keeney swore that he "knew of no officer of the United Mine Workers District Seventeen, but what was in strict accordance with the American Labor Movement as expressed by the A.F. of L." Moreover, much the same denial came from mining communities labeled hotbeds of radicalism. For example, Local 2999 of the United Mine Workers resolved that, "We are peace loving and law abiding citizens of this county and the protests (against The Constabulary Law) were not made by Bolshevists, anarchists and Industrial Workers of the World which organizations do exist in the Wendell, Flemington areas."[136] And finally, the Huntington Trades and Labor Assembly felt that it was necessary to send a committee to their City's Chamber of Commerce to clarify the central labor body's attitude on "red agitators."[137]

Labor's defense campaign was complicated by the attitude of many in union ranks. Both the State Constabulary and Red Flag bills drew heavy fire from the labor bodies. Yet there were those who had supported these measures. For example, President Rogers, of the State Federation of Labor, led lobbyists to fight the Red Flag Bill. At the same time, G. R. Blizzard, the Federation's vice president, and several other labor members of the House of Delegates supported it.[138] When the Federation met in Clarksburg and condemned the State Constabulary and Red Flag Bill, it was not without considerable discussion in which at one point Delegate Mahony demonstrated his support for the measure. "I'll never follow the red flag . . . there's only one flag in this county and that's the Stars and Stripes." Mat Greer responded that Mahony and others completely misunderstood the bill. It was really a blind that would be used to deny the worker's right of free speech and assembly. This same pattern held true for Belmont County, where the Local Trades Assembly condemned the Red Flag ordinance of the town of Bellaire, but over the objections of Delegate David Jones, who defended it.[139]

It is difficult to say exactly the extent to which the West Virginia Socialists suffered as a result of the continuing divisions within the party and the general atmosphere of rampant anti-radicalism. Some scanty evidence would suggest, however, that the losses were considerable. There was no longer much radical press to promote the party's position. *The Wheeling Majority* paid some occasional nostalgic tributes to the days when its front pages were devoted to Socialist news and it did run a Free Speech Column in a not too conspicuous space. In the main, however, the paper promoted in 1919 the American Alliance for Labor and Democracy's campaign of continuing wartime cooperation between employee and employers.[140] Interviews with old Socialists indicates that regular meetings of local branches were held only infrequently and that many chapter ceased to function.[141] This trend is partially substantiated for the Wheeling area by minutes of the Belmont County Ohio Socialist Executive Committee meetings. In December 1917 the state secretary of the West Virginia Party wrote to the Belmont County of his concern for Wheeling, which had a Socialist organization, "but that it was not very active" and suggested "that we call a meeting of the Ohio County branches and try to get them lined up for the 1918 campaign."[142] The decline in West Virginia relative to other parties in the country was reflected in the figure of the National Executive Committee, which showed that the Mountain State party was 27th in 1916 and 31st in 1917.[143]

It was unfortunate that the West Virginia Party was not in a position in late 1919 to take advantage of what seemed a heightened interest in political action by the laboring men of their state. The reason for the discontent of the workers was not hard to perceive. Wartime union gains were being reversed. Employers' actions in the Coal and Steel Strike in West Virginia seemed to foreshadow the capitalists' return to their pre-war character and made any cooperation campaign look ridiculous. As a result of this and mounting prices, workers had plunged into the municipal elections in 1919 with some gratifying results. Union men had been elected as mayors in Clarksburg and Shinnston. Labor leaders also had high hopes for duplicating these victories in Fairmont and Moundsville.[144] Moreover, workers were doing much more to create solidarity by promoting union membership for Negroes and seeking cooperation with interested farm groups.[145]

Opportunities Lost: The 1920 Non-Partisan Political Campaign

The progress of the 1920 Non-Partisan Political Campaign in West Virginia clearly illustrated the problems and lost opportunities of the local radicals. The plans for the Non-Partisan Campaign were formulated by over 250 delegates from labor organizations, which met in Parkersburg on April 1, 1920. The conference elected William Petrey, the vice president of District 17 of the United Mine Workers, as state chairman; established a campaign committee for each congressional district; secured the cooperation of central labor bodies and farmer organizations; and unanimously endorsed Samuel B. Montgomery for the Republican nomination for governor of West Virginia.[146]

The Non-Partisan primary campaign effort faced many difficulties. The Republican machinery backed Montgomery's rival, Ephraim Morgan. The only organized financial backing for Montgomery came from labor and even that proved most inadequate. This was true despite the fact that the State Federation of Labor voted that all its locals levy a fifty-cent per member assessment. The testimony of many newspaper and prominent citizens also indicate that this primary was particularly corrupt. In spite of their problems, Montgomery was defeated by only 1,868 votes out of almost 85,000 cast. The Non-Partisan Political Action Committee was encouraged by this fine showing and they determined Montgomery could lead an independent ticket in the general election.[147]

The candidacy of Sam Montgomery created further confusion in West Virginia Socialist ranks. Despite the obvious weakness of the party, some of the more radical members were not ready to give up their claim as the only real vehicle for working-class politics. These same Socialists were not sure that the Non-Partisan candidate deserved their support. The memory of Montgomery's endorsement of the Hatfield Settlement still rankled. From that point on he had become in their minds just another politician. He was no longer Samuel B. Montgomery but "B. S. Montgomery," who was taking salaries from the operators and miners at the same time.[148] In addition, Montgomery's platform was hardly radical enough to excite a Wyatt Thompson or a George Harper. James Weinstein has emphasized the similarity of the national programs of the Non-Partisans and the Socialists.[149] However, in West Virginia, Montgomery campaigned on such relatively tame issues as better schools, better pay, old age pensions, and a severance tax on coal production and royalties.[150]

Other West Virginia Socialists saw Montgomery in a more favorable light. Some thought it was foolish to waste their votes on the Socialist candidate for governor while Montgomery's showing in the primary gave every hope that a laboring man could be elected to the state's highest office.[151] In some cases local Socialists believed that their own candidacies would be aided if they could ride Montgomery's coattail. For example, in Fayette County old-line Socialists such as Gus Frish, Dennis O-Brien, H. B. Colebank, Dennis V. Argabright, Harry Lloyd, and others met in the office of Judge W. R. Bennet of Fayetteville and nominated Socialists to run with Montgomery on the Non-Partisan ticket.[152]

Montgomery had to be cautious about Socialist support. On the one hand, he welcomed votes from any source. As he told a rally in Williamson, "Well, there are independent voters by the thousands, Democrats, Socialists, single-taxers, wet and dry, without money and price . . . ."[153] On the other hand, there was the fact that although the worst of the Red Scare was over, a heritage of suspicion and distrust remained. Conspicuous Socialist support might well drive away moderate voters. The opposition did their best to do just that. Governor Cornwell warned that Montgomery's election would be understood as a victory for radical lawlessness. Republican newspapers noted that in his entourage were radicals of the worst sort. Men who had gone to the state legislature to protect the Red Flag Bill and who had circulated anarchist literature in the industrial centers of the state.[154] There were, of course, Socialists or former Socialists working directly for the Montgomery campaign. Some of the more prominent were Frank Keeney, Fred Mooney, Walter Hilton, John Gatherum, and G. W. Lavinder. Many of these radicals had apparently switched first to the Democratic Party. If they were still Socialists, they tried to keep in the background.[155] Nevertheless, Montgomery felt compelled to defend his moderation.

Sam Montgomery denied that he was a "Red." He described himself as a Mugwump and not a radical. He further explained that his family had invested in coal in northern West Virginia so why would he want to do any harm to the systems? At Huntington he told a crowd that whatever he was, he would be an improvement over Governor Cornwell, who could not have caused more trouble, unless he brought Lenin and Trotsky to West Virginia.[156] This was a far cry from the Montgomery who told the striking miners in 1912, "There is liberty enough for us all. Out in the intellectual sea there is space enough for every sail and in the intellectual air there is place for every wing . . . I believe in revolution—peaceful revolution not by the bullet, but the ballot. The workers of the world are going to unite. You have nothing to lose but your chains."[157] Certainly the Fayette County Non-Partisan Campaign Committee did not want to be linked with the Socialists. The committee made it plain that their sole interest was electing Montgomery as governor. Only the slowness of the legal system prevented the campaign committee from using the injunction it sought against the Socialist candidates being placed on the Non-Partisan ticket.[158]

Although Sam Montgomery finished a poor third in his bid for governor, the lessons of the 1920 election were clear. West Virginia workers were willing to follow a labor candidate if it looked as though he had any chance of success. Returns from Fayette County suggest that many of those Socialists, who had switched to the

Democrats in 1916, now supported Montgomery.[159] The election was a disaster for the Socialists. Debs polled 1.1 percent or less than he had in 1908 and the showing of candidates for state and local office was a little worse. The situation for the party is summed up in Fayette County where Montgomery polled 6,113 votes while the local Socialists, even though running as Non-Partisan candidates, polled less than 300 votes each.[160]

CHAPTER VI
Technological Change and the Decline of Trade Union Strength for the West Virginia Socialist Party

In a stimulating reappraisal of American socialism, James Weinstein has argued that the Socialist Party did not decline dramatically in 1912 but remained a significant economic and political force until after the First World War. During these years, he continues, the party had made even greater progress within the ranks of organized labor. Weinstein also believed that if the Socialists had not become hopelessly split into Communist and Socialist Party factions, they could have continued to grow because "popular radicalism was widespread in the first half of the 1920's."[1] While this view may have validity for some elements in the party, it neglects an important facet of the radicals' difficulty with trade unionists. The First World War and the postwar atmosphere only added greater confusion to the issue of craft versus industrial unionism, which mocked the party's efforts at labor solidarity.

This study has demonstrated that the West Virginia Socialist Party recruited most of its working-class membership from the ranks of the skilled craftsmen who were the backbone of the labor movement. The tradesmen represented a labor aristocracy whose power rested upon the monopolization of certain skills that were still vitally needed in the process of production. At the same time, these crafts were being gradually undermined when certain efficiencies were instituted by the modern industrial corporation.

During the first decade of the twentieth century, machinery had begun to make significant inroads into important handcraft industries in West Virginia. As early as 1904, almost 1,000 machines were being used in the West Virginia coal fields. This meant a little less than one-third of all coal produced with the aid of machinery.[2] In glass production even greater technological progress was being made. A device for automatically blowing glass cylinders was introduced into the window-glass plants.[3] There was also a gradual extension of the range of a semi-automatic machine for blowing glass containers.[4] Threats to eventual skill displacement were apparent in machine shops and potteries.[5]

The technical developments represented threats to the position of the skilled craftsmen. The early mining machines, which were used to undercut coal, could greatly increase production. With this device one man could make a six-foot-deep cut across a thirty foot seam of coal in thirty minutes, which previously would have taken two men at least three hours.[6] The new machines in the glass industry could eliminate the skilled glassblower. For example, with semi-automatic bottle blowers, a presser and gatherer could make 700 more quart jars in a day than three blowers could by the old hand method.[7] In railroad repair shops and foundries, machines that could be operated by unskilled labor were already performing tasks that heretofore had been the assignment of the hand craftsman.[8]

Many skilled tradesmen were not as aware as they might have been to the threat of these innovations. The fact that they only displaced part of a craft was partly to blame. As George DelForge, a big "ring blower" at the cooperatively owned Banner Window Glass Company in South Charleston, explained, "Many of the boys thought that the machines would never take their jobs but the blowers already knew better. It was only logical to me that if machines could blow glass, why couldn't they flatten and cut it?"[9] The relative slowness by which the machines came in also eased the immediate peril to the craftsmens' position. Oscar Dubois, a glass cutter at the Marilla plant in Morgantown, recalled that even some blowers were deluded by the pace of introduction. "The machine started to come in," DuBois observed, "but it came in very slowly. The companies lost money for a good many years . . . the old blowers though . . .

they said they can't do that. They will never make it. But they actually did."[10] This slowness was often the result of the patentees' wish to get maximum benefits from their rights, either by exploiting the devices themselves or by placing careful restrictions on their utilization by others. In still other instances the unions were strong enough to slow the introductions.[11]

Although the craftsmen had weathered the first wave of twentieth-century machinery, the unsettled nature of their industries and the threat to future craft security were enough to push many working men toward radical politics. Eugene Monin did not become as active a Socialist as his brother, but he explained why he believed glass workers voted for Eugene Debs in 1908. "We liked a lot of his ideas, especially the government taking over industry. The glass business was getting to a point where only something like the government could straighten it out so that everybody concerned would not be ruined."[12] A Huntington Socialist captured the feelings of many machinists in his city: "Time was when the Ensign shops (a subsidiary of American Car and Foundry) was not a part of a trust and the bulk of the work was done by hand . . . whereas now the marvelous machinery of modern times had displaced the human worker . . . "[13] Duff Scott, brother of a Socialist justice of the peace, recalled that his conversion to socialism came as the result of a speech he had heard a party organizer make in 1911. "A girl from New York came down and made a speech in the meeting hall at Mucklow. She was talking about automation. . . . She said it wouldn't be long before someone would push a button at the entrance of the mine and coal would come out automatically."[14]

It became clear to some Socialist tradesmen that their craft unions were gradually becoming ineffective in dealing with the large business enterprise. It is interesting to note that several of these radical craftsmen were in a good position to get a clearer picture of the potential impact of machinery in their trades. For example, Edwin Firth was the foreman at the Wiley Pottery Company in Huntington; Felix Dandois was a foreman at the Banner

Window Glass Company; Edward Kintzer held a similar position in Clarksburg; and Harry Leeds had been a foreman in the Benwood Steel Mill.[15] The left-wing *Huntington Socialist and Labor Star* hoped that these workers would find the logical answer to their problems. "Beaten and baffled by the masters, and internally held in check," wrote Wyatt Thompson, "the members of craft organizations are disposed to listen to the more militant and revolutionary voice of industrial unionism." In addition, Thompson tried to demonstrate through reprints of articles from union journals that glassworkers, miners, and machinists all over the country were realizing the logic of an industrial organization.[16]

On the other hand, there were Socialist craftsmen who were not nearly so enthusiastic about "diluting the trade even more by bringing every 'boomer' in the plant into the union."[17] Precisely because they were fighting against a decline in status, these tradesmen clung even more tenaciously to the security of their dwindling craft privileges. They were often in the forefront of attempts by their unions to restrict the number of apprentices in the trade; to use union policies to retard the introduction of machines; or to attempt to secure for the displaced craftsman the right to operate the new device.[18]

In the six years preceding the First World War technological improvements proceeded at such a rapid rate that many craft-oriented radicals knew that more drastic action was necessary. By 1915 two-thirds of all window glass was mechanically blown while wages for the hand blowers fell one-third. More than one-half of the blowers in the bottle trade passed into the ranks of unskilled workers. Of greater significance, new devices had been developed that could completely mechanize the glass industry. The machine shops were affected by slower but similar changes. These helped produce the type of organizational drive that came in the wake of the Paint Creek-Cabin Creek Strike.[19]

It was at this critical juncture in the fortunes of the West Virginia Socialists that the economic effects of the First World War intervened and eased some of the technological pressure on the state's craftsmen. Orders from the allied powers and interruption of normal trade created enough business to keep all types of productive methods busy. *The Wheeling Majority* was typical of other papers in the state when it explained that all over the city, plants were running at full tilt.[20] For instance in 1916, the number of hand pots in operation started to increase after four years of decline. By 1920 there were actually more hand pots in production than there had been in 1912.[21] Conditions for hand craftsmen improved correspondingly. As *The Wheeling Majority* noted:

> What's become of the old-fashioned blower who used to kick around the factory because some other blower happened to beat him a few cents on the week? What's become of the gatherer who didn't mind a few blisters because the machine makes whole reams of them? He is now a rare specimen. What's become of the flattener who used to think he couldn't make a living in eight hours? The American Window Glass Company put a crimp in that idea.[22]

The war also eased the over-produced nature of the coal industry. In 1914 many miners in southern West Virginia had been producing at 65 percent of capacity.

Much of the same picture is true for pottery plants, which were working at one-half their capacity in 1914. This meant a four-day work week. However, by the fall of 1916 conditions suddenly reversed and a runaway market began.[23]

The boom economy of the Firt World War I granted a reprieve to hand manufacturing and restored a great deal of craft consciousness. Several of the drives armed at unionizing all workers, regardless of skill, either lessened or collapsed. For instance, 500 new members had joined the bottle blowers union during their campaign to bring in machine drivers and unskilled men, but by late 1916, this impetus had disappeared.[24] A similar program advocated by window glassworkers failed to get off the ground.[25] Craft-conscious machinists in Huntington were aided by some Socialist brothers in thwarting the attempt to organize new semi-skilled and unskilled laborers.[26]

The change in attitude by some Socialists was best summarized by Walter Hilton. He claimed to be as interested as ever in organizing all workers; however, his emphasis on the permanent employment of the craft union was stronger than it had been in 1914. Recent experience had shown the worker, Hilton explained:

...that effective organization must provide for craft needs, which were, after all, individual needs. They accepted the principle of craft organization.... Now the labor movement has been settling down to the middle of the road policy of craft unionism to care for craft affairs, shop organization, and industrial organization where the craft union is not practical.[27]

The West Virginia Socialists who preached industrial unionism were discouraged. There was still the possibility that miners of Districts 17 and 29 under radical leadership might transform the United Mine Workers from within. On the other hand, there was a feeling that more work and better wages were turning many miners away from revolutionary dedication. "Too many had already sold out for a mess of pottage," was the way Duff Scott explained it.[28] Wyatt Thompson expressed what was in the minds of many left-wingers. "Some of the boys around the state were foolish enough to think that craft unionism would still work. That was ridiculous, but we also missed our chance for real industrial unionism."[29]

Wyatt Thompson's insight was better than he knew. The decade after the First World War sealed the fate of the skilled craftsman in many trades. The passage of a national prohibition law and the tendency toward the use of standardized bottles added to the sophistication of machines in replacing skilled hands. Only the fact that there was still some demand for fancy cologne and perfume bottles kept some hand-craft bottle plants in business.[30] The National Window Glass Union doggedly pursued policies by which it hoped to protect the ever-diminishing need for the skilled craftsmen. Shifts were split to share work and production was rationed more carefully among the hand plants.[31] Finally the union established its own plant in Huntington, West Virginia, in hopes of demonstrating that production by older methods was still profitable.[32] This organization also tried to prevent the machine plants from getting an adequate supply of the one skill that they needed. Heavy fines were imposed on any cutter who went to work at a plant not under the jurisdiction of the National Window Glass Workers.[33]

Nothing could be done to prevent the decline of the handcraft glass trade. Some blowers and gatherers joined the Window Glass Cutters and Flatteners Protective Association of America, the new union in the machine plant. According to some who made this transition, the new unions were much more bureaucratic and conservative. Union officials frequently made their peace with the machine plant owners, thereby securing good positions and stock grants in the company. By 1929 the National Window Glass Union was gone.[34] The pathos of what had happened was expressed perfectly by Pete Felix:

> At one time in the mountain state
> And many years ago, Pete Felix could blow window glass
> As very few could blow,
> Pete Felix in those early days
> Had manners and was neat,
> Was known for his fine living ways
> And called glass blower Pete.
> His friends and fellow mechanics
> Were workers highly paid
> And training their apprentices
> They kept the tricks of trade
> But Pete could see the machine age
> Creeping with stealthy pace,
> Yet vowed that lacking eyes or brains
> Machines couldn't win the race.
> Till changes came at a rapid rate

Altho he said, "It can't be done"
Machinery had him out of date
A dozen sheets to his one.[35]

The particular conditions in each industry often meant that the introduction of technological improvement proceeded at quite different paces and with somewhat differing effect. The pottery industry, which had provided many important members to the West Virginia Socialist Party, retained its craft nature longer than glass. In the decade of the twenties, however, innovations in casting techniques, continuous kilns, and drawing and unloading devices increased production and cut down the need for skilled employees.[36] These developments often caused the closing of some plants that had not been modernized. Such a closing of a Huntington pottery plant removed an important source of radical support from the area.[37]

The displacement of craft workers by mechanization in the 1920s caused a variety of responses that will require closer future inquiry; however, some hints of the effect were uncovered in this study. A minority of West Virginia Socialists joined the Communist Party, which temporarily seemed to provide an escape via the quick solution of world revolution. For most Socialists, however, the day when the worker had the power and will to create a Cooperative Commonwealth had disappeared. Despair and apathy were especially apparent among the older radicals, who scattered in order to find employment as janitors, policemen, truck drivers, clerks, or watchmen so they might protect what little security they had left.

Conclusion

"I sure wish the Socialist Party would have made it," sighed seventy-eight-year-old Bert Seachrist as he rocked on the porch of his miner's cottage at Holly Grove. "They had an awful lot of smart people there, and I'd like to seen them get a chance. Was a time when the miners here was all Socialists and wouldn't talk anything else."[1] Seachrist had captured the dilemma of the American Socialist Party. For a dozen or more years after the turn of the century, important segments of the working class not only talked socialism, but voted for an elected party members to political and trade union offices. Yet, within a few more years, this vital working-class base had been lost to the Socialist Party. The history of this party's relationship to the West Virginia worker may provide some insight into the failure of socialism in America.

For more than half the period covered by this study, the West Virginia Socialists followed a strategy that produced, if not spectacular, at least steady growth of labor support for the party. Basically, the local Socialist worked patiently through existing union organizations to create as much class consciousness as possible.

Building upon the unsettled conditions generated in the wake of a growing concentration of industrial holdings and the 1907 panic, union members of the West Virginia Socialist Party were particularly active in aiding their fellow tradesmen. They led attempts to achieve such practical and immediate aims as an eight-hour day, mine and factory inspections, employers' liability, and cleaner, safer, neighborhoods in which to live.

At the same time the Socialists attempted to mobilize labor behind measures that would lead to a more fundamental reconstruction of society. Municipal ownership of playgrounds, transportation facilities, and public utilities were steps in that direction. In the same light, local party members saw initiative, referendum, and recall as important functional tools of a more democratic and cooperative social order.[2]

The success of the strategy used by the young West Virginia Socialist Party is a further indication that standard views of workingmen in the Progressive Era are distorted. Historians have relied too heavily on the Wisconsin school of labor history's contention that the majority of trade unionists were pragmatic, job-conscious individuals who were not much interested in radical reforms or labor politics. By contrast, this study has revealed that workers in West Virginia often had broad social concerns and were frequently inclined toward labor politics. In fact, there were relatively few leaders in the state's labor movement who did not advocate some substantial changes in the capitalistic system.

The early success of the West Virginia Socialists also reveals much about the nature of the membership of their party. Contrary to the common assumption, the majority of radicals were not recruited from the downtrodden, immigrant laborers, but rather from the skilled craftsmen. In addition, the leadership section of this study indicates that working class Socialists were more native than their conservative peers. They also appeared to have been more intelligent and socially sensitive than those union or political leaders who remained in the regular parties. Since these members were within the workforce, they could fuse the ideology of socialism with a flexible, pragmatic program deliberately suited to appeal to the local culture. The Cabin Creek-Paint Creek coal struggle from 1912 to 1914 appears to have been critical to the future of the West Virginia Socialist Party. The thrilling solidarity of the workers as they battled the arrayed forces of capitalism convinced many local radicals that this was the answer to the dilemma that their party was facing everywhere. The increasing tempo of industrial and technological change was undermining the type of socialism that had seemed appropriate to America before 1910. The skilled and semi-skilled craftsmen had provided the basis for the party; however, it was becoming increasingly apparent that in order to realistically contend with the capitalists for the control of the vital forces of production, an industrial mass union was necessary. The 1912 coal strike further persuaded many West Virginia Socialists that direct industrial action was the best way to achieve their goal. The miners had demonstrated that the workers must fight capitalism "not as crafts but as a class."[3]

Once they embraced mass industrial action, much of the party began to manifest a certain inflexibility, which had not been characteristic of their early approach. In fact, they now began to act more like the model of the chiliastic, utopian that Daniel Bell used to characterize the Socialist Party. This was evident as early as the political campaign of 1914. All segments of the party actively campaigned, but in many places candidates no longer "made reference to local issues. They advanced not a single vote catching proposition."[4] The passage of a primary election law only served to convince the direct actionists that it was foolish to pursue political methods. Gradually electing Socialists to office would indeed seem quite pallid when it was felt that "the class conscious workers of West Virginia but await a state-wide burning issue to unite them into one undivided revolutionary army. . . ."[5]

Pursuance of revolutionary industrial action and the neglect of politics divided the local socialists at a time when they were faced with some most formidable external challenges. It weakened the party politically when the Democrats were making a successful effort to attract the labor vote. The direct actionist emphasis on speed may have prepared many party members for the unrealistic world revolutionary appeal of the Third International. Finally, the mass action approach may have helped push many radicals back into a more defensive craft attitude just at the time when the First World War seemed to slow the threat of technological change.

A Forty-Year Retrospective

Dr. Fred Barkey interviewed by Gordon Simmons

Could you talk about the context in which you undertook the research and oral histories that led to your study of the Socialist Party in West Virginia?

I was an early convert to the idea that American labor history needed to be more than just the story of unions and collective bargaining. I had been living in West Virginia for a decade or so and was struck by the disconnect between what high school and college textbooks said about labor in West Virginia and what I had picked up through conversation with my wife's family, friends, and neighbors in the Cabin Creek mining district.

At the time, I was enrolled as a doctoral student at the University of Pittsburgh, and I explored that gap by doing a seminar paper on the Paint Creek-Cabin Creek Strike of 1912 to 1914. My strongest point in that presentation was that what little literature existed on this great labor struggle tended to ignore workers' political activity. So right off, you have accounts that present what I called at the time a "partial workingman."

A new labor history was beginning to emerge at the same moment. In Great Britain it was developed by scholars like E. P. Thompson and Eric Hobsbawn, and in the United States by the late Herbert Gutman and, of course, David Montgomery, who had just been hired by Pittsburgh where, to my good fortune, he became my advisor.

When it came time to propose a dissertation topic, I secured Professor Montgomery's enthusiastic approval to exhume the record of the Socialist Party in West Virginia. As it turned out, other scholars, doubtless swept up by the same Zeitgeist that captured me, were also exploring the Socialists in the same way, from a local and regional rather than just a national party perspective.

What surprised you most in your findings?

It was surprising that, right from the beginning, the party was so American in origin and presentation. All too often, Socialist movements in this country are depicted as foreign and composed of foreign immigrants. It's true that one could find Finns, Italians, Belgians, Austro-Hungarians, and the like in the Mountain State movement, but the leadership of the party in West Virginia was overwhelmingly native-born Americans.

This composition of party membership helps explain why West Virginian socialism owed as much to working-class perceptions of traditional American history as it did any influence of Marx or Lenin. They viewed the American Revolution, for example, as an assertion of democratic rights across a broad spectrum of our society. For them, more modern economic developments constituted a kind of counter-revolution against what had been sought in the historical era from 1777 to 1787. Here were Mountain State socialists enunciating an idea that would become a major thesis of the great Progressive historian, Charles Beard.

Another surprise was how relatively influential Socialists were in organized labor in both the northern and southern parts of the state. Wherever I looked these radicals weren't just backbenchers or tolerated eccentrics. Instead, they were, very early, performing important roles as respected leaders and contenders for significant influence.

Wheeling and the surrounding area provide the best example of this, where Socialists were prominent in the leadership of the Ohio Valley Trades and Labor Assembly as early as the first decade of the twentieth century. They were not only busy pushing workers to organize, but also to commit their organizations to support a radical political agenda for American society.

This early influence of socialism wasn't confined to industrial areas such as Wheeling, Fairmont, and Clarksburg, it was also to be found in several large districts of the southern coal fields. While it is true that District 17 of the United Mine Workers was initially controlled by conservative and classical trade unionist leaders in the twentieth century's first decade, a simmering layer of younger, mostly native-born workers like Frank Keeney, Fred Mooney, A. D. Lavender, and Lawrence Dwyer were growing restless. For these young miners, a vision of society based on norms of democracy and cooperation were as key as anything in their ongoing drive to give the union new leadership.

Were there discernible differences between the Socialists in mining and manufacturing occupations?

To a certain extent, there were some differences. Miners' discontent appeared to be triggered more by the fact that so many of them lived in relatively isolated communities that a had great potential for creating a high degree of class consciousness. In a setting where the coal operators controlled all facets of communal life, as long as economic conditions were favorable, those operators could provide a benevolent environment. As conditions became less favorable, management's style could turn out to be very oppressive and, all too often, miners suffered accordingly. The periods of intense conflict in the coal fields of West Virginia have to be understood in the context of that setting.

By contrast, the radicalism of West Virginia workers in urban, manufacturing settings was shaped by management's efforts to introduce techniques and organizational schemes aimed at producing greater efficiency. The analysis of glass production in northern West Virginia made by Ken Fones-Wolf is an excellent example of this phenomenon at work.

Weren't there also important strategic differences among West Virginia's Socialists concerning the "correct" way to create a more equal and just society?

The most obvious distinction in that regard was the ongoing dispute between socialists who were labeled "gradualist" and those who were more radical or revolutionary. The "slowcialists," as they were called by their detractors, believed that reforms produced by means of electoral politics would eventually add up to a fundamental reordering of American society. The "red" socialists took their cues from syndicalists like the Industrial Workers of the World (I.W.W., or Wobblies), who advocated strikes and other direct action at the workplace as the best path to the Cooperative Commonwealth in America.

Did this difference follow the north–south distinction to which you referred?

To at least some extent, the southern West Virginia Socialists seemed more inclined to the direct action philosophy of the party's left wing. The predominance of coal miners in my sample would help to explain that. Still, one needs to be cautious when talking about coal miners. For example, when District 24 of the U.M.W.A. was founded in 1913, just about the entire executive board were acknowledged Socialists, led by Lawrence C. Rogers.

Some four years later, when District 17 was taken over by Frank Keeney, Fred Mooney, and other Socialists, Rogers was very critical of the new leadership as being more revolutionary in orientation. Like others in the Socialist Party, Rogers apparently believed that the coal industry and society as a whole could be changed by collective bargaining and legislative measures.

On the other hand, Keeney, despite his direct action orientation, was not adverse to using electoral action, no matter how cynical he and other leftwingers may have been about conventional machine politics dominated by capitalists. With Keeney, it seems to have been the case that if electoral participation can help achieve the Revolution, then, by all means, use it.

Would it be accurate to say that you are wary of taking an overly national perspective on the Socialist Party's factional debates and rigidly impose national labels on local personalities and organization?

That is what I am saying. It's important to keep an open mind in order to interpret what socialism meant to folks at what historian James Green has called the grassroots level. That's why I spent much of my time analyzing the Socialist Party vote in West Virginia's magisterial districts for nearly fifteen counties to disclose what it meant to be Socialist at the local level.

What I found was that in so many of the high Socialist voting precincts, there were independent communities where, for one reason or another, workers felt free to exercise their opinions and control their own affairs. I have elsewhere called them "islands in the stream." These were towns like Esksdale in Kanawha County, or Gatewood, Hilltop, and Powellton in Fayette County. There, local capitalists did not exercise the feudal sort of control all too common within the state at that time, the kind of control we've come to recognize as characteristic of "company towns."

Did West Virginia Socialists pay a price for their desire to change the system?

For most of the period I studied, it was acceptable to be a Socialist, at least in labor circles. With the coming of the First World War, however, and the Socialist Party's opposition to participation in that war, as well as the rise of Russian Bolshevism, Socialists and other leftists became increasingly vilified as foreign and hostile to American society.

A number of West Virginian Socialists would suffer for their views. Dr. Matthew Holt, an anti-war Socialist in Weston, felt compelled to send his sons to Canada to protect them from sure punishment for a refusal to serve in the military. Local small businesses operated by known Socialists were vandalized by super-patriot groups.

In the Red Scare and Palmer raids after the war, a variety of state Socialist Party members were swept up and put in federal prison. For example, Edwin Firth, an English worker who had been a key Socialist Party organizer in Huntington, eventually died in federal incarceration. Several such radicals were meted out the worst punishment for a West Virginian, exile from the state with no hope of returning home. The most prominent of those was Wyatt Thompson, who had been a Socialist Party newspaper editor in Charleston and Huntington, and who died in Columbus. Fred Merrick, of Parkersburg, ended up in federal captivity after editing a revolutionary Socialist newspaper in Pittsburgh.

Why revisit this tradition now?

The time is right because a great many of the problems we face are the result of unrestrained capitalism. Alternatives and solutions to these problems require us to be as open-minded as possible. The beauty of the high point of the Socialist movement in this country was that our society was more open to a broad range of ideas, and, fortunately for us, many of those proposals are an accepted part of the American system today.

Despite that, in America "socialism" has long been a politically charged term of infamy, something totally outside the box of acceptable options. Now, however, the commitment of some of our predecessors to a more cooperative collective arrangement seems unexpectedly relevant once more.

—*November 30, 2011*

Appendix A

Table I: Socialist Leadership Sample

Name	Town	County	Occupation	Leadership Position
Albert, Adrian	Wheeling	Ohio	Stogie maker	Candidate, State
Alderman, Everett	Winifrede	Kanawha	Miner	Organizer, can., local
Argabright, Daniel V.	Hilltop	Fayette	Farmer–Miner	Sec., Br. Soc. P.
Bannister, John	East Bank	Kanawha	Miner	School Board, 1912
Bauer, Albert	Wheeling	Ohio	Carpenter	Pres., OVTLA
Beazley, Isam	Mill Creek	Fayette	Miner	Branch Secretary
Boone, Darius O.	Anthony	Greenbrier	Railroader	Candidate, Local
Boswell, Charles	Charleston	Kanawha	Printer	Editor, Labor Argus
Brown, L. M.	Charleston	Kanawha	Carpenter	Organizer
Boyd, Alf	Standard	Kanawha	Miner	Pres., U.M.W., Local
Brigode, Joe	Charleston	Kanawha	Glassblower	Branch Secretary
Chewning, O. B.	Gatewood	Fayette	Miner	Candidate, Local
Cocoran, Howard	Wheeling	Ohio	Bartender	Candidate, Local

APPENDIX A

Name	Town	County	Occupation	Leadership Position
Coulter, M. B.	Mt. Hope	Fayette	Miner	Organizer and Br. Sec.
Courtney, P. C.	Ronceverte	Greenbrier	Railroader	Candidate, Local
Dandoix, Felix	So. Charleston	Kanawha	Glassblower	Candidate, Local
Daniel, J. H.	Fayetteville	Fayette	Gardener	Candidate, Local
Darlington, Geo. M.	Powellton	Fayette	Miner	Secretary, Local U. M.
Dean, Clyde	Longacre	Fayette	Miner	Candidate, Local District 29
Dwyer, Lawrence	Beckley	Raleigh	Miner	Organizer, W.M.W. Pres.
Firth, Edwin	Huntington	Cabell	Potter	Organizer, U.M.W.
Franklin, Henry	Huntington	Cabell	Barber	Officer, W.Va. S.F.L.
Frisk, Gustave	Hilltop	Fayette	Miner	School Board
Forman, Lee	Morgantown	Monongalia	Motorman	Candidate, Local
Gatherum, John	Gatewood	Fayette	Miner	Sec., District 29, U.M.W.
Gherkin, George	Charleston	Kanawha	Tailor	County Comm. Chm.
Gillispie, George W.	Huntington	Cabell	Machinist	State Exec. Comm. S.P.
Glasgow, V. B.	Fairmont	Marion	Railroader	Candidate, Local
Glass, George	Kallys Creek	Kanawha	Farmer	Sec., Local U.M.W.

APPENDIX A

Name	Town	County	Occupation	Leadership Position
Goff, Sylvanus	Gatewood	Fayette	Miner	Pres., U.M.W. Local
Griffith, Clarence	Hugheston	Kanawha	Miner	V.P., U.M.W. 17
Grounds, Henry	Boomer	Fayette	Timberman & Miner	V.P., U.M.W. 29
Guntner, Herman	Morgantown	Monongalia	Engraver	W.Va. Socialist Ex. Comm.
Harper, George W.	Charleston	Kanawha	Painter	Pres., Painters' Union
Hanes, Alva	Fairview	Marion	Carpenter	Candidate, Local, Sec.
Hecker, J. T.	Wheeling	Ohio	Stogie maker	Officer, OVTLA
Higgins, John C.	Star City	Monongalia	Laborer	State Sec., Soc. P.
Holstein, Lincoln	Coalburg	Kanawha	Miner	Candidate, Local
Hough, Oscar	Morgantown	Monongalia	Lather	Candidate, Local
Hudnall, William D.	Holly Grove	Kanawha	Miner	City Councilman
Jefferies, C. S.	Gatewood	Fayette	Miner	Sec., Br. Soc. P.
Keffer, Mat.	Glen Ferris	Fayette	Miner	Candidate, Local
Knight, L. M.	Charleston	Kanawha	Railroader	Candidate, Local
Lavinder, A. D.	Gatewood	Fayette	Miner	Organizer, Soc. P. U.M.W.
Leeds, Harry	Wheeling	Ohio	Boilermaker	Organizer, Can., State

APPENDIX A

Name	Town	County	Occupation	Leadership Position
Link, Herndon	Ronceverte	Greenbrier	Painter	Candidate, State
Linville, Bess	Dawes	Kanawha	Miner	Officer, Dist. 17
Lusk, Charles	Scarbro	Fayette	Miner	Candidate, State
Monin, Eugene	So. Charleston	Kanawha	Glassblower	Sec., Br. Soc. P.
Morgan, David	Montgomery	Fayette	Miner	Sec., Br. Soc. P.
Mooney, Fred	Cannelton	Fayette	Miner	V.P., Dist. 17
Morris, Alfred H.	Ronceverte	Greenbrier	Railroader	Candidate, Local
Morrison, S. S.	Huntington	Cabell	Car man	Organizer, Soc.P.
Notter, Oscar	Huntington	Cabell	Railroader	Candidate, Local
O'Brien, Dennis	Miami	Kanawha	Miner	Pres., U.M.W. Local
Parsons, George "Fleet"	Hansford	Kanawha	Miner	Organizer, Soc. P.
Peters, W. A.	Wheeling	Ohio	Tin Worker	Candidate, Local
Reuther, Valentine	Wheeling	Ohio	Teamster	Candidate, Congress Pres., OVTLA
Rodes, Homer	Gatewood	Fayette	Miner	Candidate, Local
Rodes, Vincent	Gatewood	Fayette	Miner	Sec., Br. Soc. P.

APPENDIX A

Name	Town	County	Occupation	Leadership Position
Roger, L. C.	Oak Hill	Fayette	Miner	Candidate, Congress Pres., Dist. 29
Rumbaugh, Warren	Winifrede	Kanawha	Miner	Candidate, Local
Schaefer, Meade	Wellford	Kanawha	Farmer	Sec., Br. Soc. P.
Schane, Carl V.	Wheeling	Ohio	Machinist	Candidate, Local Sec., Br. Soc. P.
Schuck, Jesse	Charleston	Kanawha	Printer	Candidate, Local
Seachrist, Bert	Holly Grove	Kanawha	Miner	Sec., Br. Soc. P.
Shay, William	Ronceverte	Greenbrier	Boilermaker	Mayor, Star City
Skaggs, Coy	Jodie	Fayette	Miner	Sec., W.M.W. Local
Smith, Willis	Star City	Monongalia	Glassworker	Sec., Br. Soc. P.
Stuntz, Fred	Charleston	Kanawha	Painter	Sec., Br. Soc. P.
Thompson, Wyatt	Huntington	Cabell	Printer	Editor, *Soc. and Labor Star*
Tincher, Thomas	Chelan	Kanawha	Railroader	Candidate, Local
Toney, Cleveland	Dothan	Fayette	Miner	Candidate, Local
Toney John D.	Dothan	Fayette	Miner	Candidate, Local
Wilson, C. T.	Gauley Bridge	Fayette	Railroader	Candidate, Local

Name	Town	County	Occupation	Leadership Position
Wilson, O. T.	Gauley Bridge	Fayette	Railroader	Candidate, Local
Williams, Marshall	Charleston	Kanawha	Painter	Sec., Br. Soc. P.
Wood, Walter H.	Elkridge	Fayette	Miner	Sec., U.M.W. Local
Workman, John	Eskdale	Kanawha	Miner	Exec. Bd., Dist. 17

Note: Members of both samples usually held many more leadership positions than can be listed here. Abbreviations for positions stand for:

1. W. Va. S.F.L.–West Virginia State Federation of Labor
2. CCTLA–Capitol City Trades and Labor Assembly
3. Sec. Br. Soc. P.–Secretary of Branch of the Socialist Party
4. H.T.L.A.–Huntington Trades and Labor Assembly
5. OVTLA–Ohio Valley Trades and Labor Assembly

Table II: Non-Socialist Leadership Sample

Name	Town	County	Occupation	Leadership Position
Adkins, Ira	Fairmont	Marion	Railroad Conductor	House of Delegates
Barker, C. W.	Olcott	Kanawha	Miner	
Bartlebaugh, C. E.	Wheeling	Ohio	Street Car Conductor	Pres., OVTLA
Beleal, E. L.	Charleston	Kanawha	Carpenter	Officer, CCTLA, Sec. Carpenters & Joiners
Bess, Charles	Cannelton	Fayette	Miner	Sec., U.M.W., Local Justice of Peace

APPENDIX A

Name	Town	County	Occupation	Leadership Position
Blake, Noah	Hilltop	Fayette	Railroader	City Council
Blizzard, Gordon	Edmond	Fayette	Carpenter	2nd. V.P. W.Va. S.F.L. House of Delegates
Bond, J. H.	Huntington	Cabell	Carpenter	Pres., H.T.L.A.
Bradley, E. L.	Charleston	Kanawha	Stage hand	Pres. and Sec., Stage hands
Brandum, Earnest	Huntington	Cabell	Carpenter	Pres. Carpenters and Joiners
Byrne, John J.	Wheeling	Ohio	Street car worker	V.P., OVTLA
Cairns, Tom	Olcott	Kanawha	Miner	Pres., Dist. 17
Coffey, C. P.	Charleston	Kanawha	Plumber	Sec., CCTLA
Coleman, John V.	Kimberly	Fayette	Miner	Organizer, Dist. 29
Cumberledge, W. L.	Wheeling	Ohio	Barber	Pres., OVTLA
Conner, John L.	Milton	Cabell	Railroader	House of Delegates
Craigo, William E.	Carbondale	Fayette	Miner	Sec., U.V.W. Dist. 17
Davis, Ben	Montgomery	Fayette	Miner	Pres., U.M.W., Dist. 17
Davis, E. F.	Charleston	Kanawha	Stage hand	Sec., Stage Hands
DelForge, George	So. Charleston	Kanawha	Glassblower	Sec., National Window Glass Workers
Diani, James	Boomer	Fayette	Miner	Organizer, U.M.W.
Donnally, J. D.	Charleston	Kanawha	Plasterer	Town Official Deputy Sheriff

Name	Town	County	Occupation	Leadership Position
Dooley, Jack	Gatewood	Fayette	Miner	Sec., U.M.W., Local
Dowdy, D. C.	Huntington	Cabell	Boilermaker	Business Agent
DuFour, W. W.	Elkridge	Fayette	Miner	Sec., U.M.W., Local
Edgington, Cyrus	Charleston	Kanawha	Bricklayer	House of Delegates
Elswick, William	Smithers	Fayette	Miner	1st V.P., W. Va. S.F.L.
England, William	Elkridge	Fayette	Miner	
Fitzwater, A. W.	Charleston	Kanawha	Carpenter	Pres., CCTLA
Folio, Armando	Wendel	Fayette	Miner	6th V.P., W. Va. S.F.L. Organizer, U.M.W.
Frazer, Don	Charleston	Kanawha	Pressman	Treas., CCTLA
Gatens, Pat	Plymouth	Putnam	Miner	2nd V.P., W. Va. S.F.L. V.P. U.M.W. Dist. 17
Haggerty, Lawrence	Charleston	Kanawha	Pressman	Sec., Typos.
Hastings, B. S.	Montgomery	Fayette	Miner	Mayor, Montgomery
Henry, Earl A.	Clifton	Mason	Miner	House of Delegates
Hetzell, Lewis	Huntington	Cabell	Tailor	Pres., HTLA
Huggins, G. H.	Wheeling	Ohio	Electrician	V.P., OVTLA
Hurt, J. C.	Sanger	Fayette	Miner	V.P., U.M.W. Dist. 29
Jarrett, Homer	Charleston	Kanawha	Printer	Pres., Typos 146

APPENDIX A 185

Name	Town	County	Occupation	Leadership Position
Javins, E. H.	Winifrede	Kanawha	Miner	Sec., U.M.W., Local
Kilcoyne, Thomas	Huntington	Cabell	Boilermaker	Pres., Boilermakers
Lanham, Luke	Olcott	Kanawha	Miner	V.P., U.M.W., Dist. 17
Lusk, Whit	Smithers	Fayette	Miner	Sec., U.M.W., Local
Mathis, George	Charleston	Kanawha	Electrician	Del., S.F.L.
Massau, Charles	Boomer	Fayette	Railroader	Pres., Bro. Loco. Eng.
McGraw, Anthony	Ansted	Fayette	Miner	Sec., U.M.W., Local
Mino, Joe	Kayford	Kanawha	Miner	Sec., U.M.W., Local
Monday, R. L.	Carbondale	Fayette	Miner	Sec., U.M.W., Local
Montgomery, Samuel	Kingwood	Preston	Miner	Pres., State Fed. of Labor, House of Delegates
Morris, Ben	Marmet	Kanawha	Miner	Pres., Dist. 17 Mayor, Marmet
Nugent, John	Crown Hill	Kanawha	Miner	Pres., W. Va. S.F.L. House of Delegates
Otto, Hupp	Wheeling	Ohio	Printer	Pres., Typo 79
Patrick, W. H.	Standard	Kanawha	Miner	Sec., U.M.W. 79
Pauley, James L.	Charleston	Kanawha	Bartender	V.P., W.Va. S.F.L.
Payne, Charles	Dawes	Kanawha	Miner	V.P., U.M.W., Dist. 17
Phillips, Emmett	Crown Hill	Kanawha	Miner	Sec., U.M.W., Local

Name	Town	County	Occupation	Leadership Position
Prather, Lewis	Gamoca	Fayette	Miner	Sec., U.M.W.
Ramsey, Henry	Charleston	Kanawha	Painter	Pres., Painters Local
Scaggs, Grover	Ansted	Fayette	Miner	Pres., U.M.W., Local
Scott, C. R.	Powellton	Fayette	Miner	Sec., U.M.W., Local
Simms, Edward	Wheeling	Ohio	Printer	Pres., Typos 79
Snider, Edison	Huntington	Cabell	Boilermaker	Pres., HTLA
Snyder, Frank	Charleston	Kanawha	Printer	Sec.-Treas., W.Va. S.F.L.
Staats, C. P.	Charleston	Kanawha	Carpenter	Pres., Carpenters Union, Local
Stanley, W. M.	Handley	Kanawha	Miner	Exec. U.M.W., Dist. 17
Stark, Norris	Charleston	Kanawha	Carpenter	Sec., Carpenters Union
Stover, A. T.	Elkridge	Fayette	Miner	Auditor, U.M.W. Dist. 17
Surbaugh, C. F.	Charleston	Kanawha	Plumber	Treas., Plumbers Union
Teufel, John	Wheeling	Ohio	Carpenter	V.P., OVTLA
Trail, T. H.	Ohley	Kanawha	Railroader	Sec., Carmen's Union
Vickers, E. B.	Mucklow	Kanawha	Miner	4th V.P. W. Va. S.F.L.
Walter, Charles	Thayer	Fayette	Miner	Auditor, U.M.W., Dist. 17
Ward, Everett	Cannelton	Fayette	Miner	Sec., U.M.W., Local

Name	Town	County	Occupation	Leadership Position
Waterloo, Jules	So. Charleston	Kanawha	Glass Cutter	Sec., National Window Glass Workers
Weiss, Harry A	Huntington	Cabell	Iron Worker	House of Delegates
Welch, William	Wheeling	Ohio	Street car worker	Pres., W. Va. S.F.L.
White, Dolphus	Gatewood	Fayette	Miner	Organizer, Dist. 29
Witherall, E. A.	Huntington	Cabell	Glassblower	Sec., Flint Glass
Wood, Hugh	Elkridge	Fayette	Miner	Del., W.Va. S.F.L., Sec., U.M.W., Local

Note: Members of both samples usually held many more leadership positions than can be listed here. Abbreviations for positions stand for:

1. W. Va. S.F.L.–West Virginia State Federation of Labor
2. CCTLA–Capital City Trades and Labor Assembly
3. Sec. Br. Soc. P.–Secretary of Branch of Socialist Party
4. HTLA–Huntington Trades and Labor Assembly
5. OVTLA–Ohio Valley Trades and Labor Assembly

Table III: Central Labor Body Positions Held by West Virginia Socialist Party Members

STATE FEDERATION OF LABOR

Name	Occupation	Office	Date
C. W. W. Koontz	Painter	Second vice-president	1903
William Hornsby	Miner	Third vice-president	1903

Table III: Central Labor Body Positions Held by West Virginia Socialist Party Members *continued*

Albert Bauer	Carpenter	Secretary-treasurer	1907
Harry P. Corcoran	Stogie maker	Second vice-president	1908
Orlie Fulton	Potter	Fifth vice-president	1909
E. J. Weekley	Carpenter	Fifth vice-president	1913
Harry P. Corcoran	Stogie maker	President	1914
E. O. Lloyd	Potter	First vice-president	1914
E. O. Lloyd	Potter	Third vice-president	1915
Harry Lowe	Potter	First vice-president	1916
Harry Lowe	Potter	First vice-president	1917

HUNTINGTON TRADES AND LABOR ASSEMBLY

Name	Occupation	Office	Date
G. L. Ward	Carpenter	President	1912
Sherman Lewis	Car man	Secretary	1912
Oscar Notter	Barber	Trustee	1912
George Gillespie	Machinist	Delegate to A.F.O.L.	1912
C. W. Mylar	Potter	President	1913

APPENDIX A

Sherman Lewis	Car man	Vice-president	1913
George Gillespie	Machinist	Vice-president	1913
Henry Franklin	Barber	President	1913
Harry Lowe	Potter	Secretary	1913
Oscar Notter	Barber	Treasurer	1913
C. W. Mylar	Potter	President	1914
Wyatt Thompson	Printer	Del. State Fed. of Labor	1914
Henry Franklin	Barber	Del. State Fed. of Labor	1914

OHIO TRADES AND LABOR ASSEMBLY *

Name	Occupation	Office	Date
Albert Bauer	Carpenter	President	1900
E. J. Weekley	Carpenter	Vice-president	1900
J. T. Hecker	Stogie maker	Vice-president	1900
Lewis Hayes	Stogie maker	Organizer	1900
W. A. Peters	Tin Worker	President	1902
H. P. Corcoran	Stogie maker	President	1904
J. T. Hecker	Stogie maker	Vice-president	1908
Valentine Reuther	Brewery worker	President	1909

H. P. Corcoran	Stogie maker	President	1910
E. J. Weekley	Carpenter	President	1911
E. J. Weekley	Carpenter	Vice-president	1914
Mat Greer		Vice-president	1915

* Walter Hilton, editor of the *Wheeling Majority*, and H. J. Ninness, a molder, were almost perennial organizers for the Assembly.

Appendix B

Table I:
Comparison of Socialist Vote: National and State of West Virginia

County	1904		1908	
	National Office	State Office	National Office	State Office
Brooke	3	7	57	50
Cabell	101	97	111	97
Fayette	155	129	464	461
Harrison	21	20	86	77
Kanawha	205	288	624	589
Marion	54	43	222	201
Marshall	171	125	238	189
Monongalia	26	17	187	175
Ohio	382	286	441	349
Randolph	2	2	110	109
Tucker	1	0	18	14
Wood	40	37	127	125

Table I: Comparison of Socialist Vote *continued*

County	1912		1916	
	National Office	State Office	National Office	State Office
Brooke	244	208	120	119
Cabell	480	432	229	227
Fayette	1428	1399	361	278
Harrison	1077	1027	584	603
Kanawha	3071	3380	598	520
Marion	826	795	443	429
Marshall	521	480	229	225
Monongalia	580	568	297	295
Ohio	2666	1546	509	478
Randolph	371	356	253	230
Tucker	253	254	158	94
Wood	428	406	142	130

Socialist Presidential Candidates	1904	1908	1912	1916	1920
Percentage in West Virginia	.6%	1.1%	5.7%	2.1%	1.1%

Table II: Comparative Analysis of Congressional Votes 1904–1920

1904

County	Republican Percentage	Democrat Percentage	Socialist Percentage	Other Third Party Percentage
Brooke	58	39	.3	2.7
Cabell	50	47	1.3	.7
Fayette	61	34.5	1.5	3
Harrison	56	39	.1	4.9
Kanawha	55	42.2	.3	1.5
Marion	49.7	48.3	.5	1.5
Marshall	57	36.5	2.5	4
Monongalia	63.5	33.5	.4	2.6
Ohio	58.4	38	2.6	1
Randolph	44	54	.04	1.96
Tucker	58	38.97	.03	3
Wood	54.5	43	.5	.5

Table II: Comparative Analysis of Congressional Votes 1904–1920
continued

1906

County	Republican Percentage	Democrat Percentage	Socialist Percentage	Other Third Party Percentage
Brooke	56.7	37	3.3	3
Cabell	50	47.1	1.5	1.4
Fayette	59	28	4	9
Harrison	55.6	40.4	.3	4.7
Kanawha	53.9	38.1	5.8	2.2
Marion	49.7	41	2.8	6.5
Marshall	55	36	2.68	6.3
Monongalia	62.3	34.4	1.8	1.5
Ohio	55	41	2.8	1.2
Randolph	46.6	49	3	.4
Tucker	56.5	38.4	5	.1
Wood	52	39	7.4	1.6

1908

County	Republican Percentage	Democrat Percentage	Socialist Percentage	Other Third Party Percentage
Brooke	49	41	2.4	8.6

Cabell	43	52.2	1.8	3
Fayette	50	40	2.1	7.9
Harrison	37	54.1	2.9	6
Kanawha	54	41.12	2.8	2
Marion	47	47	2.4	3.6
Marshall	55.5	38.2	3.3	3
Monongalia	60	34	3.2	2.8
Ohio	52.5	44	2.5	1
Randolph	42	53.6	2.4	2
Tucker	56	40.3	.04	3.6
Wood	51.5	46	1.5	1

1910

County	Republican Percentage	Democrat Percentage	Socialist Percentage	Other Third Party Percentage
Brooke	49	41	2.4	8.6
Cabell	43	52.2	1.8	3
Fayette	50	40	2.1	7.9
Harrison	37	54.1	2.9	6
Kanawha	42.2	44	1.8	12
Marion	31	54.7	4.3	8

Table II: Comparative Analysis of Congressional Votes 1904–1920
continued

Marshall	48.7	39	4.3	8
Monongalia	55	35.3	2.7	7
Ohio	42.1	44	.9	13
Randolph	36	56	2.0	6
Tucker	41	48.1	2.9	8
Wood	46.5	51	.5	2

1912

County	Republican Percentage	Democrat Percentage	Socialist Percentage	Other Third Party Percentage
Brooke	54.7	32.3	9.4	2.6
Cabell	46	46	4.9	3.1
Fayette	46.4	37.1	14.2	2.3
Harrison	43	45	9.3	3.7
Kanawha	39.6	39.3	19	2.1
Marion	40	47	9.2	3.8
Marshall	49.6	38.4	7.7	4.3

Monongalia	53	34	9.4	3.6
Ohio	43.3	44.2	11.4	1.1
Randolph	41.6	50.3	7	1.1
Tucker	51	40	6.6	2.4
Wood	47.4	46.6	4.9	1.1

1914

County	Republican Percentage	Democrat Percentage	Socialist Percentage	Other Third Parties Percentages
Brooke	43	49	4.9	3.1
Cabell	42.7	47.2	5.8	5.3
Fayette	37	43	13.9	6.1
Harrison	38.4	40.2	11.1	10.3
Kanawha	38	38	18	6
Marion	49.1	36.3	7.8	6.8
Marshall	39.5	47.4	6.1	7
Monongalia	40.8	44.1	7	8.1
Ohio	41.6	48.2	6.8	4.4
Randolph	55.3	30.2	9.3	5.2

Table II: Comparative Analysis of Congressional Votes 1904–1920
continued

Tucker	44.7	45.1	9.2	1
Wood	46.3	45.4	4	4.3

1916

County	Republican Percentage	Democrat Percentage	Socialist Percentage	Other Third Party Percentage
Brooke	45.7	48.5	2.4	3.4
Cabell	45.1	48.2	2.1	4.6
Fayette	49.3	46.3	3.2	1.2
Harrison	48.4	41.6	5	5
Kanawha	50.2	46.6	3.2	0
Marion	40.3	55.4	4.3	0
Marshall	51	45.7	3.3	0
Monongalia	56.2	38.7	5	1.1
Ohio	51.5	44.4	4.1	0
Randolph	55	41	4	
Tucker	49	50.5	.5	
Wood	48.3	50.6	1.1	0

1918

County	Republican Percentage	Democrat Percentage	Socialist Percentage	Other Third Parties Percentage
Brooke	51.5	46.5	2	0
Cabell	49.3	49.6	1.1	0
Fayette	43.6	49.2	7.2	0
Harrison	44.1	54.7	1.2	0
Kanawha	45.5	53.3	1.2	0
Marion	51.6	48.4	0	0
Marshall	44.3	52.6	2.1	0
Monongalia	51.2	45.2	3.6	0
Ohio	52	46.9	1.1	0
Randolph	58.6	39.2	2.2	0
Tucker	47	50.7	2.3	0
Wood	45.2	54.8	0	0

1920

County	Republican Percentage	Democrat Percentage	Socialist Percentage	Other Third Parties Percentage
Brooke	52.7	47.3	0	0

Table II: Comparative Analysis of Congressional Votes 1904–1920
continued

Cabell	48.6	51.4	0	0
Fayette	45.1	54.9	0	0
Harrison	42.3	57.7	0	0
Kanawha	45.1	54.9	0	0
Marion	49.6	50.4	0	0
Marshall	47.8	52.2	0	0
Monongalia	67	33	0	0
Ohio	51.4	48.6	0	0
Randolph	53.3	66.7	0	0
Tucker	46.5	53.5	0	0
Wood	46.1	53.9	0	0

Table III: Municipalities And Districts in West Virginia Electing Socialists to Office: 1910–1915

Date	County	Municipality or District	Office
1910	Kanawha	Washington District	1 Constable
			1 Justice of Peace
	Randolph	Mingo District	1 Magistrate
		Elkins	1 Councilman
			1 Magistrate
1911	Kanawha	Charleston	1 Councilman
	Monongalia	Star City	1 Mayor
			6 Councilman
		Morgantown	1 Councilman
1912	Kanawha	Miami	1 Mayor
		Eskdale	1 Mayor
			2 Councilmen
		Cabin Creek District	2 Justices of Peace
			2 Constables
			Board of Education
	Fayette	Falls District	2 Justices of Peace
			2 Constables
			Board of Education
	Monongalia	Morgantown	1 Councilman
		Star City	1 Mayor
			6 Councilmen
	Harrison	Adamston	1 Mayor
			1 Councilman

Table III: Municipalities And Districts in West Virginia Electing Socialists to Office: 1910–1915 *continued*

Date	County	Municipality or District	Office
1913	Greenbrier	Ronceverte	1 Councilman
	Tucker	Hendricks	1 Mayor
			6 Councilman
	Monongalia	Morgantown	1 Councilman
		Star City	1 Mayor
			6 Councilmen
	Marion	Fairmont	1 Councilman
1914	Kanawha	Cabin Creek District	2 Justices of Peace
			2 Constables
			Board of Education
	Fayette	Mill Creek	1 Mayor
	Marshall	Cameron	1 Mayor
	Monongalia	Star City	1 Mayor
			6 Councilmen
1915	Monongalia	Star City	1 Mayor
			6 Councilmen
	Harrison	Adamson	1 Mayor
			6 Councilmen

Note: No Socialists elected after 1915.

APPENDIX B

Table IV: High Socialist Voting Districts and Precincts in Fayette County: 1908, 1912, 1916*

Districts	1908			1912			1916		
	Dem.	Rep.	Soc.	Dem.	Rep.	Soc.	Dem.	Rep.	Soc.
	Percentage								
Fayetteville	34	58	5	34	54	10	49	48	3
Falls	42	52	6	29	41	29	62	45	3
Kanawha	33	57	6	32	51	16	49	47	3
Mt. Cove	47	41	8	39	41	13	50	43	7
Precincts									
Deepwater	30	42	10	35	42	23	72	26	1
Eagle	20	80	0	14	70	16	35	65	0
Fayette Station	43	49	1	29	50	16	37	46	17
Gatewood	28	46	14	27	43	24	62	28	10
Hickory Camp	32	61	1	41	34	10	32	68	0
Hilltop	27	53	20	22	50	16	48	48	4
Kincaid	33	57	8	28	57	11	32	61	7
Longacre	37	58	4	31	40	29	43	55	2

Precincts

Lowe	37	61	5	22	58	20	70	27	3
Michigan	31	59	8	24	55	21	41	51	8
Mossey	21	46	2	19	31	49	32	40	28
Mt. Carbon	32	44	22	26	21	54	66	22	12
Powellton	19	66	14	14	45	40	48	51	1
Smithers	46	47	4	16	39	46	50	48	1

* 1914 Returns for Fayette County (Official abstract available at Department of Archives and History, Charleston, W. Va.):

Democrats: 36%
Republicans: 33%
Progressive: 4%
Independent Republican: 7%
Independent Labor: 11%
Socialist: 14%

Socialist Strength

	Socialist		Ind. Labor
	1912	1914	1914
Lowe	20%	31%	4%
Mossey	44%	57%	0%

Independent Labor Strength

	Socialist		Ind. Labor
	1912	1914	1914
Oak Hill	13%	16%	17%
Hilltop	16%	24%	27%

Gatewood	24%	49%	3%	Harvey	12%	22%	35%
				Rendville	14%	33%	9%
				Wingrove	9%	9%	27%
				Kaymour	8%	25%	7%

Notes

Chapter I

1. James M. Callahan, *Semi-Centennial History of West Virginia* (Charleston, W. Va., 1913), p. 188.
2. *Ibid.*, pp. 185–187; Charles Henry Ambler, *West Virginia: The Mountain State* (New York, 1940), pp. 481–83. An interesting example of the manner in which penetration of a potential coal field by one railroad stimulated, in turn, the rapid expansion by a rival line into an adjoining field can be found in Walter R. Thurmond, *The Logan Coal Field of West Virginia* (Morgantown, W. Va., 1964), pp. 24–27.
3. Charles P. Anson, "A History of the Labor Movement in West Virginia" (an unpublished dissertation, University of North Carolina, 1940), p. 16. Based upon establishments with $500.00 more per year production. Anson also points out the diversity of industrial activity in the period. He lists sixteen different types of industrial activity in 1870 compared to seventy-four different types by 1900, p. 17. Hereafter cited as "Labor in West Virginia."
4. Callahan, *Semi-Centennial*, pp. 195–229. The development of many counties is often reflected in a great number of municipal incorporations in this period. In Fayette County, which became a great producer of coal in the southwestern part of the state, new incorporations included most of its future urban areas; Montgomery, 1890; Anstead, 1891; Mt. Hope, 1895; Powellton, 1897; Glen Jean, 1898; Scarbro, 1901; Thurmond, 1903; and Oak Hill, 1903. See also, Anson "Labor in West Virginia," p. 46.
5. *Ibid.*, p. 223.
6. The actual increase in wage earners was 19,300 to 33,727 or 72%. Anson, "Labor in West Virginia," p. 46. His figures on employment: 1890—5,523 native whites, 1,181 foreign whites, and 4,620 colored.
7. *Ibid.*, p. 17.
8. Evelyn Harris and Frank Krebs, *From Humble Beginnings: The West Virginia State Federation of Labor, 1903–1957* (Charleston, W. Va., 1960), p. xi.
9. Selig Pearlman and Philip Taft, *History of Labor in the United States* (New York, 1935), pp. 20–24.
10. *The Wheeling Intelligencer*, July 27, 1897.

11. Mrs. Carl V. Shane, interview with the wife, an active Socialist in the Mozart Section of Wheeling, March 28, 1967.
12. *The Wheeling Intelligencer*, July 9, 1897.
13. Conrad Leeds, interview with Harry Leed's eldest son, Big Wheeling Creek, July 22, 1968.
14. *Ibid.*
15. William Butscher to Harry Leeds, September 12, 1900, Butscher Letterbook, p. 138. Socialist Party Papers, Duke University, hereinafter referred to as SPP, Duke.
16. *Wheeling Intelligencer*, October 25, 1900. See also Letter, Joseph Yahn to the Ohio Valley Trades and Labor Assembly, August 22, 1903, Bk. #3, Ohio Valley Trade and Labor Assembly Minutes, West Virginia University; occupations are found in city directories for Wheeling 1898 to 1901; complete collection in the Wheeling Public Library.
17. Harris and Krebs, *Humble Beginnings*, p. 69.
18. Ira Kipnis, *The American Socialist Movement: 1897–1912* (New York, 1952), p. 79. Hereinafter as Kipnis, *American Socialist*.
19. Harris and Krebs, *Humble Beginnings*, pp. xii–xiii.
20. *The Ohio Valley Trades and Labor Assembly; City of Wheeling and the Ohio Valley Trades and Labor Assembly and its Affiliated Organizations* (By the Assembly, Wheeling, W. Va., 1902), pp. 341–42.
21. Letter, J. T. Hecker, et al. to the officers and members of the O.V.T.L.A., October 9, 1904 (O.V.T.L.A. material, West Virginia University).
22. *Ohio Valley Trade and Labor Assembly*, Minutes, OVTLA, February 6, 1900, III, 15.
23. *Wheeling Intelligencer*, April 27, 1900.
24. Especially active in this regard was Louis Hayes, Minutes, O.V.T.L.A., December 9, 1900, III, 59.
25. Kipnis, *American Socialist*, pp. 84–89.
26. Minutes, O.V.T.L.A., April 22, 1900, III, 25.
27. *Ibid.*, March 24, 1901, III, 69.
28. *Wheeling Intelligencer*, April 27, 1900.
29. *Ibid.*
30. *Wheeling Intelligencer*, November 5, 1900.
31. Minutes, O.V.T.L.A., August 25, 1901, III, 131.

32. *Ibid.*, October 31, 1901, III, 148.
33. Kipnis, *American Socialist*, pp. 84–89.
34. Bedford Smith, *Socialism and the Workers in Massachusetts, 1886–1912* (Amherst, Mass., 1966), pp. 186–89; Minutes, O.V.T.L.A., December 8, 1901, III, 151.
35. Kipnis, *American Socialist*, p. 113.
36. Minutes, O.V.T.L.A., June 13, 1901, III, 65.
37. *Journal of the Senate of the State of West Virginia for the 25th Regular Session* commencing January 9, 1901 (Charleston, W. Va., 1901), passim.
38. Minutes, OVTLA, March 24, 1902, III, 88.
39. *Ibid.*, March 3, 1902, IV, 47.
40. Kipnis, *American Socialist*, pp. 234–36. On the other hand, David Shannon has stressed the importance of local organization in deciding matters of political tactics. David Shannon, *The Socialist Party of America* (New York, 1955), pp. 6–7, 258–59.
41. Minutes, O.V.T.L.A., March 3, 1902, IV, 47. The legislative committee consisted of the Socialist Joseph John and J. T. Hecker and one old single taxer, William O'Neil, *Wheeling Intelligencer*, August 11, 1902.
42. *Ohio Valley Trades and Labor and Its Affiliated Organizations*, p. 229.
43. Minutes, O.V.T.L.A., March 3, 1902, IV, 47.
44. *Wheeling Intelligencer*, April 28, 1902.
45. Minutes, O.V.T.L.A., April 27, 1902, IV, 57. Mohoney was well characterized by his write-up in Trades and Assembly Yearbook as "young, active, progressive and conservative, considerate of the rights of employer and employee." *Ohio Valley Trades and Labor and Its Affiliated Organizations*, p. 345.
46. *Wheeling Intelligencer*, April 28, 1902. See also Minutes, O.V.T.L.A., April 23, 1902, IV, 58.
47. *Ibid.* However, the *Intelligencer* stated later that some had voted against the motion because they felt "politics should not even be recognized to that extent."
48. *Wheeling Intelligencer*, May 25, 1902.
49. Minutes, O.V.T.L.A., May 25, 1902, IV, 70.
50. *Wheeling Intelligencer*, May 25, 1902.
51. *Ibid.*, May 26, 1902.
52. *Ibid.*
53. Minutes, O.V.T.L.A., June 22, 1902, IV, 75; July 13, 1902, IV, 78.

54. *Wheeling Intelligencer*, July 14, 1902. The Socialist continued to follow the activities of Daniel Moody, who was elected to the House of Delegates. In February 1903, Albert Bauer accused him of using his power as chairman of the Labor Committee to pigeon-hole the Eight Hour Law. Minutes, O.V.T.L.A., February 22, 1903, IV, 161.

55. Kipnis, *American Socialist*, p. 146. This incident allegedly was the immediate cause of the downfall of the National Secretary Leon Greenbaum, who had suggested that other locals might try the same tactics.

56. *Ibid.*, pp. 148–49. Mailly seems to have been especially interested in organizing his own section of the county—the South.

57. William Mailly to John Slayton, April 22, 1903. Mailly Letterbook, p. 359. SPP, Duke.

58. William Mailly to George B. Kline, June 13, 1903. William Mailly to F. A. Zimmerman, June 24, 1903. Mailly Letterbook, SPP, Duke.

59. William Mailly to F. A. Zimmerman, July 8, 1903. Mailly Letterbook, SPP, Duke.

60. William Mailly to George H. Goebel, July 10, 1903, Mailly Letterbook, SPP, Duke.

61. William Mailly to W. G. Critchlow, May 6, 1903. Mailly Latterbook, SPP, Duke. Moundsville had been growing since it became a junction between the Baltimore and the Ohio River Railroad, which in turn was a connecting link between the Chesapeake and Ohio, and the Pennsylvania systems. By 1903, the growth of labor organization in the community had brought about the creation of a Central Labor Body. Callahan, *Semi-Centennial History*, p. 209.

62. Minutes, O.V.T.L.A., August 23, 1903, IV, p. 188.

63. Interview, Conrad Leeds, July 21, 1968, Wheeling, W. Va. Mr. Leeds states that Fred Merrick of Parkersburg was one of those who came in and helped out in demonstrating street meeting techniques.

64. *Wheeling Intelligencer*, August 24, 1903.

65. William Mailly to Frank P. O'Hare, August 13, 1903. Mailly Letterbook, SPP, Duke.

66. *Wheeling Intelligencer*, August 24, 1903.

67. Minutes, O.V.T.L.A., August 23, 1903, IV, 188.

68. Based on compilation of the occupation of some sixty Socialists in the "…

Belmont Trades Assembly and Stogiemakers who are allied with the Hayes faction of the A.V. of L.," *Wheeling Intelligencer*, August 24, 1903.

69. *Manual of the State of West Virginia* (Charleston, W. Va., 1907) p. 243. House of Delegates candidates were: Albert Bauer, Herman Reinhardt, John H. Gillespy, and George A. Kaiser, p. 258.

70. Debs's vote in this county increased from 117 in 1900 to 382 in 1904 with the state and country office seekers receiving a comparable figure. The House of Delegates candidates ranged from 353 to 354 and Leeds who was running for Congress drew 351. Figures in *Manual of State of West Virginia* (Charleston, W. Va., 1907).

71. Huntington grew from 3,174 in 1880 to 31,161 in 1900, Callahan, *Semi-Centennial History*, pp. 197, 229.

72. *Ibid.*, pp. 194–95.

73. Nathan Fine, *Labor and Farmer Parties in the United States: 1828–1928* (New York, 1961), pp. 251, 261. Fine cites boilermakers, machinists, railway car men as among some fifteen or so internationals within the A.F. of L. whose votes on key resolutions demonstrate their considerable Socialist strength.

74. Interview, Martin H. Maloney, August 18, 1968, Hinton, W. Va. At ninety-four, Mr. Maloney is the oldest living railroader in Hinton. He started work there in 1895 and recalls Socialist agitational activities and the wide circulation of the *Appeal to Reason*.

75. Interview, Charles Woods, June 21, 1969. Woods is a retired machinist who chaired several Socialist meetings and was later active in the Huntington Trades and Labor Assembly. Woods suggests an engineer named E. L. Sanford, who came down the line from Hinton, was quite active as were machinists R. M. Kephart, Israel A. Duncan, George W. Gillespie, J. W. "Uncle Dave" Swan, and a carpenter from Ohio, Asa Barringer. See also Letter, A. K. Notter to Fred Barkey, July 9, 1969. Notter states that his father and other railroad men came from Greasey Ridge, Ohio, to work in the C. and O. shops.

76. Interview, Price Williams, February 23, 1967, Hansford, W. Va. Mr. Williams is a retired school official and newspaper reporter who was active in Socialist circles in Huntington.

77. William Mailly to J. R. Estey, February 26, 1903. Mailly Letterbook, SPP, Duke.

78. Eugene D. Thoenen, *History of the Oil and Gas Industry in West Virginia* (Charleston, W. Va., 1964), pp. 78–79.

79. Callahan, *Semi-Centennial*, pp. 353–55.
80. Thoenen, *Oil and Gas*, pp. 153–56, 191–251.
81. Interview, Raymond Yost, July 22, 1969, Fairview, W. Va.
82. Bernard L. Butcher and James M. Callahan, *Genealogical and Personal History of the Upper Monongahela Valley, W. Va.* (New York, 1912) pp. 1152–53.
83. Letter, Alva Hanes to W. S. Moore, February 26, 1902, Manningtown, W. Va.
84. Interview, Raymond Yost.
85. Interview, Price Williams; Interview, Helen Houston King, June 20, 1969, Charleston, W. Va. Little information is available on Merrick's background; however, his father was a fairly well-known farmer and real estate salesman in Parkersburg.
86. Morris P. Shawkey, *West Virginia in History, Life, Literature, and Industry* (New York, 1928), IV, 78.
87. George W. Atkinson, *Bench and Bar of West Virginia* (Charleston, W. Va., 1909), pp. 231–32.
88. Interview, Mrs. Helen Houston King, June 20, 1969, Charleston, W. Va.
89. Morris Shawkey, *West Virginia: History and Industry*, I, 295.
90. Callahan, *Semi-Centennial History*, p. 186. Although the really large numbers of glassworkers do not arrive in West Virginia until about 1906 or 1907, the movement was well under way by 1900, especially in northern West Virginia. Interview, George Delforge, November 18, 1967, St. Albans, W. Va.
91. Interview, Mr. and Mrs. Jules Waterloo, November 16, 1967, Charleston, W. Va.
92. Interviews, George Delforge, Eugene Monin, November 1967, St. Albans, W. Va.; Edgar Michaux, November 17, 1967, South Charleston, W. Va.
93. Lloyd Ulman, *The Rise of the National Trade Union* (Cambridge, Mass., 1966), p. 507.
94. Harris and Krebs, *Humble Beginnings*, p. 517.
95. James Weinstein, *The Decline of Socialism in America, 1912–1925* (New York, 1967), pp. 116–18, 173–76.
96. Interview, George Bougamont, March 6, 1967, South Charleston, W. Va., Eugene Monin, November 17, 1967, St. Albans, W. Va.; Harold Glasgow, July 28, 1969, Fairmont, W. Va. This tendency seems especially true for the Flint glassworkers. Officials of the Ohio Flints frequently came out of their headquarters at Toledo

either to organize and speak in West Virginia or in nearby Ohio River towns. A striking example of this was reported some years later when F. W. Rowe, the state president of the Ohio Flints, spoke to the Belmont Trades and Labor Assembly. On this occasion as the *Wheeling Intelligencer* put it, "His speech was a straight agreement in favor of Socialism." And he even "... lauded some of the principles of Emma Goldman." *Wheeling Intelligencer*, March 23, 1908.

97. Interview, Ed. Shay, February 18, 1967, Star City, W. Va., Mr. Shay's father was the first Socialist mayor of Star City. They had moved into Star City in 1901 from Charleroi, Pa. Also, Rene Zabeau, July 26, 1968, Clarksburg, W. Va.

98. Interview, Warren Martin, July 22, 1968, Star City, W. Va. The Star City and Adamston platform are typical of municipal reform Socialists. Also, Shay, Interview; see lists of candidates and occupations in Minutes of the City Council of Star City, 1907–1911. Available at City Hall, Star City.

99. Callahan, *Semi-Centennial History*, pp. 185–390. Within the 1890s, the years of greatest growth were 1898 to 1899 when production climbed from 14,248 to 19,252 short tons, p. 347.

100. Clarence E. Roth, "Some Notes on Early Mining in West Virginia." *The 1967 Proceedings of the West Virginia Coal Mining Institute* (Morgantown, W. Va., 1968), pp. 53–58.

101. James M. Callahan, *Semi-Centennial History*, pp. 228–29.

102. Clarence E. Roth, "Early Mining," p. 58.

103. McAllister Coleman, *Men and Coal* (New York, 1943), pp. 59–60.

104. Harris and Krebs, *Humble Beginnings*, pp. 17–21.

105. Charles A. Ambler and Festus P. Summers, *The Mountain State* (Englewood Cliffs, N.J., 1959), p. 445.

106. I. V. Barton, *Report of the West Virginia Labor Commissioner, 1897–1898* (Charleston, W. Va., 1899), pp. 75–78.

107. West Virginia Coal Operators Association, *The United Mine Workers in West Virginia* (Operator's Special Committee to the U.S. Coal Commission, 1923), p. 6.

108. John M. Barb, "Strikes in the Southern West Virginia Coal Fields" (an unpublished Master's Thesis, Department of History, West Virginia University, 1946), p. 39.

109. Selig Perlman and Phillip Taft, *History of Labor in the United States* (New York, 1935), p. 20.

110. Morris Shawkey, *West Virginia Life and Industry*, I, 266–67.
111. *The Charleston Labor Argus*, March 10, 1910.
112. Interview, A. D. Lavinder, July 25, 1968, Gatewood, W. Va. Mr. Lavinder was a member of the Board of U.M.W. for eleven years and an organizer under three national presidents, John Mitchell, T. L. Lewis, and John L. Lewis.
113. *Ibid*.
114. Foster R. Dulles, *Labor in America* (New York, 1949), pp. 189–90.
115. *United Mine Workers in West Virginia*, p. 11; John Mitchell was opposed to a general stroke and had used funds supplied by Mark Hanna to try to prevent one. Robert H. Wiebe, "The Anthracite Strike of 1902: A Record of Confusion," *Mississippi Valley Historical Review* (September 1961), XLVIII, 229–51.
116. Anson, "History of West Virginia Labor," p. 216.
117. John M. Barb, "Strikes in Southern West Virginia," p. 39.
118. Anson, "History of West Virginia Labor," p. 216; for an account of the U.M.W. failure in Fairmont fields, see Edward M. Steel, "'Mother' Jones in the Fairmont Field, 1902," *The Journal of American History* (September 1970), LVII, 290–308.
119. *Charleston Gazette*, June 12, 13, 1902.
120. *Ibid.*, September 2, 1902.
121. Interview, John Frisk, May 11, 1968, Charleston, W. Va.
122. Interview, Sylvanus Goff, April 18, 1967, Gatewood, W. Va. Goff was thrown out of the Anstead area for supporting the union.
123. Winthrop D. Lane, *Civil War in West Virginia* (New York, 1921), p. 11.
124. Interview, A. D. Lavinder, July 25, 1968, Gatewood, W. Va.
125. *Charleston Gazette*, August 31, 1902.
126. Interview, Sylvanus Goff, April 18, 1967, Gatewood, W. Va,; H. L. Rodes, April 18, 1967, Gatewood, W. Va.; C. M. Dooley, April 17, 1967, Gatewood, W. Va.; Ulyssis Argabright, April 17, 1967, Hilltop, W. Va. These communities were selected because of the early and persistently high Socialist vote.
127. William Mailly to B. H. Hunt, March 12, 1902, Gatewood, W. Va., Mailly Letterbook, SPP, Duke, also, H. L. Rode's Interview, April 18, 1967. Hunt was Rode's brother-in-law. His father was a Virginian Democrat who came to Fayette County with a slave girl whom he sold to buy their small farm in Gatewood.
128. Interview, A. D. Lavinder.
129. *Ibid.*, also Interview, Ulysis Argabright.

130. *The Charleston Gazette*, September 28, 1902.
131. Interview, Wyatt Thompson, October 13, 1968, Columbus, OH.
132. Interview, Anna Gherken, November 4, 1968, Charleston, W. Va. Miss Gherken recalled that her father began to keep a list of miners about 1903.
133. Interview, Myatt Thompson. Thompson described Gherken as "a little bit of a German tailer and a strong Socialist. He was the one who started me on the road to Scientific Socialism. He loaned me *Das Kapital* and discussed it with me."
134. Letter, William Mailly to "Mother" Jones, April 15, 1903. Mailly Letterbook, SPP, Duke. "Mother" Jones was to receive $3.00 per day.
135. *Manual of the State of West Virginia* (Charleston, W. Va., 1907).
136. *Ibid.* The counties were Brooke, Ritchie, Tyler, Wetzel, Preston, Marion, Ohio, Marshall, Harrison, Fayette, Kanawha, Cabell, Mercer, and Greenbrier.
137. For an idea of the range of basic reforms that interested one group of workers, see *The Ohio Valley Trades and Labor Assembly and Its Affiliated Organizations* (Wheeling, W. Va., 1902), pp. 320–30.

Chapter II

1. *The Labor Argus*, November 10, 1910.
2. *Ibid.* June 23, 1910.
3. Anson, "Labor in West Virginia," pp. 28–29, 46.
4. Elizabeth J. Goodall, "History of the Charleston Industrial Area" (unpublished Master's Thesis, West Virginia University, Morgantown, 1937), pp. 41–43.
5. Interview, Mrs. Bert Seachrist, April 8, 1968, Holly Grove, W. Va.
6. *The Labor Argus*, August 2, 1901.
7. Testimony, W. L. Connell, president, Paint Creek Collieries, *Conditions in the Paint Creek District, West Virginia.* Hearings before a subcommittee of the Committee on Education and Labor, United States Senate, 63rd Cong., 1st sess., I, 1048.
8. *The Charleston Gazette*, August 28, 1906.
9. Interview, Joe Mino, May 28, 1968, Leewood, W. Va.
10. Carter Goodrich, *The Miner's Freedom* (Boston, 1925), p. 26.
11. Interview, Mrs. Elizabeth Franklin Matheny, August 21, 1969, Fairmont, W. Va.
12. *The Labor Argus*, May 21, 1906.

13. Minutes, O.V.T.L.A., October 26, 1906, V, 180. *The Labor Argus*, October 11, 1906.
14. Ibid., February 28, 1907, *Wheeling Intelligencer*, May 9, 1906.
15. Robert K. Holliday, *Politics in Fayette County* (Montgomery, W. Va., 1956), p. 133; Interview, Julius DeGruyter, August 18, 1969, Charleston, W. Va.; *The Charleston Gazette*, January 31, 1907.
16. *The Code of West Virginia, 1906* (St. Paul, 1906), pp. 442–43.
17. Holiday, *Politics in Fayette County*, p. 160.
18. Harris and Krebs, *Humble Beginnings*; Minutes, O.V.T.L.A., V, October 16, 26, 28, 1906.
19. *Labor Argus*, July 26, 1906, August 23, 1906; *Wheeling Intelligencer*, July 28, 1906.
20. *Ibid.*, August 30, 1906.
21. Thomas E. Posey, "The Labor Movement in West Virginia, 1900–1948" (Doctoral Dissertation, University of Wisconsin, Madison, 1948), p. 16.
22. *Labor Argus*, July 26, 1906.
23. *Wheeling Intelligencer*, May 9, 1906.
24. Marc Karson, *American Labor Unions and Politics, 1900–1918* (Boston, 1965), p. 45.
25. *The Labor Argus*, July 26, 1906.
26. Minutes, O.V.T.L.A., October 28, 1906, V, 181.
27. *The Labor Argus*, November 9, 1906.
28. *Journal of the Senate of the State of West Virginia for the 28th Regular Session Commencing January 12, 1907* (Charleston, W. Va., 1908), pp. 432, 589.
29. *The Labor Argus*, February 28, 1907.
30. Minutes, O.V.T.L.A., October 14, 1906, V, 177.
31. *Ibid.* December 23, 1906, V, 200.
32. *The Labor Argus*, February 28, 1907.
33. Interview, George W. Harper, February 7, 1968.
34. Harris and Krebs, *Humble Beginnings*, p. 17.
35. *Ibid.* pp. 12–26.
36. *The Charleston Gazette*, November 5, 1907; Minutes, O.V.T.L.A., October 18, 1907, V, 212.
37. Minutes, O.V.T.L.A., October 25, 1907, V, 213.

38. *The Labor Argus*, May 16, 1907.
39. Harris and Krebs, *Humble Beginnings*, p. 16.
40. *The Labor Argus*, September 19, 1907.
41. Minutes, O.V.T.L.A., October 25, 1907, V, 214.
42. *The Wheeling Intelligencer*, November, 1907. See also, *The Charleston Gazette*, November 5, 1907.
43. Interview, Hupp E. Otto, March 18, 1968, Wheeling, W. Va. Mr. Otto is one of the oldest members of the Ohio Valley Trades and Labor Assembly, also *Wheeling Intelligencer*, November 6, 1907. Harris and Krebs, *Humble Beginnings*, p. 22.
44. Oscar Barck and Blake, *Since 1900* (New York, 1952), p. 58.
45. *The Charleston Gazette*, January 19, 25, 1908.
46. *The Wheeling Intelligencer*, February 3, 1908.
47. *The Huntington Herald Dispatch*, October 6, 1908.
48. *The Charleston Gazette*, February 21, 1908.
49. Interview, Cleveland Toney, July 19, 1968, Dothan, W. Va.
50. Letter, Feltz to Collins, March 22, 1908, Bluefield, W. Va. Collins Papers West Virginia University Archives.
51. *The Labor Argus*, December 3, 1908.
52. Interview, Fred Smith, August 28, 1969, Clendenin, W. Va.
53. Interview, George W. Harper, February 7, 1968, Charleston, W. Va.
54. Interview, Alfred D. Lavinder, July 25, 1968, Gatewood, W. Va.
55. *Clarksburg Telegram*, April, 23, 1909.
56. Harris and Krebs, *Humble Beginnings*, p. 51.
57. *The Charleston Gazette*, October 23, 1907. Also, *The Labor Argus*, July 18, 1907.
58. *The Labor Argus*, December 3, 1908.
59. *The Charleston Gazette*, April 12, 1908.
60. *The Labor Argus*, July 24, 1908.
61. *The Charleston Gazette*, April 12, 1909.
62. *The Wheeling Intelligencer*, May 25, 1909.
63. Interview, Hugh Woods, November 5, 1968, Mt. Carbon, W. Va. That the operators took such action is also suggested in Letter, Feltz to Collins, October 28, 1908. Collins Correspondence Series II, (Archives of West Virginia University).
64. Interview, Sylvanus Goff, April 18, 1967, Gatewood, W. Va. For a similar explanation by Morrison in written form, see, *Labor Argus*, March 12, 1908.

65. *The Wheeling Intelligencer*, March 23, 1908; Minutes, O.V.T.L.A., October 25, 1908, IV, 50.
66. Minutes, O.V.T.L.A., February 23, 24, 1908, VI, 11.
67. *The Wheeling Intelligencer*, June 1, 1908.
68. *The Labor Argus*, April 23, 1908; May 7, 1908.
69. *The Charleston Gazette*, March 3, 1908.
70. *The Wheeling Intelligencer*, June 1, 1908. Identification of Socialist members of the Belmont Assembly was made by Fred Walchli, a longtime secretary of the Belmont County Socialist organization. Interview, June 25, 1969, Bellaire, Ohio.
71. *The Wheeling Intelligencer*, April 12, 1908; Minutes, O.V.T.L.A., February 23, 1908, VI, 11.
72. *The Wheeling Intelligencer*, August 17, 1908.
73. Minutes, O.V.T.L.A., October 11, 1908, VI, 48; October 25, 1908, VI, 50. The A.F. of L. later struck back at the Radicals in both Assemblies. Belmont was told to drop its stogie-makers and flint glassworkers. Wheeling was denied a chatter until it purged itself of stogie-makers: *Wheeling Intelligencer*, May 17, 1990; Minutes, O.V.T.L.A., February 28, 1909, VI, 65.
74. *The Labor Argus*, August 20, 1908.
75. *The Labor Argus*, December 3, 1908.
76. *Ibid.* August 10, 1910.
77. *Ibid.* September 1, 1910.
78. *Ibid.* September 2, 1906; March 2, 1910.
79. Interview, Price Williams, February 24, 1967, Hansford, W. Va.
80. U.S. Senate, *Conditions in the Paint Creek District, West Virginia* (Hearings before a subcommittee on Education and Labor), 63rd Cong., 1st sess., 1913, I, 2009.
81. *The Parkersburg Socialist*, August 31, 1912 (Copy in West Virginia University Archives).
82. *The Labor Argus*, February 18, 1909; August 18, 1910.
83. Socialist Party of West Virginia, *Monthly Bulletin*, September 1910, p. 1. SPP, Duke.
84. *The Appeal to Reason*, May 1, 1909.
85. Interview, William Smith, August 20, 1969, Winifred, W. Va.
86. Interview, George W. Harper, February 7, 1968, Charleston, W. Va.
87. *The Labor Argus*, January 23, 1907.

88. *Ibid.* September 1, 1910; September 22, 1910; Socialist Party of West Virginia, *Monthly Bulletin*, September, 1910.
89. *Ibid.* February 20, 1907.
90. Herndon Link, "A Socialist Vision" (an unpublished Poem by an at-large member of the West Virginia Socialist Party, Original—Mrs. S. Wise, Ronceverte, W. Va.), *circa* 1911.
91. *The Labor Argus*, October 20, 1910.
92. Letter from Victor Reuther to Fred Barkey, October 22, 1969.
93. Interview, Fred Smith, August 28, 1969.
94. *The Labor Argus*, October 27, 1910.
95. Interview, Wyatt Thompson, October 13, 1968, Columbus, OH.
96. *Manual of the State of West Virginia 1907–1908* (Charleston, W. Va., 1907), pp. 277–78.
97. *The Labor Argus*, January 7, 1909; October 6, 1910.
98. Socialist Party of West Virginia, *Monthly Bulletin*, September, 1910. SPP, Duke.
99. *Ibid.*
100. Samuel P. Hays, *The Response to Industrialism, 1885–1914* (Chicago, 1957), p. 151.
101. Minutes, O.V.T.L.A., March 26, 1911, VI, 152.
102. *The Labor Argus*, April 22, 1907, May 20, 1909.
103. Interview, George W. Harper, February 7, 1968.
104. Interviews, Wyatt Thompson, Sylvanus Goff, Homer Rodes.
105. *The Labor Argus*, October 6, 1910.
106. West Virginia Socialist Party, *Monthly Bulletin*, 1910, SPP, Duke.
107. *The Labor Argus*, October 27, 1910; March 23, 1911.
108. *The Huntington Socialist and Labor Star*, October 16, 1914.
109. *The Labor Argus*, July 15, 1909.
110. Minutes, Local 302 Carpenters and Joiners Union, Huntington, W. Va., 1916 Minute Book, p. 43 (available at the Union Hall, 7th Ave., Huntington, W. Va.).
111. Interview, George Glass, October 22, 1969 (Mr. Glass has an extensive collection of Socialist pamphlets, Charleston, W. Va.).
112. *The Appeal to Reason*, January 2, 1909. *The Labor Argus* grew out of a small workingman's publication called *The Wasp*, which was also edited by the Snyders. Interview, Homer Jarrett, May 12, 1969, Charleston, W. Va.

113. Interview, Hupp E. Otto, March 18, 1968.
114. West Virginia Socialist Party, *Monthly Bulletin*, September, 1910, p. 2.
115. See Appendix B, Table II.
116. *The Labor Argus*, April 28, 1910.
117. Marc Karson, *American Labor Unions and Politics 1900–1918* (Boston, 1956), ch. 10.

Chapter III

1. This includes those who show-up several times as secretaries of local branches. The names were taken from information relating to the years 1908–12 when it appears most of the local branches in the party had been established.
2. For a list of socialist and control group workers, see Appendix A, Table I.
3. The only *Who's Who* for West Virginia Labor covers important members of Ohio Valley Trades and labor Assembly for 1901–2. *The Ohio Valley Trades and Labor Assembly and Its Affiliated Organizations*, Wheeling, W.Va, 1902.
4. *The Thirteenth Census of the United States Taken in the Year 1910, Vol. IV, Population*, Government Printing Office, Washington, D.C., 1916.
5. Interview, Henry Boone, August 28, 1968, Anthony, W. Va.
6. Interview, Cleveland Toney, July 19, 1968, Dothan, W. Va.
7. Interview, Wyatt Thompson, October 13, 1968, Columbus, OH.
8. Samuel P. Hays, *The Response to Industrialism* (Chicago, Ill., 1963), p. 151.
9. Interview, John Frisk, May 11, 1968, Charleston, W. Va.; Mrs. John Guntner, February 8, 1968, Morgantown, W. Va.
10. *Huntington Socialist and Labor Star*, February 20, 1914.
11. Interview, George DelForge, April 25, 1968, St. Albans, W. Va.
12. Interview, Warren Martin, February 5, 1968, Star City, W. Va.
13. Interview, Edward Shay, February 6, 1968, Star City, W. Va.
14. Interview, Wyatt Thompson.
15. John Brown, *Constitutional Government in West Virginia* (a pamphlet written at the time of the Cabin Creek-Paint Creek strike, ca., 1913), pp. 40–41.
16. Interview, Bezra Atkins, November 20, 1970, Keith, W. Va.
17. Interview, Homer Rodes, May 28, 1968, Gatewood, W. Va.
18. *State Party Bulletin*, September, 1910, SPP Duke University.
19. Interview, Earnest Brandum, November 17, 1969, Huntington, W. Va.

20. For a more elaborate argument along these lines, see David Montgomery, "Trade Union Practices and Syndicalist Thought," memo copy at History Department, University of Pittsburgh.
21. *Constitution and By-Laws of the National Window Glass Workers*, Cleveland, OH, 1908, pp. 27–32, Labor Archives, West Virginia University.
22. *Ibid.* p. 33.
23. Interview, Oscar DuBois by Sue Miller, May 6, 1965, Morgantown, W. Va.: Labor Archives, West Virginia University.
24. "The Passing of the Window Glass Workers," *Monthly Labor Review*, Vol. XXIX (October, 1929), pp. 1–17.
25. Interview, John Brandum, October 28, 1969, Huntington, W. Va.
26. Interview, Wilbur Stone, August 25, 1970, Clarksburg, W. Va.; Interview, Jim Lowe, May 25, 1968, Chesapeake, W. Va.
27. David Montgomery, "Syndicalist Thought."
28. U.S. Senate, *Conditions in the Paint Creek District, West Virginia*, (Hearings before a subcommittee on Education and Labor, 63rd. Cong., 1st sess., 1913).
29. Winthrop Lane, *Civil War in West Virginia*, p. 88.
30. *Huntington Socialist and Labor Star*, June 6, 1913.
31. Donald Egbert and Stow Parsons, *Socialism and American Life*, pp. 581–82.
32. Interview, Corbet A. Toney, April 24, 1968, Mossey, W. Va.
33. Interview, E. L. Bradley, April 26, 1968, Charleston, W. Va.
34. Interview, Scott Cantly, May 1, 1968, Hansford, W. Va.
35. Interview, Wyatt Thompson.
36. Interview, George Harper.
37. Herndon Link's books are in the possession of his daughter, Mrs. V. Wise, Swathmore Ave., Ronceverte, W. Va.
38. See example; Meade Schafer's books at Wellford, W. Va.
39. Interviews, Duff Scott, February 23, 1968, Chelyan, W. Va.; Grover Scaggs, June 23, 1968, Ansted, W. Va.
40. Interview, Hupp Otta, March 18, 1968, Wheeling, W. Va.
41. Interview, Mrs. C. G. Holstein, May 15, 1968, Chesapeake, W. Va.
42. *The Huntington Socialist and Labor Star*, February 27, 1914.
43. Interview, Mr. C. G. Holstein, May 15, 1968, Chesapeake, W. Va.
44. Interview, Alvin Grounds, March 25, 1968, Montgomery, W. Va.

NOTES 221

45. Howard Quint, "Socialism and Communism in the United States," in *Main Problems in American History* (Homewood, Ill., 1968).
46. This phenomenon is discussed more fully in Herbert G. Gutman, "Protestantism and the American Labor Movements: The Christian Spirit in the Gilded Age," *American Historical Review* (October 1966), pp. 74–101.
47. *Huntington Socialist and Labor Star*, June 27, 1913.
48. *Ibid*. February 6, 1914.
49. *The Labor Argus*, June 6, 1913.
50. *The Miner's Herald*, October 3, 1913.
51. Interview, H. F. Parson, August 28, 1968, Chesapeake, W. Va.
52. Interview, A. D. Lavinder, July 28, 1968, Gatewood, W. Va.
53. Interview, Isom Beasley, October 28, 1968, Miliken, W. Va.
54. Interview, Mrs. Carl V. Shane, March 28, 1967, Wheeling, W. Va.
55. Interview, Wyatt Thompson.
56. Interview, Marshall V. Williams, May 23, 1969, Charleston, W. Va.
57. Summary of lodge affiliation (Based on only 25% of sample):

	Masons	IOOF	K.O.F.P.	Elks, Moose, Eagles	Redmen
Socialist	10%	10%	10%	25%	45%
Non-Socialist	36%	16%	22%	18%	8%

58. *The Appeal to Reason*, February 21, 1914.

Chapter IV

1. Evelyn Harris and Frank J. Krebs, *From Humble Beginnings, West Virginia State Federation of Labor, 1903–1957* (Charleston, 1960), pp. 67–68; see also *Proceedings State Federation of Labor, May, 1912*.
2. *Wheeling Intelligencer*, May 5, 1912.
3. Among those opposing were Beleal and Caldwell, carpenters; Ferguson and Padden, streetcar workers; Semner, a printer; Pauley, a bartender; Wilson, a potter;

Taylor, a laborer; and Scroggins, a stogie-maker. *Proceedings—6th Convention of the State Federation of Labor*, pp. 72–79.

4. Selig Perlman and Philip Taft, *History of Labor in the United States* (New York, 1935), Vol. IV, p. 330.

5. Charles B. Crawford, "The Mine War on Cabin Creek and Paint Creek, West Virginia in 1912–13" (unpublished Master's Thesis, University of Kentucky 1939), pp. 22–23; *Huntington Socialist and Labor Star*, August 4, 1912. See also, *Huntington Herald Dispatch*, September 17, 1912.

6. Perlman and Taft, *Labor*, p. 329.

7. Lawrence Lynch, "The West Virginia Coal Strike," *Political Science Quarterly* (December 1914), p. 630.

8. Harris and Krebs, *Humble Beginning*, p. 73.

9. U.S. Congress, Senate, 63rd Cong., 1st sess., Committee on Education and Labor. *Conditions in the Paint Creek District, West Virginia*. Hearings before a subcommittee of the Committee on Education and Labor, Washington, 1913, 3 Vols., Quinn Morton testimony, I, 953. Hereinafter cited testimony will be referred to as *Senate Hearings*.

10. Crawford, "Mine War," p. 41.

11. M. Michelson, "Feudalism and Civil War in the United States," *Everybody's Magazine* (May 1913), pp. 32–34; *New York Call*, July 28, 1912.

12. Crawford, "Mine War," p. 41.

13. Fred Mooney, *Struggle in the Coal Fields: The Autobiography of Fred Mooney*, ed. by J. W. Hess (Morgantown, 1967), pp. 27–28.

14. Mary "Mother" Jones, *Autobiography of Mother Jones*, ed. by Mary Field Parton (Chicago, 1925), pp. 1–30.

15. Crawford, "Mine War," pp. 37–39; Paul Brissenden, The I.W.W., *A Study in American Radicalism* (New York, 1919), p. 60.

16. Testimony, Charles Pratt, *Senate Hearings*, II, 1760. See also J. H. Bradford, "Digest of The Report of The Senate Hearings on Education and Labor Relative to The Investigation of Conditions in The Paint Creek Coal Fields of West Virginia, April, 1914" (unpublished MS. Bureau of Labor Statistics, July 29, 1914, General Records of the Dept. of Labor, National Archives).

17. Letter, Wyatt Thompson to Price Williams. (Though sparse, this correspondence is an invaluable source on Thompson's life and attitude on a variety of

subjects. Originals in possession of Price Williams, Hansford, West Virginia—copies in author's collection.)

18. *Senate Hearings*, Testimony, Frank Gwin, I, 1197; A. W. Laing, II, 1594; Dr. Williams, III, 2247.

19. *Ibid.* Speech of Harold Houston, August 4, 1912, III, 2258–59.

20. *Ibid.*

21. *Charleston Gazette*, August 2, 1912.

22. *New York Call*, November 12, 1912.

23. Harold E. West, "West Virginia Coal Strike," pp. 44–45; Kyle McCormick, *Kanawha River Mine War* (Charleston, 1959), p. 141; *Huntington Dispatch*, July 28, 1912.

24. *Parkersburg Dispatch and News*, October 29, 1912; *Huntington Advertiser*, November 4, 1912; *Morgantown News Dominion*, November 16, 1912; *Labor Argus*, September 3, 1912. (Clipping Files, Glasscock Papers, West Virginia University).

25. John W. Brown, *Constitutional Government Overthrown in West Virginia*, ca. 1913. (Original in possession of Mrs. S. Ricca, East Bank, West Virginia. Copy in author's collection) pp. 25–26.

26. *Clarksburg Telegram*, September 16, 1912.

27. *Fayette Sun*, October 11, 1912. Glasscock Clippings.

28. John Brown, *Constitutional Government*, p. 8.

29. *Charleston Gazette*, June 2, 1912.

30. Cabell Testimony, *Senate Hearings*, II, 1450–51. See also poster in West Virginia University Collection of labor materials.

31. *Wheeling Register*, October 21, 1912. Glasscock Papers, Clipping File.

32. Goff Interview; Seachrist Interview; *Wheeling Intelligence*, October 21, 1912.

33. *Charleston Daily Mail*, October 26, 1912.

34. *The Wheeling Majority*, October 31, 1912.

35. Interview, Ed Shay, March 2, 1968, Morgantown, W. Va.

36. *Wheeling Intelligencer*, September 3, 1912; *Moundsville Echo*, September 7, 1912.

37. For a true indication of this, one needs to examine various county election books to determine Socialist candidates for minor offices. See especially those available in Fayette, Kanawha, Cabell, and Ohio counties.

38. *Appeal to Reason*, January 4, 1913. The Debs vote compiled from totals listed in the W. Va. Blue Book of 1916.

39. Ten leading coal producers and their Socialist Party vote, 1912. 1. McDowell: .6% 2. Fayette: 14% 3. Kanawha: 18% 4. Marion: 9% 5. Harrison: 9% 6. Raleigh: 7% 7. Mercer: .2% 8. Logan: .8% 9. Mingo: 14% 10. Preston: 30% For figures on producers, see James H. Thompson, "Significant Trends in the West Virginia Coal Industry, 1900–1957" (Bureau of Business Research, West Virginia University, Morgantown, W. Va., 1958), p. 8. A percentage of Socialist votes are computed from congressional returns recorded by the office of the Secretary of State of West Virginia. Local candidates' votes run slightly ahead of the Debs percentage in most counties with a high Socialist vote. See Appendix B, Table 1.

40. *The Charleston Daily Mail*, November 9, 1912.

41. Unfortunately, only fragmentary returns are available for Kanawha County for 1912; see *Charleston Daily Mail*, November 6, 1912 for the best of these.

42. *Huntington Socialist and Labor Star*, November 13, 1912.

43. Herbert G. Gutman, "The Workers Search for Power," in H. Wayne Morgan, ed., *The Gilded Age* (Syracuse, 1963), p. 43.

44. *The Charleston Gazette*, September 26, 1912.

45. Peters and Carden, *A History of Fayette County*, p. 533. Dothan residents probably voted at Lick Fork, where the Socialist vote was 45% in 1912.

46. Interview, Ulysses Argabright, May 18, 1968, Hilltop, W. Va.; see also Minute Book, City of Hilltop (Mrs. Argabright's possession).

47. Roxie Trent, "Hard Up" in *Huntington Socialist and Labor Star*, September 12, 1913.

48. Armstrong Creek Area. 1912 Socialist Party Vote: Powellton 40%, Kimberly 22%, Mt. Carbon 54%; Hawks Next to Ansted area-Hawks Nest 36%, Ansted 13%.

49. *Peters and Carden*, Fayette County, p. 491.

50. Robert Holliday, *Politics in Fayette County* (Montgomery, W. Va., 1956), p. 102.

51. *Charleston Gazette*, July 4, 6, 24, 1902; Interview, Charles Walters, April 23, 1968, Oak Hill, W. Va.

52. Letter, Henderson Kelly to J. A. Renahan, Davy, W. Va., October 27, 1911. Justus Collins Papers, West Virginia University Archives.

53. For example: McDonald 3%, Scarbro 5%, Stuart 1%, Parall 0%. The only Dixon property to draw a substantial Socialist vote was the incorporated community of Harvey 12%.

54. *Appeal to Reason*, May 17, 1913.

55. *The Labor Argus*, April 27, 1911.

56. Returns available in the Records of the Cabell County Court, Court House,

NOTES 225

Huntington, W. Va.; Interview, John Brandum, October 24, 1969, Huntington, W. Va.
57. *Clarksburg Telegram*, November 12, 1914.
58. *Morgantown Post Chronicle*, April 1, 1913.
59. Interview, Adrian Albert, June 25, 1969, Wheeling, W. Va.
60. The exceptions were Cabell County, which had been Republican in 1908, and Marion County, which was an old Democratic stronghold since the most powerful capitalists, the Watsons, were Democrats. The Republican counties were Brooke, Hancock, Harrison, Marshall, Ohio, Monongalia, Fayette, Kanawha, and Randolph; see Callahan, *Semi-Centennial*, p. 247.
61. Selected from election returns for city of Huntington for 1912. Available at City Hall, Huntington, W. Va.

A: High Socialist Votes

Precinct	Democratic	Progressive	Republican	Socialist
21	39%	39%	5%	10%
25	38%	40%	9%	10%
26	31%	48%	5%	13%
27	28%	47%	13%	11%
31	47%	29%	14%	7%

B: High Republican Votes

Precinct	Democratic	Progressive	Republican	Socialist
5	42%	25%	31%	1%
8	50%	19%	31%	9%

B: High Republican Votes *continued*

12	43%	25%	24%	2%
10	42%	27%	27%	3%
6	45%	26%	26%	6%

62. Minutes, O.V.T.L.A., October 7, 1912, IV.
63. See Appendix B, Table IV.
64. Interview, Price Williams (Williams joined the staff of the Huntington paper shortly after Wyatt Thompson became its editor).
65. *The Parkersburg Socialist*, August 31, 1912.
66. Interview, George Glass.
67. Crawford, "Mine War," p. 46; *Charleston Gazette*, November 15, 1912.
68. Brown, *Constitutional Government*, p. 13.
69. Testimony, George Williams, *Senate Hearings*, II, 1859.
70. "Report of the West Virginia Mining Investigation Commission Appointed by Governor William E. Glasscock on the 28th day of August, 1912" (Charleston, 1912), p. 10; Mooney, *Struggle*, p. 20. See also McCormick, *Kanawha River and Mine War*, pp. 134–37.
71. *Socialist and Labor Star*, January 2, 1913; *The Labor Argus*, January 2, 1913; *Baltimore Sun*, September 5, 1912, Glasscock Clippings.
72. Brown, *Constitutional Gov't*, p. 14, Bruce Reed, Testimony, *Senate Hearings*, I, 25. Reed said Nance got a seven-year sentence for the incident, which occurred ten days before martial law was declared and that Nance swore at the officer and threatened him with reprisal.
73. *The Charleston Gazette*, November 21, 1912; *Wheeling Intelligencer*, November 21, 1912. "Few Clothes" had allegedly taken part in the shootings of Brownsville, Texas. See *Mooney Struggle*, p. 29.
74. Merrick, "Betrayal of the West Virginia Rednecks," *International Socialist Review* (July 1913).
75. *The Wheeling Majority*, December 5, 1912. (*The Majority* from August 1912

through July 1914 is available from the State Historical Society of Wisconsin at Madison).

76. Cora Older, "The Last Day of the Paint Creek Court Martial," *Independent*, Vol. LXXIV (May 15, 1913), p. 1085; Brown, "Constitutional Gov't.," pp. 18–20.

77. *The Labor Argus*, January 2, 1913: Judge Ira Robinson dissented from the opinion of the court and felt that such broad assumption of power was very dangerous. However, Colonel Wallace of the state militia had hoped for this vindication as he wrote to Glasscock: "If the Supreme Court declares a state of war and suspends the Constitution within the theatre of military operations then every act claimed by ourselves follows as a necessary conclusion." Wallace to Glasscock, December 20, 1912. Glasscock Papers.

78. *Ibid.*

79. *Ibid.* January 19, 1913.

80. Minutes, *Huntington Trades and Labor Assembly*, September 23, 1912, p. 21 (from author's collection).

81. *The Labor Argus*, January 2, 1913; January 30, 1913.

82. Brown, *Constitutional Government*, p. 13.

83. *Ibid*, pp. 45–57; *The Wheeling Majority*, November 28, 1912; November 21, 1912. Peter J. Brien and Ben C. Mentz were recruited the same day as timekeeper and cook. They were brought to Kayford, where they discovered there was a strike in progress. They subsequently escaped to Eskdale, where Lawrence Dwyer bought them dinner and paid their transportation back to New York.

84. Interview, Duff Scott, February 23, 1968, Chelyan, W.Va.

85. J. H. Lowe, conductor in the baggage car, affidavit describes the activities of the Baldwin-Felts "guard" who fired the machine gun at the tent encampment at Holly Grove. *General Records*, Department of Labor, National Archives; *Appeal to Reason*, June 7, 1913. See also M. Michelson, "Sweetland of Liberty; Feudalism and Civil War in the U.S. of A. Now," *Everybody's Magazine* May 1913, pp. 615–28; Brown, *Constitutional Government*, p. 58; *Wheeling Majority*, February 20, 1913; Mooney, *Struggle*, pp. 36–38.

86. Brown, *Constitutional Government*, pp. 58–62; U. S. Cantley testified, "I was arrested on February 13th with sixty-six others rounded up at Holly Grove and marched to Pratt, searched, and put into a military train." Cantley testimony.

87. *The Wheeling Majority*, February 20, 1913; Mooney, *Struggle*, pp. 20–21;

Brown, *Constitutional Government*, p. 62; *Charleston Gazette*, February 14, 1913.

88. Interview, Wyatt Thompson.

89. Perlman and Taft, p. 333; Brown, *Constitutional Government*, pp. 65, 67, 74; *Appeal to Reason*, June 21, 1913.

90. Interview, A. D. Lavinder; Interview, Bert Seachrist.

91. Wyatt Thompson, "Victory to Settlement," p. 13; *International Socialist Review*, (July, 1913); Perlman and Taft, pp. 334–335.

92. *Appeal to Reason*, June 21, 1913.

93. Fred H. Merrick, "The Betrayal of the West Virginia Rednecks," *International Socialist Review* (July, 1913), pp. 20–21.

94. *Appeal to Reason*, June 21, 1913; Wyatt Thompson's version was that the miners' proposal of nondiscrimination was read along with Hatfield's compromise so that the delegates believed it was accepted by the convention. Wyatt Thompson "How Victory Was Turned into a Settlement," *International Socialist Review* (July 1913), p. 14.

95. Wyatt Thompson, "Victory unto Settlement," p. 13; Brown, *Constitutional Government*, pp. 68–69.

96. *The Wheeling Majority*, April 17, 1913.

97. Wyatt Thompson, "Victory unto Settlement," p. 13, *Wheeling Majority*, May 1, 1913; *Appeal to Reason*, May 10, 1913.

98. Charles Boswell, Testimony, *Senate Hearings*, III, 2108.

99. *Appeal to Reason*, May 10, 1913.

100. *Ibid.* June 21, 1913.

101. *The Wheeling Majority*, May 8, 1913. The Socialist found evidence that one of the men was a notorious guard by the name of Mayfield.

102. Wyatt Thompson testimony, *Senate Hearings*, II, 2090–96.

103. Interview, Duff Scott (Brandt Scott's younger brother and a participant in the strike action), Chelyan, W.Va., May 15, 1968; Brandt Scott testimony, Senate Hearings, I, 483–99.

104. *Appeal to Reason*, January 21, 1913.

105. *Ibid.* June 14, 1913.

106. Socialist Party Press Release, May 28, 1913, July 2, 1913, SPP Duke; *Huntington Socialist and Labor Star*, June 14, 1913.

107. W. H. Thompson, "How a Victory Was Turned into a Settlement in West Virginia," *International Socialist Review* (Aug. 1913), p. 15.

108. *Appeal to Reason*, June 28, 1913.
109. *The Wheeling Majority*, May 8, May 15, 1913.
110. Interview, H. Lee Rodes, June 6, 1968, Gatewood, W.Va.; for a similar statement see his letter to the *Appeal to Reason*, June 28, 1913.
111. Interview, Kyle Kintzer, October 30, 1969, Parkersburg, W.Va.; State Party Bulletin, August, 1913 (author's collection); the number of locals in 1910 was about fifty-three and by August 1913 they had gone to eighty-six, *Huntington Socialist and Labor Star*, August, 1913.
112. *The Wheeling Majority*, June 12, 1913 (*The Majority* ran the text of the committee's report June 12 and 19).
113. *Appeal to Reason*, May 31, 1913; June 14, 1913; June 14, 1913.
114. *The Wheeling Majority*, June 12, 19, 1913.
115. Thompson, "Victory into Settlement," p. 15. An opinion that Debs shared as he wrote to Germer. "Had the National Executive Committee acted as it had the power to do and as it was its duty to do two months ago, there would be a different situation in West Virginia. Had it been Berger and Spargo in the bullpen instead of Mother Jones and John Brown, the N. E. C. would not have waited until the whole country was seething. . . ." Letter, E. V. Debs to R. Germer, May 14, 1913, Castleton Papers, Tamiment Institute, N.Y.
116. *Huntington Socialist and Labor Star*, June 7, 1913; Thompson, "Victory to Settlement."
117. *Huntington Socialist and Labor Star*, June 7, 1913.
118. Fred Merrick, "Betrayal of the West Virginia Radicals," *International Socialist Review* (July 1913), p. 22. Thompson was a little more charitable and felt that Debs was too sentimental and easily duped; Interview, Wyatt Thompson. For a slightly different interpretation, see Weinstein, *The Decline of Socialism*, pp. 34–35.
119. Eugene V. Debs, *International Socialist Review* (August 1913).
120. Weinstein, *Decline*.
121. Letter, Eugene Debs to Adolph Germer, January 20, 1912, Castleton Papers, Tamiment Institute, New York.
122. "Debs Denounces Critics," *New York Call*, August 2, 1913; Eugene Debs to Adolph Germer, July 24, 1913, Castleton Papers, Tamiment Institute, New York.
123. Wyatt Thompson, "A Reply to Debs," *International Socialist Review* (August 1913) p. 197; Thompson Interview; Certainly Thompson knew that Merrick had

gone to edit *The Pittsburgh Justice*, an I.W.W. paper, and that Elmer Rumbaugh and Paul Camplin were Wobblies. See Paul Camplin, *Wobbly, the Rough-and-Tumble Story of an American Radical* (Chicago, 1948), pp. 116–20.

124. *Huntington Socialist and Labor Star*, August 1, 1913; July 26, 1913; Nov. 4, 1913.

125. Thompson, "Victory to Settlement," p. 17.

126. Interview, George W. Harper, April 28, 1968; *Huntington Socialist and Labor Star*, February 14, 1914; May 1, 20, 1914; June 6, 1914.

127. *The Wheeling Majority*, May 1, 15, 1913. The situation was so acute that according to *The Majority*, "*The Labor Argus*, the Charleston paper edited by Charles H. Boswell...could call a strike with any one issue of the paper." *The Wheeling Majority*, June 29, 1913.

128. *Ibid*. November 14, 1912.

129. *Ibid*. April 10, May 22, 1913. Peters and other important Ohio County Socialists are listed in *The Wheeling Majority*, June 11, 1914.

130. *Ibid*. June 18, 1914.

131. *Ibid*. April 24, 1913.

132. Letter, Adolph Germer to Theodore Debs, September 13, 1913, Castleton Papers, Tamiment Institute.

133. Press Release, Socialist Party of America, June 26, 1913, SPP, Duke.

134. *Socialist and Labor Star*, June 6, 1913.

135. Press Release, Socialist Party of America, June 26, 1913, SPP, Duke; *The New York Call*, July 3, 1913.

136. *International Socialist Review* (August 1913), p. 88.

137. Mooney, *Struggle*, p. 39.

138. *International Socialist Review* (July 1913) p. 22.

139. *The Fayette Tribune*, October 29, 1914.

140. *Miner's Herald*, September 19, 26, 1913.

141. *Ibid*, September 27, 1913; *Wheeling Intelligencer*, September 19, 1913.

142. *Ibid*. September 6, 1913.

143. *Ibid*. January 23; March 20, 1914.

144. Mooney, *Struggle*, pp. 44–45.

145. *Ibid*, pp. 42–45; Goff Interview.

146. Minutes, O.V.T.L.A., March 9, 1913 XVI, 370; *The Wheeling Majority*, May 8, 1913.

147. *Ibid.* April 27, 1913, XVI, 373.
148. Minutes, O.V.T.L.A., February 8, 1914, XVI, 471.
149. *Wheeling Majority*, November 20, 1913.
150. *Clarksburg Telegram*, July 3, 1913; *The Wheeling Majority*, July 3, 1913.
151. *Wheeling Majority*, July 17, 24; August 14, 1913; *Clarksburg Telegram*, August 21, 1913.
152. Minutes, O.V.T.L.A., October 22, 1913, XVI, 6 (details the efforts of the Organizing Committee); *Wheeling Majority*, July 17, 1913.
153. *The Wheeling Majority*, November 9, 30; December 4, 1913.
154. *Ibid.* August 14, 1913.
155. Minutes, O.V.T.L.A., February 10, 1914, XVI, 42.
156. *Ibid.* June 28, 1914; August 23, 1914, VI, 7–14. Leo LaFlem claimed the A. F. of L. would not provide any organizers to help unions that belonged to the O.V.T.L.A. and that was the reason the Assembly conducted its own organizing campaign.
157. Minutes, O.V.T.L.A., February 10, 1914, XVI, 48.
158. *The Wheeling Majority*, September 19, 1912; January 5, 1913.
159. Interview, George DelForge.
160. *Wheeling Majority*, January 5, 1914. For some insight into the influence of I.W.W. in Pittsburgh's stogie-makers, see *The Pittsburgh Justice*, October 18, 1913, Tamiment Institute.
161. Interview, Conrad Leeds. Kintzer said he and Houston were believers in sabotage and voted no on recall of Billy Haywood in 1912, *Wheeling Majority*, January 9, 1913; *Huntington Socialist and Labor Star*, October 9, 1914.
162. *Huntington Socialist Star*, May 8, 1914.
163. Interview, Duff Scott, June 25, 1968, Chelyan, W.Va.
164. Letter, John Brown to W. A. Peters, April 10, 1913, printed in *The Wheeling Majority*, April 24, 1913.
165. Ira Kipnis, *American Socialist*.
166. *Wheeling Majority*, October 23, 1913; *Socialist and Labor Star,* Sept. 19, 1914.
167. *Huntington Socialist and Labor Star*, March 27, 1913; August 18, 1914; *Wheeling Majority*, February 29, 1914; Interviews, Ed Shay, John Frisk.
168. *Clarksburg Telegram*, July 8, 14, Oct. 8, 1914; *Huntington Socialist and Labor Star*, July 17, 24, 1914.
169. In 1912 Debs received 2,666 votes while local candidates received about

1,496. Compiled from returns in the West Virginia Blue Book. Statistics for 1914 are based upon comprehensive congressional election returns provided by the office of Secretary of State of West Virginia.

First Congressional District

	1912	1914
Brooke	9%	5%
Hancock	6%	3%
Harrison	9%	11%
Lewis	4%	4%
Marion	9%	7%
Marshall	7%	6%
Ohio	11%	6%
Wetzel	4%	3%

Second Congressional District

	1912	1914
Monongalia	10%	7%

Randolph	7%	9%
Tucker	7%	9%
Taylor	4%	4%

Third Congressional District

	1912	1914
Fayette	14%	14%
Greenbrier	3%	3%
Kanawha	18%	18%

Fourth Congressional District

	1912	1914
Wood	3%	5%

Fifth Congressional District

	1912	1914
Boone	12%	11%

Fifth Congressional District *continued*

Cabell	5%	5%
Putnam	8%	6%

170. *The Huntington Socialist and Labor Star*, Feb. 14, 1914, October 23, 1914.

171. *The Labor Argus*, December 11, 1913 (copy in author's collection); *Huntington Socialist and Labor Star*, October 23, 1913.

172. Interview, Homer Rodes.

173. *The Charleston Labor Argus*, February 23, 1911; Interview, Homer Jarrett, Charleston, Aug. 14, 1969; Charleston, W. Va.

174. Interview, George Glass.

175. J. F. Peters and Carden F., *History of Fayette County*, pp. 73–75; increase in population figures compared to Socialist vote:

	Population				% of Socialist Vote		
	1890	1900	1910	1920	1908	1912	1914
Mining-rural							
Nuttall		3,180	3,388	3,584	19%	4%	3%
Sewall Mt.	3,100	3,618	3,331	3,315	.4%	3%	2%
Mining-urban							
Fayetteville	4,110	9,889	20,605	23,288		10%	14%
Falls View	1,099	1,597	6,775	8,784		29.1%	29%
Kanawha	4,451	6,078	7,790	11,192		16%	19%

176. *The Huntington Socialist and Labor Star*, June 13, 1913.
177. *The Charleston Labor Argus*, July 15, 1990.
178. *The Huntington Socialist and Labor Star*, Sept. 11, 1914; Oct. 9, 1914.
179. See blacklist in John Brown's *Constitutional Government*, p. 44.
180. Percent average of Socialist vote of predominantly Negro polling places for Election of 1914 computed from County Abstracts: Huntington, Negro Precincts:12–2%, 13–10%, 14–2%, 15–3%. Charleston, Garnet School: Republican–71%, Democrat–32%, Socialist–.3%. Only Hilton, MacDonald, and Kaymoor in Fayette County out of eighteen precincts with Negro votes had strong Socialist votes. Negro schools and the number of rooms in each can be found in *The Fayette Tribune*, March 5, 1914.
181. *Huntington Socialist and Labor Star*, August 8, 1913.
182. *The Pioneer Press*, May 25, 1912 (West Virginia Department of Archives and History, Charleston, West Virginia).
183. Richard Hadsell, "Justus Collins and the Role of the Baldwin-Felts Detective Agency," April 1969, pp. 71–75. (Copy in author's collection).
184. *Appeal to Reason*, March 27, 1913.
185. *The Wheeling Majority*, July 3, 1913.
186. Press Release, SPP, Duke University.
187. *The Huntington Socialist and Labor Star*, July 3, 31, 1914.
188. Letter, Wolf to Collins, February 27, 1913, Collins Papers.
189. Minutes, Huntington Trades and Labor Assembly, February 17, 1913 (author's collection); Interview, Thompson.
190. Interview, Charles Woods.
191. Holliday, *Politics in Fayette*, pp. 3–5, Holliday covers the formation of the Fusion Party but fails to deal with the Republican Labor Alliance Party.
192. *The Fayette Tribune*, October 17, 1914; Interview, A. D. Lavinder.
193. *The Fayette Journal*, October 1, 8, 1914.
194. *Ibid*. October 22, 29, 1914.
195. *Huntington Socialist and Labor Star*, July 3, 1914.
196. *Fayette Tribune*, October 8, 17, 22, 1914.
197. *Ibid*. October 1, 1914.
198. See Appendix B, Table IV, Footnote a.
199. Minutes, *Huntington Trades and Labor Assembly*, pp. 75, 130, 154, 157, 182; Minutes, O.V.T.L.A., October 13, 1913, XVI, 406.

200. *Ibid.*, September 23, 1912, p. 121.
201. Interviews, Ed Shay, John Frisk, A. D. Lavinder.
202. See Appendix B, Table III.
203. Interview, Wyatt Thompson.

Chapter V

1. *The Argus Star*, May 13, 1915 (author's collection).
2. *Ibid.*
3. Interview, George W. Harper.
4. *Huntington Socialist and Labor Star*, May 29, 1914.
5. *The Argus Star*, May 6, 1915 (author's collection).
6. *The Charleston Gazette*, July 3, 1916.
7. *Proceedings of the State Federation of Labor*, 1916, p. 26.
8. *Report of the Attorney General of West Virginia, 1917–1918* (Charleston, W. Va., 1918), pp. 21–22.
9. *Wheeling Majority*, September 21, 1916.
10. *Clarksburg Telegram*, August 11, 14, 1916.
11. *The Charleston Gazette*, November 3, 1916.
12. *Wheeling Majority*, September 21, 1916.
13. *Report of the Attorney General of West Virginia, 1917–1918*, p. 56.
14. *The Wheeling Majority*, October 5, 1916.
15. *Ibid.* September 21, 1916.
16. *The Argus Star*, February 10, 1916.
17. *The Argus Star*, January 13, 1916.
18. *The Argus Star,* February 10, 1916.
19. Interview, Charlie Walters, May 18, 1968, Oak Hill, W. Va.
20. Mooney, *Struggle*, p. 45; *Argus Star*, February 13, 1916.
21. *Argus Star*, May 6, 1915, April 13, 1916.
22. *The Fayette Journal*, July 1, 1915.
23. *Argus Star*, February 10, 1916.
24. *Fayette Tribune*, February 8, 1916.
25. *Argus Star*, February 10, 1916.
26. *Morgantown Daily Post*, January 20, 1916.

27. *Argus Star*, March 30, 1916. The following daily wage rates were used to show how much better mine organizations' contracts were.
28. *Ibid*. April 13, 1916.

U.M.W.A.		W.V.M.O	
	Per Day		Per Day
Day Laborers	$2.00	Lay [sic] Laborers	$2.10
Driver (1 mile)	$2.05	Driver (1-mile)	$2.20
Driver (team)	$2.16	Driver (team)	$2.27
Track Layer	$2.43	Track Layer	$2.55
Motormen	$2.55	Motormen	$2,68

29. *Ibid*.
30. Interview, Wyatt Thompson.
31. Mooney, *Struggle*, p. 45.
32. *The Argus Star*, March 30, 1916. Mooney stayed in the U.M.W.A. because "did not believe that a man or group of men can put their house in order by going outside and throwing bricks through windows," Mooney, *Struggle*, p. 45.
33. *Ibid*. February 10, 1916; April 13, 1916. The operators at Kayford sought an injunction against the harassment of U.M.W. District 17 while the Boomer Coal Company sued Tom Cairns because his union was unable to provide workers as stipulated in the last contract. *Boomer Coal Company vs. Tom Cairns*, May 8, 1914. Record of the Court of Kanawha County.
34. Mooney, *Struggle*, p. 52, and *The Wheeling Majority*. Mooney was elected to the office of secretary of District 17. See also Harris and Krebs, *Humble Beginnings*, pp. 103–4.
35. *The Argus Star*, April 13, 1916.

36. *The Argus Star*, March 30, 1916.
37. Letter, W. Ice Poling to J. J. Cornwell, October 5, 1916. Cornwell Papers, West Virginia University, Morgantown, W. Va.
38. *The Charleston Gazette*, October 31, 1916.
39. *The Argus Star*, March 30, 1916.
40. *The Wheeling Intelligencer*, October 27, 1916.
41. Minutes, O.V.T.L.A., November 12, 1916, VII, 167; Letter David C. Reay to J. J. Cornwell, May 7, 1916. Cornwell Papers, West Virginia University.
42. Letter, E. A. Hamilton to J. J. Cornwell. Cornwell Papers, October 16, 1916.
43. *The Charleston Gazette*, November 3, October 30, 1916.
44. Interviews, Bill Smith, August 20, 1969, Winifrede, W. Va.; Joe Mino, May 28, 1968, Kayford, W. Va.; A. D. Lavinder and *The Wheeling Majority*, November 9, 1916.
45. *The Socialist and Labor Star*, June 19, 1914; October 2, 1914.
46. The Pistol Act allowed only law officers to carry firearms. *The Argus Star*, January 13, 1916.
47. Letter, W. J. Hall to J. J. Cornwell, May 16, 1916. Cornwell Papers.
48. Letter, Jess L. Hern to John J. Cornwell, July 10, 1916. Cornwell Papers.
49. Letter, W. "Ice" Poling to John J. Cornwell, October 5, 1916. Cornwell Papers.
50. Letter, G. Burgess Taylor to J. J. Cornwell, July 17, 1916. Cornwell Papers.
51. Letter, Percy Byrd to J. J. Cornwell, August 19, 1916. Cornwell Papers.
52. Letter, W. W. Kenny to J. J. Cornwell August 18, 1916. Cornwell Papers.
53. Letter, J J. Cornwell to W. W. Keeney, August 22, 1916. Cornwell Papers.
54. *The Charleston Gazette*, October 25, 1916.
55. *The Charleston Daily Mail*, October 25, 1916.
56. Letter, George A. Borders and J. R. Mills to Cornwell, September 27, 1916. Cornwell Papers.
57. Interview, Charlie Woods.
58. *The Charleston Gazette*, October 30, 1916.
59. *The Socialist and Labor Star*, November 17, 1914.
60. Interview, H. L. Rhoes, Gatewood, W. Va. However, others select different points, such as American involvement in the First World War, economic changes, or repression during the "Red Scare."

61. Minutes of the County Court for 1916, Fayette County Court House.
62. *Manual of the State of West Virginia, 1916.*
63. Socialist Vote:

Counties	1912 Percentage	1914 Percentage	1916 Percentage
Ohio	11	6	4
Marshall	7	6	3
Marion	9	7	4
Monongalia	10	7	5
Harrison	9	11	5
Wood	5	3	1
Cabell	5	5	2
Boone	12	10	4

64. Computed from abstracts in *Clarksburg Telegram.*

	1912 Percentage	1914 Percentage	1915 Percentage
Monticello S. H.	19.5	34	16
Alta Vista S. H.	14.2	14	4
Carlisle S. H.	9.5	4	1

64. *continued*

Industrial S. H.	38	37	19
Adamston	25.5	24	10
Mayor's Office	25.5	24	8
City Bldg., Salem	18.7	10	3
Bristol	13	17	16

65. For comparison of Democratic, Republican, and Socialist parties at congressional level, see Appendix Table I (B).
66. Other high Socialist votes in precincts in Fayette County.

	1914	1916		1914	1916
Lowe	31	3	Powellton	27	1
Gatewood	44	10	Gauley Bridge	20	1
Oakhill	16	6	Mahan	22	3
Hilltop	24	4	Smithers	20	1
Fayette Sta.	47	17	Longacre	26	2
Victor	26	10	Gamoca	61	16
Hawk's Nest	42	17	Michigan	42	8
Kay Moor	25	1			

67. Computed from scattered returns from *The Charleston Daily Mail*, November

16, 1916, and a survey of county votes by districts in *Huntington Socialist and Labor Star*, November 13, 1914.

68. Computed from abstracts in *The Clarksburg Telegram*

	1912 Percentage	1914 Percentage	1916 Percentage
Enterprise S. H.		15	8
Shinnston S. H.		11	2
Hamilton Block	7	12	1
Gydsey	9	8	3
Point Comfort 5th	12.4	8	2
North View	23	22	7
Mount Clare	38	35	15

69. *West Virginia Legislative Handbook and Manual and Official Register* (Charleston, W. Va., 1922), p. 324.

70. *The Charleston Post*, December 4, 1916.

71. Cabin Creek District:

	1914 Percentage	1916 Percentage
Democrats	26	49 (+24)
Republicans	28	41 (+13)
Socialists	47	10 (–37)

Based on scattered returns in *The Charleston Daily Mail*, November 16, 1916, and summary of magisterial districts in *Socialist and Labor Star*, November 13, 1914.

Although there are no returns available for Cabin Creek district in the early years of this study, *The Charleston Gazette* stated that it had been traditionally Republican, with the Democrats making gains until the parties were about even. Then the Socialists broke but, "having received the benefits of a Democratic Administration, it looks like the district will go Democratic." *Charleston Gazette*, November 6, 1916.
72. Percentages based on official abstracts from *Fayette Journal* and *West Virginia Department of Archives and History*.

Districts	1906 Percentage			1908 Percentage			1912 Percentage			1916 Percentage		
	D*	R	S	D	R	S	D	R	S	D	R	S
Fayetteville	25	66		34	58	5	34	54	10	49	48	3
Falls	40	53		42	52	6	29	41	29.1	62	45	3
Kanawha	20	63		33	57	6	32	51	16	49	47	3
Mt. Cove	45	49		47	41	4	39	41	13	50	43	7
Precincts	D*	R	S	D	R	S	D	R	S	D	R	S
Lowe				34	61	5				70	27	3
Mossey				21	46	2				32	40	28
Gatewood				28	46	14				62	28	10
Hilltop				27	53	20				48.3	48	4
Fayette Sta.				43	41	1				37	46	17
Mt. Carbon				32	44	22				66	22	12

Michigan	31	59	8	67	23	8
Gamoca	23	61	16	49	35	16
Smithers	46	47	4	50	48	1
Longacre	23	61	4	43	55	2
Deepwater	30	42	10	72	26	1
Mahan	51	43	5	63	34	3

*D, R, S = Democratic, Republican, Socialist.

73. *The Wheeling Majority*, November 9, 1916.
74. For example, Richland Magisterial District:

Precinct No.	1912 Percentages			1914 Percentages			1916 Percentages		
	D	R	S	D	R	S	D	R	S
1	42	48	10	40	49	11	45	50	5
2	35	53	12	40	55	5	44	53	3
3	47	39	14	39	49	11	45	51	3
4	50	46	4	39	57	3	45	52	3
5	47	32	21	51	42	7	55	41	7

Based on returns in *Wheeling Intelligencer* and *New Register*.

75. Computed from returns in the *Clarksburg Telegram*:

Precincts	1912 Percentage			1916 Percentage		
	D	R	S	D	R	S
Monticello	23	58	19	26	57	17
Court House	44	52	4	45	54	1
Industrial S. H.	26	36	38	38	46	14
Fair Grounds	41	47	10	43	47	9
Adamston S. H.	30	44	25	41	48	10
Northview S. H.	28	49	23	34	58	7
Carlisle S. H.	29	66	5	35	63	2
City Bldg. Salem	44	38	13	54	41	5
Depot Sore	43	47	10	45	49	6
Graselli	49	38	13	54	41	5

76. *Huntington Socialist and Labor Star*, May 15, July 20, 1914.
77. *Proceedings of the State Federation of Labor, Fairmont*, W. Va., p. 31.
78. *The Socialist and Labor Star*, August 1914; *The Argus Star*, January 13, 1916.
79. *Ibid*. August 28, 1914.
80. Minutes, O.V.T.L.A., November 28, 1915, VII, 30–31.
81. *The Huntington Herald Dispatch*, May 11, 1915.
82. *Wheeling Majority*, February 15, 31, 1916.
83. *The Charleston Gazette*, February 12, 1917.

84. *Wheeling Majority*, February 22, 1917.
85. Interview, Charlie Walters, August 20, 1969, Oak Hill, W. Va.
86. Interview, Reverend Fred Smith, August 20, 1969, Clendenin, W. Va.
87. *Wheeling Majority*, April 18, 1918.
88. Socialist Party Bulletin, SPP, Duke; *The Clarksburg Exponent*, April 14, 1917.
89. *Wheeling Majority*, April 5; May 10, 1917.
90. James Weinstein, *Decline of Socialism*, pp. 130–31.
91. *Wheeling Majority*, March 7, 14; April 18; July 14, 1918.
92. *Appeal to Reason*, December 17, 1917, for example, George Harper recalled that he felt it would be a real irony if a war started by capitalists could end up bringing in socialism. Interview, George W. Harper.
93. *Wheeling Majority*, August 15; September 12, 1918.
94. Interview, John N. Brandum, May 25, 1969, Huntington, W. Va.
95. *Wheeling Majority*, August 29, 1918.
96. Mooney, *Struggle*, pp. 58–60. See also "The United Mine Workers in West Virginia," p. 5.
97. *Wheeling Majority*, August 22, 1918.
98. Letter, George Wolfe to Justus Collins, May 15, 1917. Winding Gulf Papers, West Virginia University, Morgantown, W. Va.
99. *Wheeling Majority*, March 22; November 8, 1917.
100. Interview, Houston G. Young, March 20, 1968, Charleston, W. Va.
101. Interviews, George Glass, Wyatt Thompson, and *Wheeling Majority*, February 21, 1918.
102. Minutes, Belmont County Socialists (author's collection), p. 107, February 3, 1918, and Interview, Wyatt Thompson.
103. *Proceedings of the 1918 Convention of the State Federation of Labor*, p. 9, and *Wheeling Majority*, June 26, 1918.
104. *The Charleston Gazette*, April 6, 7, 1918.
105. *Wheeling Majority*, March 28, April 4, June 6, August 8, September 12, October 24, 1918. See also Minutes of the City of Star City, p. 174.
106. James Weinstein, *Decline of Socialism*, p. 164, and *Wheeling Majority*, September 26, July 2, 1918.
107. *Wheeling Majority*, January 9, May 1, 8, September 25, October 9, 1919.
108. Interview, George Glass.

109. Interview, George W. Harper. The speech Harper had reference to was probably "Mother" Jones's address to workers at Mingo Junction in which she further stated, as only she could, "The minister say Jesus won't even look at you if you are a Bolshevist. Jesus has been looking down at me for 90 years and I have been raising hell all the time." *Wheeling Majority*, September 18, 1919.

110. *Wheeling Majority*, March 13, November 6, 1919.

111. Letter, R. L. Thompson, S. Freeman to National Executive Committee, June 15, 1919, SPP, Duke; C. W. Kirkendall, Jay Allen to National Executive Committee, July 6, 1919, SPP, Duke.

112. David Shannon, *The Socialist Party of America* (Chicago, 1957), pp. 141–46.

113. Minutes, Belmont County Socialist Executive Committee, February 3, April 7, June 2, 1919, pp. 143–60.

114. Letter, H. W. Houston to Seymour Steadman, February 9, 1918, SPP, Duke; Letter, Jesse Bird to A. Wagenecht, June 12, 1919, SPP, Duke and Interview, Price Williams.

115. Gneiser captured the oppressive atmosphere of the times when he described the charges as absolutely ridiculous "and yet when we consider the temperament of the nation and the judge, it would not be surprising if I (am) convicted on general principle." G. A. Gneiser to Adolph Germer, February 7, 1918, SPP, Duke.

116. *Wheeling Majority*, May 24, 1917, August 8, 1918, and Interview, Williams.

117. Stanley Cobden, "A Study in Nativism: The American Red Scare of 1919–20," *Political Science Quarterly*, LXXIX (March 1964), pp. 52–75.

118. Letter, Agent 37 to C. E. Smith, October 29, 1919, C. E. Smith Papers, West Virginia University.

119. Letter, Agent 35 to C. E. Smith, October 18, 1919.

120. *The Clarksburg Telegram*, November 13, 1919.

121. *Ibid.* November 16, 21, 1919.

122. *Wheeling Majority*, July 17, February 20, September 25, 1919.

123. Harris and Krebs, *Humble Beginnings*, p. 131.

124. *The West Virginia Federationist*, February 20, 1919.

125. Joseph Raybock, *A History of American Labor* (New York, 1959), p. 286.

126. *Wheeling Majority*, May 8, September 25, 1919.

127. *The Clarksburg Telegram*, September 29, 1919.

128. Joseph Raybock, *A History of American Labor*, p. 286; *Wheeling Majority*, October 9, 23, 1919. The Finnish Cooperative store in Weirton attacked and a no-

tice left behind, "Beware! This is America! No interference of the Finnish Red or IWW of Weirton will be tolerated! The Vigilance Committee," *Wheeling Majority*, November 6, 1919.

129. *The Clarksburg Telegram*, October 16, 1919.
130. *Wheeling Majority*, October 16, 1919. In Wheeling itself, the use of deputized members of the Ohio Valley Trades and Labor Assembly kept the atmosphere much saner. Harris and Krebs, *Humble Beginnings*, p. 160.
131. Letter, C. F. Keeney to John J. Cornwell, October 27, 1919, Cornwell Papers.
132. Harris and Krebs, *Humble Beginnings*, p. 150.
133. Harris and Krebs, *Humble Beginnings*, pp. 151–55. See also Winthrop Lane, *Civil War in West Virginia* (New York, 1921).
134. *The Clarksburg Telegram*, October 9, November 16, 1919. There is evidence that several mine leaders of radical reputation often acted in a moderate manner. Until events in the mine fields incited the miners beyond his control, Frank Keeney appears to have been very cooperative with Governor Cornwell's efforts to head off trouble in the coal fields. See, for example, Letter, Cornwell to Keeney, September 9, 1919, and Keeney to Cornwell, October 19, 1919; also, "Mother" Jones's attempt to prevent the second "Miners March" with a telegram from President Harding, which she faked, *New York Times*, August 28, 1921.
135. *The Wheeling Majority*, September 25, 1919.
136. *Ibid.* April 10, July 24, November 6, October 23, 1919.
137. Minutes, Huntington Trade and Labor Assembly, December 21, 1919, p. 35.
138. Harris and Krebs, *Humble Beginnings*, pp. 130–31.
139. *Wheeling Majority*, May 29, September 11, 1919.
140. *Ibid.*
141. Interviews, Bill Smith, July 24, 1968, Winifrede, W. Va.; A. D. Lavinder; George Glass.
142. Minutes, Belmont County Socialist Executive Committee Meetings, December 2, 1917, p. 100.
143. SPP, Duke (West Virginia Folder).
144. *Proceedings, State Federation of Labor*, May 1919, pp. 2–3; *Wheeling Majority*, March 13, 1919.
145. *Wheeling Majority*, August 21, 1919.
146. Harris and Krebs, *Humble Beginnings*, p. 175.

147. Thomas Posey, "Labor in West Virginia," pp. 105-8.
148. *The Argus Star*, February 18, 1915.
149. Weinstein, *Decline*, pp. 236-37.
150. *Huntington Herald Dispatch*, October 16, 1920.
151. Interview, Duff Scott, Jim Lowe, A. D. Lavinder, and George Glass.
152. *The Fayette Tribune*, October 21, 1920.
153. *Huntington Herald Dispatch*, October 22, 1920.
154. *Proceedings, State Federation of Labor*, 1920, pp. 94, 141; *Herald Dispatch*, October 16, 1920.
155. It seems likely that Mooney was by then a Democrat, Hilton had moved that way, and other former Socialists like Harry Wright were described as "Democratic Politicians," *Wheeling Majority*, November 27, 1919.
156. *The Huntington Herald Dispatch*, October 16, 17, 1920.
157. Sam Montgomery's speech in testimony, *Senate Hearings*, II, 2284.
158. *The Fayette Tribune*, October 14, 1920.
159. High Socialist vote precincts—Fayette County:

	1916 Percentages			1920 Percentages		
	Dem.	Rep.	Soc.	Dem.	Rep.	N.P.
Lowe	70	27	3			
Mossey	32	40	28	25	29	46
Gatewood	62	28	10	40	33	20
Hilltop	48.3	48	4	21	54	25
Fayette Sta.	37	46	17	7	20	65
Mt. Carbon	66	22	12	7	28	68

Michigan	67	23	8	20	35	44
Gamoca	49	35	16	16	20	65
Smithers	50	48	1	6	35	59
Longacre	43	55	2	10	43	47
Deepwater	72	26	1	47	18	36
Mahan	63	34	3	1	50	40

160. Vote for governor: Morgan, Rep. 46%, Koontz, Dem. 38%, Montgomery, 15.5%, Holt, Soc. .5%, *West Virginia Legislative Hand Book and Manual* (Charleston, W. Va., 1922), pp. 324, 372.

Chapter VI

1. James Weinstein, *The Decline of Socialism, 1912–1925* (New York, 1967), pp. 324–39.
2. Walter Thurmond, *The Logan Coal Fields of West Virginia* (Morgantown, 1964), p. 69.
3. Pearce Davis, *The Development of the American Glass Industry* (New York, 1949), pp. 182–90.
4. George E. Barnett, *Chapters on Machinery and Labor* (Carbondale, 1969), p. 69.
5. Harry Jerome, *Mechanization in Industry* (New York, 1934), p. 77; Interview, John Brandum.
6. W. P. Tams, *The Smokeless Coal Fields of West Virginia* (Morgantown, 1963), p. 40.
7. Davis, *American Glass*, pp. 182–83; Barnett, *Machinery and Labor*, p. 69.
8. Interview, Earnest Brandum, November 17, 1969; October 6, 1969.
9. Interview, George DelForge, November 18, 1967.
10. Interview, Oscar DuBois by Martha DuBois, May 6, 1965, Morgantown, W. Va., p. 17. (Available at West Virginia University Library.)

11. Barnett, *Machinery and Labor*, National Window Glass Workers, *Constitution and By-laws of the National Window Glass Workers* (Cleveland, 1908), pp. 26–31.
12. Interview, Eugene Monin, November 17, 1967.
13. *Huntington Socialist and Labor Star*, March 20, 1914.
14. Interview, Duff Scott, February 23, 1968, Chelyan, W. Va.
15. Interview, Price Williams; Interview, Charles Dandois; Interview, Kyle Kintzer; Interview, Conrad Leeds.
16. *Huntington Socialists and Labor Star*, April 3, 1914, July 3, 1914.
17. Letter, John Lindsey to Fred Barkey, July 28, 1970.
18. Interview, E. A. Witherall, July 18, 1968, Huntington, W. Va.; Interview, Harvey Falkenstein, March 24, 1968, Morgantown, W. Va.
19. See Chapter IV, p. 158.
20. *Wheeling Majority*, September 7, 1916.
21. Jerome, *Mechanization*, pp. 100–1.
22. *Wheeling Majority*, October 24, 1919.
23. Tams, *Smokeless Coal*, p. 69; Thurmond, *Logan Coal Fields*, p. 49.
24. Barnett, *Machinery and Labor*, pp. 105–6.
25. Interview, E. A. Witherall, July 18, 1968.
26. Letter, Lindsey to Barkey.
27. *Wheeling Majority*, November 21, 1918.
28. Interview, Duff Scott; Interview, Sylvanus Goff.
29. Interview, Wyatt Thompson, October 13, 1968.
30. Barnett, *Machinery and Labor*, p. 114.
31. Interview, George DelForge, November 18, 1967.
32. *National Window Glassworkers*, January 21, 1925.
33. Interview, George DelForge.
34. Interview, Jules Waterloo; Interview, George DelForge.
35. Pete Felix, "Poems of Pete Felix," Labor Archives, West Virginia University, Morgantown, W.Va.
36. Jerome, *Mechanization*, pp. 75–78.
37. Interview, John Brandum, November 17, 1969; October 6, 1969.

Conclusion

1. Interview, Bert Seachrist.
2. *Wheeling Majority*, February 13, 1919.
3. *The Huntington Socialist and Labor Star*, July 26, 1913.
4. *The Huntington Socialist and Labor Star*, November 13, 1914.
5. *Ibid*. November 14, 1913.

Bibliography

BOOKS

Abrams, Richard M. *Conservatism in a Progressive Era: Massachusetts Politics, 1900–1912.* Cambridge, Mass.: Harvard University Press, 1964.

Ambler, Charles Henry. *West Virginia: The Mountain State.* New York: Prentice-Hall, 1940.

Ambler, Charles H. and Festus P. Summers. *West Virginia: The Mountain State.* Englewood Cliffs, N.J.: Prentice-Hall, 1958.

Angle, Paul. *Bloody Williamson: A Chapter in American Lawlessness.* New York: Knopf, 1952.

Atkinson, George W. *Bench and Bar of West Virginia.* Charleston, W. Va.: Virginia Law Book Company, 1909.

Barck, Oscar and Nelson Blake. *Since 1900.* New York: Macmillan, 1959.

Barnett, George E. *Chapters on Machinery and Labor.* Carbondale, Ill.: Southern Illinois University Press, 1969.

Bedford, Henry F. *Socialism and the Worker in Massachusetts, 1886–1912.* Amherst, Mass.: University of Massachusetts Press, 1966.

Brissenden, Paul. *The I.W.W., A Study in American Radicalism.* New York: Russell and Russell, 1919.

Brody, David. *Steelworkers in America: The Nonunion Era.* Cambridge, Mass.: Harvard University Press, 1960.

Burns, James M. *Roosevelt: The Lion and the Fox.* New York: Harcourt, Brace and World, 1956.

Butcher, Benard L. and James M. Callahan. *Genealogical and Personal History of the Upper Monongahela Valley, West Virginia.* New York: Lewis Historical Publishing Company, 1912.

Callahan, James M. *Semi-Centennial History of West Virginia.* Charleston, W. Va.: Semi-Centennial Commission of West Virginia, 1913.

Cartlidge, Oscar. *Fifty Years of Coal Mining.* Charleston, W. Va.: Rose City Press, 1936.

Chaplin, Paul. *Wobbly: The Rough-and-Tumble Story of an American Radical.* Chicago: University of Chicago Press, 1948.

Coleman, McAllister. *Men and Coal.* New York: Farrar and Rinehart, 1943.
Davis, Pearce. *The Development of the American Glass Industry.* New York: Russell and Russell, 1949.
Dulles, Foster R. *Labor in America.* New York: Thomas J. Crowell, 1949.
Egbert, Donald D. and Stow Persons. *Socialism in American Life*, Vol. I, II. Princeton, N.J.: Princeton University Press, 1952.
Evans, Chris. *History of the United Mine Workers of America.* Indianapolis: The United Mine Workers of America, 1918.
Fine, Nathan. *Labor and Farmer Parties in the United States: 1828–1928.* New York: Russell and Russell, 1961.
Ginger, Ray. *The Bending Cross: A Biography of Eugene Victor Debs.* New Brunswick, N.J.: Rutgers University Press, 1949.
Goodrich, Carter. *The Miner's Freedom.* Boston: Marshall Jones, 1925.
Grob, Gerald N. *Workers and Utopia.* Evanston, Ill.: Northwestern University Press, 1961.
Harris, Evelyn and Frank Krebs. *Humble Beginnings.* Charleston, W. Va.: West Virginia Labor History Publishing Fund, 1960.
Hays, Samuel P. *The Response to Industrialism.* Chicago: University of Chicago Press, 1963.
Hinricks, A. F. *The United Mine Workers and the New Union Coal Fields*, Vol. CX. New York: Columbia University Series, 1923.
Holliday, Robert K. *Politics in Fayette County.* Montgomery, W. Va.: Montgomery Herald, Inc., 1958.
Jerome, Harry. *Mechanization in Industry.* New York: National Bureau of Economic Research, 1934.
Karson, Marc. *American Labor Unions and Politics: 1900–1918.* Carbondale, Ill.: Beacon Press, 1958.
Kipnis, Ira. *The American Socialist Movement: 1897–1912.* New York: Columbia University Press, 1952.
Lane, Winthrop. *Civil War in West Virginia.* New York: B. H. Huebsch, 1921.
Lantz, Herman R. *People of Coal Town.* New York: Columbia University Press, 1958.
Link, Arthur S. *American Epoch.* New York: Macmillan, 1955.
McCormick, Kyle. *The New-Kanawha River and the Mine War of West Virginia.* Charleston, W. Va.: Mathews Printing and Lithographing Company, 1959.

Mooney, Fred. *Struggle in the Coal Fields*. Edited by J. W. Hess. Morgantown, W. Va.: West Virginia University Press, 1963.

Morgan, H. Wayne, ed. *The Gilded Age*. Syracuse: Syracuse University Press, 1963.

Mowry, George. *The California Progressives, 1900–1920*. Berkeley, Calif.: University of California Press, 1951.

Ohio Valley Trades and Labor Assembly. *The Ohio Valley Trades and Labor Assembly: City of Wheeling and the Ohio Valley Trades and Labor Assembly and Its Affiliated Organizations*. Wheeling, W. Va.: The Ohio Valley Trades and Labor Assembly, 1902.

Parten, Mary F., ed. *The Autobiography of Mother Jones*. Chicago: C. H. Kerr, 1925.

Perlman, Mark. *Labor Union Theories in America: Background and Development*. Evanston, Ill.: Row-Peterson, 1958.

Peters, J. F. and F. Carden. *A History of Fayette County*. Charleston, W. Va.: Jarrett Printing Company, 1926.

Quint, Howard. *The Forging of American Socialism: Origins of a Modern Movement*. Columbia, S. C.: University of South Carolina Press, 1953.

Quint, Howard, ed. *Main Problems in American History*. Homewood, Ill.: Dorsey Press, 1968.

Rayback, Joseph G. *A History of American Labor*. New York: Macmillan, 1959.

Ross, Malcolm H. *Machine Age in the Hills*. New York: Macmillan, 1933.

Sappos, David J. *Left Wing Unionism*. New York: International Publishers, 1926.

Schlesinger, Arthur M., Jr. *The Crisis of the Old Order*. Boston: Houghton-Mifflin, 1957.

Shannon, David. *The Socialist Party of America*. New York: Macmillan, 1955.

Shawkey, Morris P. *West Virginia in History, Life, Literature, and Industry*, Vol. I, II, III, IV. New York: Lewis Company, 1928.

Taft, Phillip. *The A. F. of L. in the Time of Gompers*. New York: Harper and Row, 1951.

Taft, Phillip. *Organized Labor in American History*. New York: Harper and Row, 1964.

Tams, W. P. *The Smokeless Coal Fields of West Virginia*. Morgantown, W. Va.: West Virginia University Library, 1963.

Thoenen, Eugene D. *History of the Oil and Gas Industry in West Virginia*. Charleston, W. Va.: Education Foundation, 1964.

Thurmond, Walter R. *The Logan Coal Field of West Virginia*. Morgantown, W. Va.: West Virginia University Library, 1964.

Ulman, Lloyd. *The Rise of the National Trade Union.* Cambridge, Mass.: Harvard University Press, 1966.

Weinstein, James. *The Decline of Socialism in America, 1912–1925.* New York: Monthly Review Press, 1967.

Yellowitz, Irwin. *Labor and the Progressive Movement in New York State, 1897–1916.* Ithaca, N.Y.: Cornwell University Press, 1965.

GOVERNMENT PUBLICATIONS

Barton, I. V. *Report of the West Virginia Labor Commissioner, 1897–1898.* Charleston, W. Va.: Forsyth Publishing and Printing Company, 1899.

Committee on Education and Labor. *Conditions in the Paint Creek District, West Virginia.* Washington, D.C.: U.S. Government Printing Office, 1913.

Department of Labor. *General Records.* Washington, D.C.: U.S. Government Printing Office, 1914.

Mine Investigation Commission. *Report of West Virginia Mine Investigation Commission.* Charleston, W. Va.: Tribune Printing Company, 1912.

West Virginia. *The Code of West Virginia, 1906.* St. Paul, Minn.: West Publishing Company, 1906.

West Virginia. *Journal of the Senate of the State of West Virginia: 25th Session; 26th Session.* Charleston, W. Va.: Tribune Printing Company, 1901–1903.

West Virginia. *Manual of the State of West Virginia.* Tribune Printing Company, 1907.

West Virginia. *Report of the Attorney General of West Virginia, 1917–1918.* Charleston, W. Va.: Tribune Printing Company, 1917–1918.

West Virginia. *West Virginia Legislative Handbook and Manual and Official Register.* Charleston, W. Va.: Tribune Printing Company, 1922.

Wheeling. *Directories for City of Wheeling. 1898–1901.* Complete collection found in Wheeling Public Library.

U. S. *The Thirteenth Census of the United States Taken in the Year 1910; Vol. IV, Population.* Washington, D.C.: U.S. Government Printing Office, 1916.

INTERVIEWS

Argabright, Ulysis. Personal interview. April 17, 1967.

Arthur, Mrs. George Smith. Personal interview. August 22, 1968.
Atkins, Bezra. Personal interview. November 20, 1970.
Baker, Mrs. C. L. Personal interview. March 20, 1970.
Beasley, Isom. Personal interview. October 28, 1968.
Beasley, Mrs. John. Personal interview. May 20, 1968.
Blizzard, Mrs. Frank. Personal interview. June 16, 1969.
Boone, Henry. Personal interview. August 28, 1968.
Bosher, Harry. Personal interview. July 22, 1968.
Bougamont, George. Personal interview. March 6, 1967; August 26, 1967.
Brandum, Earnest. Personal interview. October 6, 1969; November 17, 1969.
Camp, Evanson. Personal interview. February 5, 1970.
Cantley, Scott. Personal interview. May 1, 1968.
Carpenter, Mrs. Carrie. Personal interview. January 20, 1969.
Coffee, Mrs. Grace. Personal interview. September 15, 1970.
Dandois, Charles. Personal interview. June 22, 1967.
Daniels, Mrs. James. Personal interview. March 14, 1968.
Darlington, Ted. Personal interview. March 14, 1968.
DelForge, George. Personal interview. November 18, 1967.
Donnally, Dr. Shirley. Personal interview. May 18, 1967.
Dooley, C. M. Personal interview. April 17, 1967.
Dowdy, D. C. Personal interview. July 9, 1968.
Dubois, Oscar. Interview by Martha Dubois and Sue Miller. Labor Archives, West Virginia University. May 6, 1965.
Du Gruyter, Jules. Personal interview. January 9, 1969.
Edington, Charles. Personal interview. April 14, 1969.
Ellis, Bosie S. A. Personal interview. January 13, 1969.
Falkenstein, Harvey. Personal interview. March 24, 1968.
Frisk, John. Personal interview. May 11, 1968.
Fooman, Neal. Personal interview. July 29, 1968.
Gherken, Anna. Personal interview. November 4, 1968.
Glasgow, Harold. Personal interview. July 28, 1969.
Glass, George. Personal interview. October 22, 1969; February 10, 1970.
Goff, Sylvanus. Personal interview. April 18, 1967.
Grounds, Alvin. Personal interview. May 25, 1968.

Guntner, Mrs. John. Personal interview. February 8, 1968.
Haggerty, L. Personal interview. February 21, 1969.
Harper, George W. Personal interview. February 7, 1968; April 28, 1968.
Hastings, Mrs. T. Personal interview. December 11, 1968.
Holstein, Mrs. Alice. Personal interview. May 15, 1968.
Holstein, Charles G. Personal interview. May 15, 1968.
Howery, Frank. Personal interview. October 12, 1967.
Hye, Mrs. D. W. Personal interview. November 4, 1968.
Jarrell, Luther. Personal interview. November 4, 1969.
Jarrett, Homer. Personal interview. May 12, 1969.
Keffer, Hester. Personal interview. March 4, 1968.
Keyser, Mrs. Gene Gillispie. Personal interview. July 9, 1968.
King, Helen Houston. Personal interview. June 20, 1969.
Kintzer, Kyle. Personal interview. July 29, 1969; October 30, 1969.
Knight, Charles. Personal interview. November 10, 1970.
Lavinder, A. D. Personal interview. July 25, 1968.
Leeds, Conrad. Personal interview. July 21, 22, 1968.
Linville, Sam. Personal interview. October 2, 1967.
Lowe, James. Personal interview. May 25, 1968.
Lush, Mrs. W. Personal interview. August 5, 1969.
Mahoney, Mrs. Sam Rogers. Personal interview. March 8, 1968.
Maloney, Martin H. Personal interview. August 18, 1968.
Martin, Warren. Personal interview. February 4, 5, 1968; July 22, 1968.
Matheny, Mrs. Elizabeth Franklin. Personal interview. August 21, 1969.
McGraw, Robert. Personal interview. August 21, 1969.
Michaux, Edgar. Personal interview. May 22, November 17, 1967.
Mino, Joe. Personal interview. May 28, 1968.
Monday, A. L. Personal interview. March 20, 1968.
Monin, Eugene. Personal interview. November 17, 1967.
Morris, Alva. Personal interview. March 21, 1968.
Morris, Eugene. Personal interview. November 12, 1969.
Morris, Paul. Personal interview. August 25, 1968.
Morris, Russell. Personal interview. November 15, 1969.
Nelson, Mrs. Pauline Vickers. Personal interview. February 6, 1968.

Newcomer, Mrs. Mildred. Personal interview. April 19, 1969.
Notter, C. K. Personal interview. July 16, 1968.
Nuskell, John J. Personal interview. May 21, 1970.
O'Brien, Mrs. Dennis V. Personal interview, September 9, 1969.
Otto, Hupp. Personal interview. March 18, 1968.
Parsons, H. F. Personal interview, August 28, 1968.
Pauley, Blanche. Personal interview. July 8, 1967.
Payne, Charles. Personal interview. June 10, 1969.
Phillips, John. Personal interview. February 4, 1968.
Prother, Louis. Personal interview. May 6, 1967.
Richards, Mrs. Dolly. Personal interview. January 1, 1968.
Rodes, H. L. Personal interview. April 18, 1967; May 28, 1968.
Rodes, Vincent. Personal interview. April 21, 1969.
Rumbaugh, Fred. Personal interview. January 29, 1968.
Saunders, William. Personal interview. June 11, 1969.
Scaggs, Grover. Personal interview. June 23, 1968.
Schaefer, Mrs. Maude. Personal interview. July 12, 1969.
Schulch, Bert. Personal interview. October 8, 1968.
Scott, Duff. Personal interview. February 23, 1968.
Seachrist, Mrs. Bert. Personal interview. April 8, 1968.
Shane, Mrs. Carl V. Personal interview. March 28, 1967.
Shay, Edward. Personal interview. February 18, 1967; February 6, 1968.
Smith, The Reverend Fred. Personal interview. August 28, 1969.
Smith, William. Personal interview. August 20, 1969.
Snider, Fred. Personal interview. June 11, 1968.
Staats, C. P. Personal interview. July 6, 1968.
Steele, Theodore. Personal interview. April 4, 1967.
Stone, Eugene. Personal interview. August 2, 1968.
Stone, Wilbur. Personal interview. August 25, 1970.
Stork, Morris. Personal interview. May 24, 1969.
Summers, Luther. Personal interview. September 24, 1968.
Surbaugh, Charles. Personal interview. October 10, 1967.
Thompson, Wyatt. Personal interview. October 13, 1968.
Tickle, Dallas, Personal interview. February 18, 1969.

Toney, Cleveland. Personal interview. July 18, 1969.
Trail, T. A. Personal interview. January 16, 1969.
Walchli, Fred. Personal interview. June 25, 1969.
Walters, Charles. Personal interview. April 23, 1968.
Waterloo, Jules. Personal interview. November 16, 1967.
White, Thomas. Personal interview. June 16, 1969.
Williams, Marshall. Personal interview. May 23, 1969.
Williams, Price. Personal interview. February 23, 24, 1967.
Wilson, Mrs. Reva. Personal interview. February 6, 1968.
Wise, Mrs. Virginia. Personal interview. August 20, 1968.
Witherall, E. A. Personal interview. July 18, 1968.
Woods, Charles. Personal interview. June 21, 1969.
Yost, Raymond. Personal interview. July 22, 1969.
Young, Houston. Personal interview. March 20, 1968; August 12, 1969.
Zabeau, Rene. Personal interview. July 26, 1968.

MANUSCRIPT COLLECTIONS

Duke University. Socialist Party Papers, Butsher Letterbook.
Duke University. Socialist Party Papers, Mailly Letterbook.
Duke University. Socialist Party Papers, West Virginia File.
Tamiment Institute. Castleton Papers.
West Virginia University. C. E. Smith Papers.
West Virginia University. Cornwell Papers.
West Virginia University. Glasscock Papers, Clipping File.
West Virginia University. Justus Collins Papers, Series I and II.
West Virginia University. Ohio Valley Trades and Labor Assembly Minutes Collection, 1898–1920 (Handwritten).
West Virginia University. Poems of Pete Felix (Typewritten).

PAMPHLETS

Brown, John. *Constitutional Government in West Virginia*. Pamphlet written during Cabin Creek-Paint Creek strike. 1913.

National Window Glass Workers. *Constitution and By-laws of the National Window Glass Workers.* Cleveland: Wilson Printing and Publishing Company, 1908.
Thompson, James H. *Significant Trends in the West Virginia Coal Industry, 1900–1957.* Bureau of Business Research pamphlet. Morgantown, W. Va.: West Virginia University Library, 1958.
West Virginia Coal Operators Association. *The United Mine Workers in West Virginia.* Operator's Special Committee Report to the U.S. Coal Commission, 1923.

PERIODICALS: ARTICLES

Glaab, Charles N. "The Failure of North Dakota Progressivism." *Mid America,* XXXIX (October 1957), 198–209.
Gutman, Herbert G. "Protestantism and the American Labor Movement: The Christian Spirit in the Gilded Age." *American Historical Review* (October 1966), 77–101.
Hathmacner, J. Joseph. "Urban Liberalism and the Age of Reform." *The Mississippi Valley Historical Review,* XLIX (September 1962), 231–41.
Heath, Frederick M. "Labor and Progressive Movement in Connecticut." *Labor History,* XII (Winter 1971), 52–67.
Lynch, Lawrence. "The West Virginia Coal Strike." *Political Science Quarterly,* XXIX (December 1914), 626–63.
Meredith, H. L. "Agrarian Socialism and the Negro in Oklahoma, 1900–1918." *Labor History,* II (Summer 1970), 277–84.
Merrick, Fred H. "The Betrayal of the West Virginia Rednecks." *International Socialist Review,* XIV (July 1913), 13–19.
Michelson, M. "Feudalism and Civil War in the United State." *Everybody's Magazine,* XXIII (May 1913), 615–28.
Older, Cora. "The Last Day of the Paint Creek Court Martial." *Independent,* LXXIV (May 15 1913), 20–21.
Steel, Edward M. "Mother Jones in the Fairmont Fields, 1902." *The Journal of American History,* LVII (September 1970), 290–308.
"The Passing of the Window Glass Workers." *Monthly Labor Review,* XXIX (October 1929), 1–17.
Thompson, Wyatt. "A Reply to Debs." *International Socialist Review,* XIV (August 1913), 107.

Thompson, Wyatt. "How Victory Was Turned into Settlement." *International Socialist Review,* XIV (July 1913), 13–19.
West, Harold E. "Civil War in Wet Virginia Coal Mines." *Survey,* XXX (April 1913), 37–50.
Wiebe, Robert H. "The Anthracite Strike of 1902: A Record of Confusion." *Mississippi Valley Historical Review,* XLVIII (September 1961), 229–51.

PERIODICALS: NEWSPAPERS

Appeal to Reason, 1900–20.
Baltimore Sun, September 5, 1912.
Charleston Daily Mail, 1900–20.
Charleston Gazette, 1900–20.
Charleston Labor Argus, 1906–11.
Charleston Post, February 1915–January 1917.
Clarksburg Exponent, 1910–20.
Clarksburg Telegram, 1902–20.
Fayette Sun, 1911–14.
Fayette Tribune, 1911–13; 1915–17.
Huntington Advertiser, 1900–20.
Huntington Herald Dispatch, 1900–1920.
Huntington Socialist and Labor Star, May 1912–March 1914.
Montgomery Herald, September 1913–March 1914.
Morgantown Daily Post, July 1904–June 1908.
Morgantown News Dominion, October 1913–December 1920.
Morgantown Post Chronicle, 1913–17.
Moundsville Daily Echo, 1911–23.
New York Call, November 12, 1912.
New York Times, August 28, 1921.
Nineteen-Nineteen, September, 1910.
Parkersburg Dispatch and News, October 29, 1912.
Pioneer Press, May 25, 1912.
Pittsburgh Justice, October 18, 1913.
Socialist Party Monthly Bulletin, September 1910.

Wheeling Intelligencer, 1897–20.
Wheeling Majority, September 1916–December 1919.
Wheeling News Register, 1917–21.

PROCEEDINGS

Roth, Clarence E. "Some Notes on Early Mining in West Virginia" in *The 1967 Proceedings of the West Virginia Coal Mining Institute*. Edited by Charles T. Holland. Morgantown, W. Va.: Morgantown Printing and Binding Company, 1968.
West Virginia Federation of Labor. *Proceedings of State Federation of Labor, 1912*. Available at West Virginia University Archives, Morgantown, W. Va.

UNPUBLISHED MATERIALS

Anson, Charles P. "A History of the Labor Movement in West Virginia." Unpublished Ph.D. dissertation, University of North Carolina, 1940.
Barb, Joseph M. "Strikes in the Southern West Virginia Coal Fields, 1912–1922." Unpublished M.A. thesis, West Virginia University, 1949.
Belmont County Socialist. Minutes of the Belmont County Socialist. Private collection of Fred Walchli, Bel Air, Ohio (Handwritten).
Crawford, Charles B. "The Mine War on Cabin Creek and Paint Creek, West Virginia in 1912–1913." Unpublished M.A. thesis, University of Kentucky, 1939.
Fayette County. Minutes of the County Court. Available at Fayette County Courthouse, Fayetteville, W. Va. (Handwritten).
Goodall, Elizabeth J. "History of the Charleston Industrial Areas." Unpublished M.A. thesis, West Virginia University, 1937.
Hadsell, Richard. "Justice Collins and the Role of the Baldwin-Felts Detective Agency." Unpublished term paper, West Virginia University.
Hanes, Alva to W. S. Moore, Letter. Private collection of Randolph Yost, Fairview, W. Va. (Handwritten).
Hilltop City Council. Minutes of City of Hilltop. Private collection of Ulysses Argabright, Hilltop, W. Va. (Handwritten).

Huntington Trades and Labor Assembly. Minutes of Huntington Trades and Labor Assembly. Author's collection (Handwritten).

Lindsey, John to Fred Barkey, Letter. July 28, 1970. Author's collection (Handwritten).

Link, Herndon, "A Socialist Vision." Unpublished poem in private collection of Mrs. S. Wise, Ronceverte, W. Va. (Handwritten).

Local 302 Carpenters and Joiners Union. "1916 Minute Book of Local 302 Carpenters and Joiners Union." Available at Union Hall, Huntington, W. Va. (Handwritten).

Montgomery, David. "Trade Union Practices and Syndicalist Thought." Unpublished article, University of Pittsburgh (Mimeographed).

Posey, Thomas E. "The Labor Movement in West Virginia, 1900–1948." Unpublished Ph.D. dissertation, University of Wisconsin, 1948.

Reuther, Victor to Fred Barkey, Letter. October 22, 1969. Author's collection (Handwritten).

Star City City Council. Minutes of the Meetings of City Council of Star City, 1907–1911. Available at City Hall, Star City, W. Va. (Handwritten).

Thompson, Wyatt to Price Williams, Letter. Private collection of Price Williams, Hansford, W. Va. (Typewritten).

West Virginia Socialist Party. State Party Bulletin, 1913. Author's collection (Mimeographed).

Index

Adamston, WV, xxiv, 23
Amalgamated Association of Iron, Steel, and Tin Workers, 46, 59, 112
American Alliance for Labor and Democracy, 142, 146–47, 154
American Federation of Labor, xviii, 2, 4, 39, 49, 113–14, 123, 140, 150, 153
American Flint Glass Workers, xv, 23, 49, 114
American Rifle Association, 82
Appeal to Reason (Girard, Kansas), 11, 54, 59, 77, 89, 100, 142
Argus Star (Charleston), 124, 132, 148

Baldwin-Felts Detective Agency, 35, 80, 84, 86, 89, 101, 110, 119
Baltimore and Ohio Railroad, 9, 21, 46
Banner Glass Company, 114, 160–1
Bauer, Albert, 10–11, 13, 15, 42–43, 49, 64, 111, 115
Bauer, Raymond, 64, 117, 147
Beasley, Isom, 70, 75
Beckley, WV, 29, 108, 122
Belgians, xv, xxii, xxx, 62–63, 86
Bellamy, Edward, 30
Belmont County Trades Assembly, 48–50, 106, 140, 143, 147, 153
Berger, Victor, x, xxv–xxvi, 101–2, 109
Bittner, Van, 52

Bituminous Coal strike of 1919, 151–52, 154
Blacks, xviii, xxiii, xxvii, 59, 93, 118–19, 121
Blair Mountain, xii, 152
Blue, Fred O., 92
Boes, Jacob, 15, 142
Bolsheviks, 144–50, 152–53
Boomer, WV, xxii, 73, 82, 91
Boone, Darius O., 62, 70, 117
Boswell, Charles, 46, 59, 71, 83, 94, 96–97, 99, 104, 110, 117, 125, 132
Boy Scouts of America, 139
Bradley, E. L., 70
Brown, John, 56, 83, 86, 94, 96–97, 115, 119, 131, 135, 141, 145
"Bull Moose Special," 95–97

Cabell County, WV, 18, 134
Cabin Creek, 35, 47, 50, 73, 80–2, 87, 92, 95, 111, 127, 130–1, 137
Cabin Creek strike (see Paint Creek-Cabin Creek strikes)
Cairns, Thomas, 109–11, 128, 130–1
Cantley, Ulysses, 70, 83, 85, 96
Chain, Dan "Few Clothes," 93
Charleston, WV, xxiv, 13, 22, 24, 30–1, 36, 38, 41, 44, 58, 64, 74–75, 81, 84, 86, 90, 114, 118, 126, 140
Charleston Gazette (Charleston, WV), 28

INDEX

Chesapeake and Ohio Railroad, 18–19, 67, 85, 90, 92, 120
Child labor, xxviii, xxxii, 13, 37
Chilton, Ned, 135
Christianity, xx–xxi, xxiii–xxiv, 53, 55–56, 72–75
Churches, xxiii–xxiv, 72
Clarksburg, WV, xxiv, xxvii, 23, 37, 42, 46, 62, 82, 91, 99, 112, 115, 119, 122, 155
Coal industry, xvi–xviii, xxv–xxvi, xix–xxx, 24–25, 34–36, 87–89, 98–102, 119– , 163–
Coal miners, xvi–xviii, xxv–xxvi, xxix–xxx,
  spread of socialism among, 28–32, 68–69
  working conditions of, 24–28, 35–36, 44–45
  militancy of, 45–48, 79–85, 148–49
  politics of, 87–90, 92–102, 136–38, 155–57
  and radicalism, 102–11, 119–20, 127–33, 151–54, 164
  and First World War, 141–43, 163
Coal Strike of 1897, xiii, 8, 25
Coal Strike of 1902, xvi, 26–32
Collins, Justus, 28, 34, 89, 119–20
Communist Party, 159, 166
Consolidation Coal Company, 85, 119
Constabulary Bill, 149–50, 153
Cooperative Commonwealth, 53–56, 58–59, 105, 127

Corcoran, Harry F., 79, 86, 133
Cornwell, Gov. John J., xxvii, xxix–xxxii, 134–35, 137, 141, 143, 149, 152, 156
Crawford, Charles, 81, 92
Cross, Samuel C., 45, 54

Dawson, Gov. William M. O., xv, 47
Dayton, Alston G., xx–xxi, 46, 134
Deal, Walter, 83, 110
Debs, Eugene Victor, x, xiii, xv–xvi, xxii, xxiv–xxvi, xxix–xxx, 1, 8–11, 21, 26, 60, 86–87, 101–5, 109, 116, 132, 136, 146, 158, 161
DelForge, George, 62, 160
Democratic Party, xxviii–xxxii, 30, 36, 49–50, 57, 63, 91, 122, 134–35, 137, 143
Diehl, Walter, 96
Dixon, Samuel, 34, 36, 43, 89
Donahue, Bishop P. J., 92
Dothan, WV, 45, 69–70, 87
DuBois, Oscar, 160–1
Dwyer, Lawrence "Peggy," 100, 129–30, 132, 143

Elections, 33, 38–40, 48–50, 60
  1912, 85–91
  1914, 116–22
  1916, 127, 133–38
  1920, 155–58
Employers' liability, 13, 79
Engdahl, J. L. , 100
Eskdale, WV, 68, 82–83, 93, 95, 130–1

Ettor, Joseph, 106–7

Fairmont, WV, xxiv–xxv, xxvii, 20, 85, 116, 119, 149, 155
Fairmont coal field, 24, 28, 34, 87, 119, 143
Fairview, WV, 20–1
Fayette County, xxiv, 24, 26, 34, 37, 42, 60–1, 70, 75, 85–91, 101, 117–18, 121–22, 128, 134–37, 157
Fayetteville, WV, 26, 29
Finns, xxx, 62–63, 150–2
First World War, xxii, xxxii, 124, 134, 138, 159, 162–63, 169
Firth, Edwin, 91, 103, 127, 141, 161
Franklin, Henry, 35–36
Free thinkers, 72–73
Frisk, Gustave, 28–29

Germans, xiii–xiv, xxii, xxx, 10, 26, 28, 63–64, 89
Germer, Adolph, xxv–xxvi, 101–3
Ghent, William J., 142, 146–47
Gherken, George, 30, 64, 110
Glass, George, 70, 117, 147
Glass industry, 22–24, 164–66
Glasscock, Governor William, 81–82, 85, 91–93, 96
Glassworkers, xxii, 23–24, 48, 62–63, 66–67, 86, 90, 160–1, 164–66
Goebel, George H., 17, 101
Gompers, Samuel, xviii, 49–50
Gneiser, Gus A., 64, 148
Greenbrier County, 19, 64, 134

Haggerty, Thomas, 25, 102–3, 108, 111, 121, 127–31, 133
Hardie, J. Keir, 86
Harper, Dana, 91, 148
Harper, George W., 45–46, 125, 156
Harpers Ferry, WV, 56
Harrison County, 135, 137
Hatfield, Governor Henry D., xxvi, 97–100, 102–3, 121, 133
Hatfield Agreement, 105, 107–8
Hayes, Frank J., 129, 144
Hayes, Louis, 11–12, 17
Hayes, Max, 12, 86
Haywood, William "Big Bill," x, 83, 115
Hecker, J. T., 10, 15–17, 49
Hilltop, WV, 29, 70, 87–88, 123
Hilton, Walter, 59, 72, 86, 99, 105–7, 111–15, 140–2, 144–46, 148, 157, 164
Hitchman Coal and Coke, xx, xxix, 46
Holly Grove, 81, 83, 95, 167
Holt, Matthew W., 126, 141
Houston, Harold W., 21–22, 47, 51, 83, 85, 97–98, 110, 118, 122, 127, 133, 136, 144–45
Hubbard, William P., xvi, 39
Huntington, WV, xxvii, 18–19, 27, 35, 67, 90, 103, 116, 118, 120, 136, 139, 166
Huntington Socialist and Labor Star, 56, 91, 100, 104, 115, 118, 122
Huntington Trades and Labor Assembly, 50, 94, 100, 123, 153

Immigrants (see also particular groups), xviii, 31, 148
Independent Labor Party, 120-2
Industrial unionism, xxviii, 164
Industrial Workers of the World (I.W.W.), ix, xxi, xxvi, 68, 82, 92, 104–7, 111, 115, 149–50, 152
Industrialization, 7–8, 19–24
Italians, xxii, 35, 51, 63–64, 91, 108, 149

Jones, Mary Harris "Mother," xv, xix, xxiii, xxv–xxvi, xxix–xxx, 8, 25, 31, 82–84, 86, 93–94, 96–97, 129, 131,
135, 145, 147

Kanawha Coal field, 26–28, 46, 79, 107
Kanawha County, 24–26, 30, 33, 41, 61, 72, 85, 88, 117, 126–27, 133, 136–37
Keeney, C. Frank, xxvi–xxx, 81–82, 110, 127, 129–30, 132, 141, 143, 145, 157
Keeney, W. W., 135, 153
Kerensky, Alexander, 146
Kintzer, Edward H., 101–2, 112, 115, 126, 133, 135, 162
Kline, George B., 10, 18
Knights of Labor, 26, 41

Labor Argus (Charleston, WV), 33, 38, 43, 45, 50–1, 59, 71, 84, 93, 100, 110, 117, 122
Labor theory of value, 51–52
Labor unions (see also individual unions), 8–10, 18, 31, 37–40, 78–79, 85, 90, 111–16, 150–55
Lane, Winthrop, 69
Lavinder, A. D., 26–27, 30, 46, 96, 157
Leeds, Harry, 9, 12, 17, 115
Lenin, Vladimir, 146–47, 157
Lewis, John L., 113
Lilly, A. A.. 126–27, 133
Lincoln, Abraham, 53
Link, Herndon, 55, 64
Local Assembly 300, Knights of Labor, 23
Logan coal field, 35, 151
Logan County, 25, 151

Machinists Union, 67–68
Mailly, William, 16–17, 31
Maley, Anna, 101, 119, 126
Marion County, 20, 36
Marshall County, 78, 126
Martial law, 81, 92–94, 96, 133
Marxism, 5, 12, 53
Matewan, WV, 151
McDonald, Duncan, 86
McDowell County, 34–35, 118, 120
McKell, William, 89, 120
Merrick, Frederick "Fritz," xxi, 21, 41, 100, 103–4
Millennialism, 73–75

Mine guards, xxv, 8, 40, 82, 85, 93, 119

Miner's Herald (Montgomery, WV), 108, 110

Mitchell, John, 31, 43, 46

Mitchell, Rome, 26, 30, 100, 108

Montgomery, Samuel B., 40, 48, 109–10, 152, 155–58

Montgomery, WV, 25, 47, 108, 128

Mooney, Fred, xxvi–xxviii, 69, 92, 96, 108, 110, 127, 131, 143, 157

Morgan, Gov. Ephraim, 155

Morgantown, WV, 20, 23, 64, 86, 90

Morris, Robert, 72, 100

Morrison, Samuel, 47–48

Moundsville, WV, 17, 51, 155

Mount Carbon Coal Company, 47, 89

Mount Hope, WV, 29–30, 89–90, 128

Mucklow, WV, 34, 81, 96, 128, 161

Municipal Reform League, 57–58

Nance, Silas, 68, 82, 93

National Window Glass Workers, 66–67, 165

Natural gas industry, 20, 22

Neely, Matthew M., xxix, 134

New River Coal Company, 34, 36, 43, 89

New River coal field, 24, 26, 28–29, 35, 63, 80, 88–90, 101, 107, 131, 143

Niehas, Andrew, 78–79

Ninness, Herbert J., 78, 111, 113

Norfolk and Western Railroad, 26, 107

Non-Partisan Political Campaign of 1920, 155–58

Nugent, John, xvii–xviii, 37–44

Oak Hill, WV, 29–30, 89–90, 101

O'Hare, Frank, 17

Ohio County, 18, 126–27, 134

Ohio Valley Trades and Labor Assembly, xiv–xv, 10–11, 13–16, 39–41, 43, 48–49, 57–58, 91, 106, 111–14, 122, 133, 139–40, 142–43, 145, 152

Oil industry, 20–22

Operator's Protective Association, 78, 109

Paint Creek, 34–35, 46–47, 79–85, 96, 109

Paint Creek-Cabin Creek strikes, xxvi, 79–85, 91–102, 108, 162, 168

Parkersburg, WV, xxi, 20–22, 91, 122

Parsons, George T., 30, 74–75, 83, 94, 96–97, 117

Peters, W. A., 106, 115

Phelps Stokes, J. G., 146

Pocahontas coal field, 24, 28

Poles, 62–63

Pope, A. O., 19, 64, 77

Pottery industry, 68, 166

Pratt, WV, 93, 97

Primary election law, 124–27, 138

Progressive (Bull Moose) Party, xxviii, 91, 122

Prohibition, 37, 120, 164

Pullman Strike, xiii, 21, 26
Putman County, 24, 33

Railroad workers, 9, 19, 21, 64, 90
Raleigh County, 29, 63–64, 101, 133
Rathburn, George, 31, 46, 70–1
Red Flag Bill, 150–53
"Red Scare," xxx–xxxi, 146–56
Red Star, WV, xxvii, 87, 116
Reed, Stuart B., 126
Republican Party, xiv–xv, xxviii, xxxii, 23, 27, 30, 36, 39–41, 45–46, 48–49, 57, 63, 90–1, 120–2, 128, 133–34, 155
Reuther, Valentine, 10, 49, 64, 79, 94
Reuther, Victor, 55–56
Robinson, Ira, 133
Rodes, Homer Lee, 29, 101, 136
Rogers, L. C., 90, 101, 108, 121–22, 128–30, 133
Ronceverte, WV, 19, 55, 71
Russell, Charles Edward, 142, 146–47
Russian Revolution, xxxi, 124, 144–46

Salem, WV, xxvii, 86
Scott, Brant, 35, 94, 100, 115, 161
Sellins, Fanny, 120
Shay, Edward, 63, 86
Simons, Algie M., 142, 146–47
Skilled workers, 13–18, 66–68, 111–16, 150–55, 159–66
Smith, C. E., xxx, 149
Snyder, Frank, 43, 45, 49, 59

Social Democratic Party, 8–13
Social Rebel, The (Parkersburg, WV), 21, 41
Socialist Party of America, x–xiii, xix–xx, xxiii, xxvii, 1, 4–5, 12, 17–19, 21, 60, 63, 109, 118, 159, 161, 167
National Executive Committee, 31, 101
National Investigating Committee, xxv–xxvi, 101–6
Socialist Party of West Virginia, xiv, xx, xxx–xxxii, 3–5, 18, 22, 30–2, 38, 60, 78–79, 86, 90, 101–2, 124, 136, 154, 159, 166–69
Star City, WV, xxiv, xxvii, 23, 63, 86, 115–16, 123, 149
Steel strike of 1919, xxx–xxxii, 150–1, 154
Stover, Everett, 128, 133
Strickland, Fred, 101, 149
Strikes (see also, particular strikes), 46–47, 112
Swinburn, Tom, 31, 70

Taft, President William Howard, xxiv
Teufel, John, 14, 16
Thompson, Wyatt, 30, 56, 62–63, 70–1, 75, 83, 99, 103–5, 107, 120, 123, 125, 156, 162–64
Tincher, T. L. "Doc," 85–86
Toney, Cleveland, 45, 62
Tracey, M. E., 10–11
Tucker County, 116, 134

United Labor Party, 48–50
United Mine Workers, xii, xx–xxi, xxiii, xxvii, 25–26, 31, 41, 45–46, 52, 79–80, 85–86, 89, 92, 97–98, 103,
107, 109, 121, 129–32, 141, 143–44
UMW District 17, xvii, xxv–xxvi, xxviii, xxx, 25, 41–42, 69–70, 81, 102, 108, 110–11, 121, 127–29, 132, 153, 155, 164
UMW District 29, xxviii, 101, 107–8, 121, 128, 132, 164
UMW District 30, 111, 128–30
United States Department of Labor, xxviii, 143
United States War Labor Board, 143–44
Upton, Rev. Del, 116

Vasey, Joseph, 103, 108, 121

Walters, Charlie, 140–1
Watson, Clarence W., xxv, xxix, 85, 143
Watson, George T., 34, 36
Weirton, WV, xxx, 112, 150, 152
West Virginia House of Delegates, xvii, 41–42, 136
West Virginia Mine Workers Organization, 130–2, 138
West Virginia Socialists
and politics, 33–41, 48, 60, 85–91, 116–22, 133–38, 155–58

Ideology of, xix–xxi, 4–5, 50–60
Profile of, xxi–xxiv, 61–77
in the coalfields, 24–33, 79–85, 92–102, 127–32
and religion, xx–xxi, xxiii–xxiv, 55–56, 71–75
Ethnic background, xiii–xiv, xxi–xxiii, 62–64
and government repression, 124–27, 146–54
and organized labor, 4, 37–53, 111–16, 122–23, 150–4, 159–66
Radicalism among, 102–11
Roots of, xiii–xviii, 8–24, 65
and First World War, 138–44
and the Russian Revolution, 144–46
West Virginia State Federation of Labor, xvii, 3–4, 37–38, 40–44, 50, 78–79, 122, 126, 139, 145, 153, 155–56
West Virginia State Legislature, 13, 124
West Virginia State Militia, 84, 92–93, 100–1
West Virginia Supreme Court, 94
Wheeling, WV, xiii–xv, xxvii, xxx, 8–18, 36–39, 42–44, 46, 57, 62, 72, 78, 86, 90, 106–7, 111–16, 133, 139
Wheeling Intelligencer, 17, 44, 49
Wheeling Majority, 59, 78, 105, 122, 138, 141–42, 146, 148, 152, 154, 163
Wheeling Stogie Workers, 79, 86, 113, 115

Whiskey Ring, 58, 122
White, John P., 97, 108, 121, 129
Williamson coal field, 28
Wilson, President Woodrow, xxiv, xxviii–xxix, 134–35, 138–40, 145

Winding Gulf coal field, 28, 143
Women, xxii–xxiii, 38, 114

Zimmerman, Fred A., 10, 18

Fred Barkey earned his Ph.D. in History (major concentration U.S. Labor History) from the University of Pittsburgh. He earned both his M.A. and B.A. from Marshall University. Dr. Barkey has taught history at the University of Charleston, Marshall University, the Institute for Labor Studies at West Virginia University, and was named professor emeritus at the West Virginia Graduate College. He has also been selected as a Danforth associate in recognition of his outstanding college teaching. He is presently the chairman of the Coal Heritage Trail Authority and chairman emeritus of the West Virginia Labor History Association, which he co-founded in 1976.

In 1988, Barkey was knighted by the King of Belgium (Order of Leopold II) for promoting greater awareness of Belgian immigrant workers to the development of West Virginia and the nation. Barkey was made a 2007 WV History Hero for his lifetime of writing, teaching, and promoting West Virginia labor and ethnic history.

Barkey has published articles in a number of journals, including *West Virginia History, Mountain Messenger,* and *Goldenseal* and is the author of *Cinderheads in the Hills: Belgian Window Glass Workers in West Virginia* and *Rednecks: The West Virginia Socialist Party 1898–1920.*

Ken Fones-Wolf is the Stuart and Joyce Robbins chair and professor of history, West Virginia University, where he teaches American working-class and Appalachian history. Fones-Wolf is the author or editor of six books, including, *Glass Towns: Industry, Labor, and Political Economy in Appalachia, 1890–1930s* (University of Illinois Press, 2007) and *Culture, Class, and Politics in Modern Appalachia: Essays in Honor of Ronald L. Lewis* (West Virginia University Press 2009).

Gordon Simmons is an adjunct professor of philosophy at Marshall University, president of the West Virginia Labor History Association, and a field organizer for the West Virginia Public Workers Union, UE Local Local 170.

www.ingramcontent.com/pod-product-compliance
Lightning Source LLC
Chambersburg PA
CBHW032034150426
43194CB00006B/277